In Defense of the Family

IN DEFENSE OF THE FAMILY

Raising Children in America Today

RITA KRAMER

Basic Books, Inc., Publishers   *New York*

Library of Congress Cataloging in Publication Data

Kramer, Rita.
  In defense of the family.

  Includes index.
    1. Family—United States. 2. Child rearing—
United States. 3. Child development—United States.
I. Title.
HQ536.K72   1982   649'.1'0973   82-72399
ISBN   0-465-03215-X

For Yale

ACKNOWLEDGMENTS

I am grateful to R. Randoph Richardson and Leslie Lenkowsky for the inspiration and support that made this book possible, and to Midge Decter and Jane Isay for the encouragement and effort that brought it into print. Diane Ravtich began it all and, as always, provided interesting suggestions and valuable criticism along the way. Thanks are also due to all of the scholars and clinicians cited in the notes, on whose observations and ideas I drew so freely.

CONTENTS

Contents

In Defense of the Family

1

The Family

Introduction

In recent years, the American family has been subject to increasing scrutiny by experts in widely divergent fields, all of them contending that the family as we know it is threatened with imminent demise, a kind of endangered species among social institutions. Historians of the family have traced its evolution from an extended band of rural kinfolk to a conjugal pair living in suburban isolation with its off-spring—the much-maligned nuclear family. Sociologists have explained the changing nature of the family as a social institution from a producing group to a consuming one. Political activists have deplored the traditional family's failure to foster women's rights, racial integration, tolerance of homosexuality or of economic justice, depending on their particular interests. And various kinds of health and welfare professionals, supported in one way or another by government, are ready to provide services they maintain families can no longer provide for their own members—in particular, their children.

It is hard to pick up a newspaper or magazine, look over the titles in a bookstore, or turn on the television set without being offered diagnoses and prescriptions for the ailing family. The media, a world in constant search of novelty, where one idea is presumed to be as good as any other, gives us reports as up-to-date and as constantly changing as weather reports on what is about to replace the family as we know it—homosexual or lesbian couples with adopted children, open marriages that may or may not be childless ones, cohabiting unmarried singles, groups living together in communes.[1]

The beleaguered couple united in a heterosexual marriage and concerned about its children's well-being has a hard time of it these days. Not only are they assured that the present situation of the American family is precarious and its prospects dim, but who can they trust among the many experts proferring them advice? The trouble is, the experts disagree. And when the authorities say different, and often even opposite things, whom do you listen to?

When writers raise that rhetorical question, the answer, of course, is usually "me." But while this book is addressed to the parents in average middle-class American families today, its aim is not to give them specific advice on the problems of child rearing but to make a more general statement: Parents are not helpless before social, political, and cultural forces beyond their control and they need not be overwhelmed by them.

It will begin by considering some of what has been said about the past and present situation of the family in a brief survey of histories of family life and statements about the contemporary needs of the nation's families, because asking where we have come from is usually helpful in understanding how we got where we are, and it will go on to deal with recent thinking about child development, child care, and children's education, asking what we actually know about children's needs. What is the best evidence we have, and what can we conclude from it?

This is not a how-to book. Its aim is to provide information thoughtful parents can use in their own way to answer their own questions about their children and themselves.

"Experts" can't tell you anything that applies in specific detail to you or your child; they can only stimulate your own use of reason and intuition. In the end you must trust yourself, be guided by your own values, apply the test of common sense to what you do.

If you listen to everyone you'll find sooner or later that they cancel each other out. The obvious conclusion is to listen to yourself. Yes, but who am I? asks the modern parent. You know who you are in other areas of your life—how you feel about your work, your politics, your religion or lack of it, your expectations in marriage, in friendship, what you owe, or don't, to your own parents. Why not as a parent? Why the fear of inadequacy, of getting it wrong, of failure, of the irreparable moment? What counts in parenthood is not any one action at any given moment. It is the kind of person you are and how that is expressed to your child.

The perniciousness of so much of the advice from experts that pervades the media is that it undermines the confidence of parents in their own abilities and their own values, overemphasizes the significance of specific child-rearing techniques, and grossly misrepresents the contribution the expert in psychiatry or education can make to the conduct of ordinary family life.

The only reason you should read something is to enlarge your world, not to restrict it. This book, too, should be taken in that spirit. Use what you can, discard the rest. It offers no prescriptions, but an array of ideas that may prove useful in gathering the courage to find and to follow your own convictions.

Advice is only useful when it comes in Socratic form, an attempt to help you define virtue yourself, by raising questions and leading you to self-knowledge. The best an author of a book addressed to parents can do is avoid the temptation to pontificate, dictate, or legislate for all parents and be content to help some of them to muddle through on their own as caring individuals have through human history, offering a few guiding principles the knowledge of which might help men and women of good will to make decisions affecting their children's lives and their own.

The theme of this book is that parents can and should make a difference in their children's lives and that the most effective way to do so is through the family as it has traditionally been defined—a married couple of different sexes living with their own children by blood or adoption and having certain hopes and expectations for their characters, their education, and their futures. Of course, there are variations on this ideal, especially in the many single-parent families resulting from increasing rates of divorce, and we have to consider ways in which to compensate for the absence of two parents in a child's life, as we do ways of compensating for other kinds of handicaps or deficits. But the traditional nuclear family as we have defined it remains the chief agency—and the best one—for developing character in the individual and for transmitting the values of the culture.

Why and how this is so follows from the way of looking at childhood and the way of looking at the world that is the subject of the pages that follow.

The family of childhood—heaven or hell, paradise or prison? It is hard to look back on life in the past as an unrelieved idyll. Famine and plague, fear and ignorance colored too much of it. And while fear and ignorance are still with us, exploration, discovery, trade, and invention have led to better ways of controlling nature and arranging our lives. Technology and information have created possibilities for a better world, if not a perfect one, given the inescapable realities of human nature.

Still, we long for something we sense was lost somewhere in the far-off past, although we're not sure exactly what it was. Gaiety, companionship, a sense of belonging, a sense of purpose? The nostalgia school of social thought has various answers, but always the present is measured against the past and in some telling way found wanting.

Where is the view of the past and present that might best serve us as a guide to the future? Is the nuclear family "besieged," as historian and social critic Christopher Lasch tells us?[2] Is it undergoing a fundamental transformation, "wracked in some kind of final tubercular spasm," as social historian Edward Shorter would have it?[3] Or is it "here to stay," as policymaker Mary Jo Bane maintains?[4]

Shorter's demographic portraits of French peasants' lives in the seventeenth century, Bane's analysis of census bureau statistics on working women and single-parent families today, and Lasch's impressive intellectual critique of historical theories and present practices in the light of psychoanalysis are but three of the many attempts made to address the plight of the child and the crisis of the family in the past twenty years. One way of surveying the history of family life in the Western world might be to look at some of the individual periods and themes that have been taken up by various writers on the family in other times and places as well as here and now.

The Old World: Childhood Betrayed or Bettered?

Historians have described the widespread brutality practiced against children in the ancient world and, although they differ, as we shall see, in their judgment of medieval life, they agree that it included little segregation of the generations. All ages mixed freely in the daily activities of the marketplace, the workshop, the kitchen, and even the bed, of which there was often only one for a family.

It was a rude life for almost everyone, master and apprentice, soldier and servant, and probably most of all for children of all but the higher social orders. If children and grownups did everything together, eating the same foods, wearing the same clothes, and, after finishing their work side by side, drinking the same grog and playing the same games, enjoying the same riddles and rhymes[5], it is doubtful whether it was because children were so mature but undoubtedly because grownups, most of them illiterate and seldom exposed to much travel or training, were so childlike.

In the sixteenth century in Western Europe a new sentiment about children began to emerge that encouraged a view of them as different from adults. They would no longer be dressed in miniature versions of grownups' clothes or expected to pursue grownups' activities. Toys and games were invented especially for them, and for the first time childhood was perceived as an entity, a special time of life with problems different from those of adulthood. More thought went into how to educate children and care for them, and the invention of the printing press made possible the publication of the first English book on child care, *The Regiment of Life, whereunto is added a treatise of pestilence, with the boke of children,* written by a physician, Thomas Phayre, exactly four hundred years before Dr. Spock published his advice to parents.

It was the surprising if not eccentric thesis of a French social historian, in a book that had enormous influence on the thinking about childhood that followed its publication in the early 1960s, that the life of the child had not only changed forever at the end of the Middle Ages, it had changed for the worse. According to Philippe Ariès's *Centuries of Childhood*[6], the invention of the idea of childhood as a distinct stage of life ended forever a happy age of freedom in which children were treated with a "gay indifference" by the adults with whom they worked side by side at the bench and mixed freely in the market square until the triumph of the forces that ushered in the tyranny of the nuclear patriarchal family, when the shades of the schoolhouse began to close round the child.

Ariès's views were given the attention that only the idiosyncratic statements and cryptic style of a true French intellectual can inspire in academia, and they influenced the content of a decade of doctoral dissertations. One of these grew into a widely reviewed book, David Hunt's *Parents and Children in History*[7]. The author set out to consider the French historian's views on children in the light of those of psychoanalyst Erik Erikson[8] and wound up taking issue with Ariès's nostalgia for a life of spontaneity in which parents allowed children to grow up as they would rather than trying to control their development in the family and the school. Was a child's life in the medieval community really less regimented than modern domestic life in any way that can possibly mean that it was a better life?

Erikson had described the way in which the events of the successive stages of life were related to certain personality traits. In the first three stages of Erikson's scheme, how the infant is fed is related to his later sense of basic trust in, or mistrust of, the world and others; his experiences in connection with holding on to and letting go of the products of his own body relate to the development of autonomy or of feelings of shame and doubt; and when the child begins to move around and to explore his own body and the outside world the stage is set for developing initiative or a sense of guilt.

Hunt starts with the idea that a set of beliefs about the nature of infants and how they should be encouraged to develop lies behind the child-rearing practices of every culture and both reflects and serves its particular social and political realities and ideals[9], and then zeros in on the issue of individual autonomy as the aspect of childhood most directly related to social/political life. How the adult world responds to its children's efforts to assert themselves is a function of whether what is valued is personal freedom and self-assertion or group solidarity and compliance. If adults encourage and support early efforts at independence and self-determination, the child will develop a sense of his own competence. If in his efforts to control his own body the child is overwhelmed and defeated, he will be shamed and full of self-doubt.

As Hunt explains it, childhood obedience was essential to the survival of a rigid hierarchical society, and thus the ancien régime rested on the foundation of a domestic life that terrorized children, swaddling, purging and whipping them for their own good in order to inculcate unquestioned obedience to the authority of the ruler, whether the father or king.

"Punished for attempting to establish selfhood, and deprived of control over their bodies, they were left with a pervasive sense of shame and doubt." The outcome of such tutelage is a person who "will never be able to demand what is his due. In this way, a repressive status quo is anchored in the conflicts of the anal stage."[10]

Of course, the alternative is not unbridled instincts and domestic chaos, which would do no better to ensure autonomous adults, but social scientists have traditionally been less concerned with warning against the perils of excess than against those of repression. However, we may assume that a free society, if it is to persist and not destroy itself with each new generation, depends on child-rearing patterns that will balance the restraints that make for honesty and self-control with the indulgence that leads to creativity and the capacity for risk-taking—kindness with courage.

Childhood Revisited: A History of Horrors

A dozen years after the publication of Ariès's book in this country, psychohistory had established itself as a new discipline and the history of childhood was being reexamined under a new glass. In it, Lloyd deMause[11], for one, saw an entirely different picture from that Ariès had described.

To deMause the life led by children in the past was far from the happy fellowship with the adults around them that Ariès saw, but an unremitting history of brutality and neglect at the hands of those adults, who had victimized and terrorized and even murdered their children throughout the ages—from the exposure and other forms of infanticide practiced in antiquity, especially on female children, through the vicious beatings administered to encourage learning and drive out devils in the Middle Ages, to the cruel restraints used to curb masturbation up to the very doorstep of our own time.

These were adults, according to deMause, whose own lives had failed to prepare them to empathize with their children. Instead, they projected their own feared impulses onto them and saw them as evil and insatiable and to be subdued by any terrors that could be perpetrated on mind or body: frightened, bound, whipped, starved, even killed if they could not otherwise be tamed.

Many of them, it must be remembered, would die in infancy anyway. Parents simply failed to form any attachment to their infants, whom they sent away at birth to be cared for by wet nurses, in whose indifferent hands many failed to survive the year. Or, if they could

not afford to send them away, overworked mothers mercilessly swaddled their infants into paralyzed—and trouble-free—stupor. Feeding
children was just another routine task of the daily life of those too
poor to hire servants. It was thought of as an onerous burden, debili-
tating and degrading, much as it is by those radical feminists today
who want to free women from child-care responsibilities, which they
see as circumscribing and demeaning.

Thus, in deMause's view, generations of battered children grew
up to batter their own children, beating and purging them for their
own good until, some time around the eighteenth century, child
abuse began to decline. Where Ariès sees the carefree child entering
the prison created for him by family and school, deMause sees the
miserable child emerging into the daylight of parental empathy and
concern. This evolution occurred as parents and children came closer
together in a life less fraught with danger and less haunted by death.
The pall of mortality began to lift from childbed and crib, and, encouraged by a new religious cult of the child as an innocent, parents
stopped separating from their children at birth and kept them at
home, where early contact stimulated sympathy and encouraged a
more humane attitude. So did the creeping effects of a science and
technology that were developing as commerce spread learning and
spurred invention. Men and women no longer living at the limits of
subsistence could begin to afford tenderness and compassion.

And so, according to deMause, the stage was set for conjugal affection and domestic intimacy. Another historian was waiting to tell us
what would become of those.

The Fallen Nest

In the past decade an increasing number of academics turned their
attention to the plight of the family. One, Canadian historian Edward Shorter[12], traced the rise—and predicted the fall—of the mod-

ern nuclear family in terms of its transformation from an agency of production in which all members worked the soil or helped in the business, and through which property and position were transmitted, to a merely private arena of domestic intimacy. No function was left to it but providing affectional relationships for its members. No longer a basic economic institution, it had become an emotional retreat from the unfriendly workplace.

In the mid-seventies, Shorter saw all around him a radical reshaping of the family characterized by marital instability and the loss of control by parents over their children. More than a threat or a trend, he saw as an accomplished reality the falling away of "the ties which bind one generation to the next." Adolescents (not *some* adolescents) no longer think of themselves as

links in a familiar chain stretching across the ages. Who they are and what they become is independent, (at least so they believe) of what their parents are. And they themselves are responsible for what their children become only to the point of seeing that they march into the future with straight teeth. The chain of generations serves no larger moral purpose for adolescents, and therewith the moral authority of parents over their growing children collapses.

Other agencies now socialize and control the young. The continuity between the generations falls.[13]

That, according to Shorter, is "the crisis of the postmodern family."

How did individual self-realization come to replace the traditional allegiance to the continuity of the community?

Once upon a time, as Shorter tells it, there was a rigidly stratified system in which men's and women's roles in work and sex were sharply demarcated, outside the home and within it, but when courtship ceased to be a community-arranged matter of the land, the lineage, and the pocketbook and became a private affair of the heart, a revolution in premarital sexual behavior was underway. The late eighteenth century also saw a turning away, inspired by Rousseau's romanticism, from the widespread practice of boarding out infants to wet nurses and a revival of nursing and mothering one's own babies. The resultant mother-child intimacy became the basis of the privatistic nuclear family, replacing the traditional family which had served as an organic part of a larger community.

Thus romantic love and maternal love created what Shorter calls "a sentimental nest" closed off from the surrounding world, and, with the industrial revolution, market capitalism encouraged an ethic of egoism with its emphasis on individual gratification and autonomy.

The nest is no longer a refuge, he tells us, only a brief stopping place, as the peer group increasingly assumes the former functions of the family. The mother-child tie that bound the nuclear family has been loosened as women have used their greater degree of personal freedom to pursue a greater degree of personal fulfillment—through outside employment. With mother out of the home, the adolescent subculture takes over; in still other "marital dyads" of free-floating couples, there are no encumbrances in the form of children at all. The result: "The nuclear family is crumbling."

Before we start looking around for the pieces to pick up, we might ask whether what Shorter was describing was indeed a universal condition in our society or, rather, a trend highly visible in some parts of it—not only partial but reversible.

The outlook of an increasingly visible number of Americans in the decade that has followed publication of Shorter's fashionable promise of unprecedented things to come in how we will arrange our personal lives is very different from the counter-culture view which received so much attention in the decade that preceded it. The youth culture has not taken over, and closed marriages still abound. Despite a continuing increase in the number of working mothers and single-parent families, there is evidence of a growing interest in preserving the traditional family.

Where Have All the Mothers Gone?

Is it a lost cause?

If, as the demographers tell us, "young adults are establishing quite different life styles from their parents, with later marriage, fewer children, more divorce, more working wives,"[14] and if "this diversity in households will increase as we move toward 1990,"[15] we have to ask ourselves about the psychological implications for children of having single parents, older parents, fewer siblings, working mothers, other-than-parent grownups living in, two sets of parents, and so on. We have to ask about the consequences if, as family-policy authority Mary Jo Bane tells us, "projections of the 1990 female labor force . . . indicate a new life course pattern for women, one of high and continuing attachment to the labor force even through the childbearing period."[16]

According to the experts, "Married women, especially those with children, show the sharpest increase in participation rates [in the labor force]. Within the group with children, the greatest increase in participation is among those with young children,"[17] and "projections call for growth . . . in working compared to non-working single-parent families."[18] In other words, many of the nation's children will soon have only one parent, a mother who works.

While mothers turn to factory jobs or clerical work, who will mind the children? As Nathan Glazer points out[19], we no longer have the large family's older siblings, the live-in grandparents, or the dedicated religious orders and "simple village girls" who used to care for other people's children. The irony is that the same feminist logic that sends mothers of young children out of the home to fulfill themselves in the labor pool makes it unlikely that anyone but those at the very bottom of the heap would be willing to take their place in the home. It also makes it unlikely that most working women—excepting, of course, the well-educated and well-connected class from which most published feminist writers

14

come—can earn much more than they would need to pay for adequate substitute-mother care.

Is publicly-funded and publicly-provided child care the answer? The authors of the MIT-Harvard report on the state of the American family tell us that the traditional "suburban nuclear-family life style" ("families with children, male workers and female homemakers") is rapidly becoming obsolete.[20] What they expect to take its place is "a new combination of work and family life that uses nursery schools, day care centers and paid child-care help more extensively." They add, "it seems likely that families in 1990 will be looking to non-family sources for help with the care of children," by which they mean that some child-care services "may become the responsibility of government."[21]

Is this the direction family life in America will take in the near future? If so, it seems ironic in view of how it all began.

The New World: Childhood Redefined

In colonial America, an adventurous spirit was in the air, antiauthoritarian, and by necessity flexible enough to adapt to new and always changing conditions. There was a palpable concern with the future in the minds of those who came to the New World, where the history of children becomes the history of education—of the schools as well as family life. By the mid-seventeenth century a law had been passed in the Massachusetts Bay Colony providing for town schools to teach local children to read, write, and do sums. But in colonial times children were still primarily workers, not students.

In Cotton Mather's day, church and school preached and taught submission to divine will and parental authority, and any lurking self-assertion or willfulness indulgent parents might have tolerated in the home, where most education took place, was probably subdued by the experiences of apprenticeship and service, which took children out of the parental household as early as six years of age, when they also began to dress as adults did.[22]

In eighteenth-century America there began to be economic advantages to having children. For most members of the agricultural society of the Old World more children had meant more mouths to feed and less to be inherited. The family's amount of land and its produce usually remained fixed when it did not decline. Poor diet, unsanitary living conditions, and disease carried off many of those infants who survived the birth process. And of those who survived the perils of childhood and a nurture often as harsh and inattentive as nature itself, relatively few can have grown up as healthy adults in terms of today's standards, either free of physical defects or psychologically capable of autonomy and self-direction. Most of the world's population was grindingly poor, and most parents lived and worked under conditions that discouraged the development of a rich emotional life and the cultivation of sentimental ties.

The separation of children from their parents at birth, the failure of mothers to nurse their own young, and the practice of sending them out to work or school at an early age, made them strangers.

Now, with so much land and so much mobility and opportunity, the common practice of "putting out" young children with nurses or relatives or sending them off to a master at an early age began to die out. Mothers began to have more contact with their young and to form closer ties with them, although constant vigilance was still recommended to instill discipline—obedience, manners, and study and work habits. Children were never to be idle; when not at their tasks or their books they should be "thinking of Christ, while they are at their play."[23]

Not only in America but throughout the Western world during the eighteenth century the idea of the independence of the individual was spreading, along with a growing tendency to replace hierarchy with equality. The opposite claims—of individuality and equality, freedom and justice—would have repercussions within the family as well as in the other institutions of society as parental values came to replace traditional ones.[24]

The Family

The widely read, discussed, and translated writings of John Locke introduced a humane and reasonable attitude toward the nurturing and training of the young. And the publication of Rousseau's *Emile* in 1762 signaled a revolution in thinking about children—how they should live and how they should be educated. The idea of the happy childhood, a time of natural innocence to be allowed its fullest possible freedom to flower, was born.

The reality was very different, however, from the romance. Another revolution, the industrial one, was having its effect on the lives of children employed in places like the textile mills and mines of England. Throughout the nineteenth century a number of parliamentary acts were passed in an attempt to regulate the conditions under which children would work. Laws were designed to ensure that no child below the age of nine would work in factories or underground. Adoption of a ten-hour day with no night work was urged. It was not uncommon in the first half of the nineteenth century for five-year-olds to spend twelve hours working in the mines for a few pennies.

In America, child labor persisted through the nineteenth century in northern factories and southern mills until it was finally outlawed by federal legislation in 1938.

A process underway for several hundred years had introduced solicitude for infants as a characteristic of life in the average family. The special needs of children, with their helplessness and vulnerability, became a focus of parents' thinking as it did of the larger society.

In colonial times, everyone in the family worked to make a living out of the new land and the child was expected to do his part. The home was a "little commonwealth"[25] and children were introduced to intellectual skills and vocational training there. As social organizations and economic institutions became more differentiated and more complex, as more people left the lands they had grown up on to found new families of their own in new places, a son was less likely to do the same kind of work his father had done. With rapid technological change, a father was less likely to know what his son needed to learn. The growth of specialized educational institutions was inevitable, as was the extension of the time young people would spend in schools before they finally left them as adults in the "real world."

In a patriarchal agricultural society, everyone had a clearly defined role. Women and children lived almost entirely within the family. With America's transformation in the nineteenth century into an urban industrial society came profound changes. In the early years of the century over 90 percent of the population was rural; by the Civil War, 20 percent lived in cities; by the turn of the century the percentage of city dwellers had doubled and would continue to rise. In the process of moving from the land to the town, the family became a consuming rather than a producing unit.

By the mid-nineteenth century, as increasing numbers of families left the country for the crowded anonymity of the city, where they were joined by tidal waves of immigrants, the traditional sources of discipline—the family and the church—were weakening. As they began to lose their grip on the young, a new class of child-care professionals stepped in to combat delinquency and the other effects of urban poverty.

With fathers increasingly absent as the workplace was separated from the home, mothers became primarily responsible for child rearing. The school and other agencies of the state gradually assumed more and more of the functions that once had belonged to the family.

Teachers, nurses, and guidance counselors stepped in via the school; the health professionals, pediatricians and psychiatrists, offered their expertise; the welfare professionals sent the social worker and the courts to enter the life of the poor. The remaining functions were carved up between the peer group—as the young strove to do what "everybody else" did, whether everybody else belonged to a street gang or a suburban sorority; and the increasingly powerful and pervasive mass media—the movies, newspapers and magazines, radio, and, eventually, television.

The social sciences and psychology had produced a new breed of health and welfare experts, many of them eager to disseminate their advice through the growing influence of the media. Every decade, if not every year, brought a new point of view for parents to absorb and hasten to make use of. The rigid training of Watson's behaviorism in the twenties gave way to its exact opposite in the decade that followed, when Freud's emphasis on the importance of the vicissitudes of early emotional life for later development was misinterpreted to support an education designed to leave the instincts untrammeled and a family life in which parents would become pals in order not to cripple their children in their formative years.[26]

We have asked institutions—the government, the schools—to undertake to direct human nature. The paradox is that as our aims have become increasingly humanitarian, our means have become increasingly controlling.

Perhaps we have had too much of a good thing. Perhaps it is time to return child care to the home, responsibility to the family, and authority to parents.

Mothers' Helpers

During the nineteenth century, urbanization and the emancipation of women broke down the extended family and reduced it, in the phrase of sociologist Ernest W. Burgess, "from institution to companionship." What Talcott Parsons, the influential structural theorist of society, called a "transfer of functions" had relieved the family of its responsibilities for educating, instructing in work, and protecting its own. All that was left to the remnants of the family was to provide an emotionally satisfying intimacy no longer available at work or elsewhere in life, and to socialize its children.

Our own century has seen the conjugal tie weaken under the impact of liberalized divorce laws and the further removal of women from the traditional role of homemaker and mother at the same time there has been a gradual takeover of the family's function as child rearer by what Christopher Lasch calls "the helping professions."

It began in the decade after World War II, when the social sciences came into their own in American academia and the world of government and the foundations and, in exchange for a promise to discover cures for all the ills of society, received unprecedented amounts of public and private funding for a literature and a set of programs one aim of which was to improve the nation and its youth by democratizing the family. Relativism and personal fulfillment would be the hallmarks of a permissive child rearing that urged parents to "relate" to their children instead of telling them what to do. Old-fashioned middle-class morality with its stifling repressions must fall by the wayside. Child rearing was seen as a profession that, like any other, required proper training (by neo- and pseudo-Freudians who had forgotten that Freud once ruefully called parenthood, along with government and psychoanalysis, an impossible profession).

Its privacy invaded by an army of experts in the fields of mental health and education, the family no longer mediated between culture and instinct, in Christopher Lasch's phrase, to socialize children. Other agencies would replace the agencies of familial attachment and the process by which the child responded to those attachments.

In one of the most thoughtful of the recent discussions of the fate of the family, Lasch deplores the influences that have invaded "the protected space formerly provided by the family for the young" and blames the erosion of domestic ties on the loss of parental authority, as "elders retreat from painful confrontations by not forcing their own standards on the young."[27]

Once he became only provider and giver of love but not of discipline, the father was no longer a figure to be struggled with and there need be no effort to live up to him as an ideal, no commitment to his standards or society's. Whatever feels good, whatever seems convenient, whatever everyone else does becomes the guide.

Lasch contends that with no authority to struggle with and succeed to, the generational conflict avoided in overt behavior persists in emotional content—in an infantile personality that has never been tested, checked, redirected in ways that could make parental rules the basis for an inner life. The result is the hollow man, the narcissist concerned only with gratifying his desires now, with no feeling for the past and no confidence in the future.

Here, then, is the cliffhanger. Will society return control of children to the family, where character can best be structured in relation to loving and at the same time restraining parents? Can we return self-assurance to mothers and fathers, along with confidence in how they raise their young? Or is it too late to stop the inexorable movement led by professionals, justified by academics, funded by the government, and publicized by the media, that claims society knows best—and is ready to tell mothers and fathers how to do it, and even to do it for them?

Private Lives and Public Policies

Mary Jo Bane was one of the co-authors of *Inequality*[28], the much-discussed "reassessment" of American education in the early seventies that concluded that "neither family background, cognitive skill, educational attainment, nor occupational status explain much of the variation in men's incomes." Since schooling cannot be correlated statistically with economic success, in order to achieve "distributive justice" in society we must forget about indirect antipoverty programs, doomed to failure. "The only way to eliminate poverty is to redistribute income directly."[29] Goodbye, equality of opportunity; hello to a social policy dedicated to ensuring equality of results.

A few years after the publication of *Inequality*, when Mary Jo Bane turned her attention to the American family, she concluded that it was "here to stay." Taking issue with the "myth" of the happy, stable, extended family of the past described by so many writers on the family, Bane found evidence in the reams of statistics from which she quotes to indicate that Americans remain as deeply committed as ever "to the notion that families are the best places to raise children."[30] She has noticed that "when left to their own devices, and even in the face of some severe discouragements, Americans continue to marry, have children, create homes, and maintain family ties."[31]

However, she thinks it inevitable that other social commitments—to sexual equality and economic equality—will require changes in the family.

To understand what kind of brave new world the academic policy makers funded by government and foundations envision for us and for our children, we must ask about the nature of those changes and the bases for them.

Bane maintains that the nuclear family—a couple and their children—has always been the predominant family form in America, although families are smaller today because couples have fewer children. Her figures also indicate that families are no more mobile now than they were in the last century.

Despite rising divorce rates, which she sees as one inevitable concomitant of women's freer position in society, she sees a continuing commitment to marriage, which remains "a pervasive and enduring institution."[32] Like Henry V, who assured his French bride that he loved her country so well he would not part with a village of it, Americans today are all for marriage—and indicate their enthusiasm by marrying as often as they can. For while couples may be committed to marriage, they are not necessarily committed to each other, a situation that must have repercussions in the lives of their children. Most of those who divorce remarry again within five years, thus enacting what Dr. Johnson called "the triumph of hope over experience" and also incidentally creating parental permutations in which children of two formerly married partners become one family. (This practice may turn out to be the answer to declining family size.)

The other inevitable concomitant of women's liberation, according to Bane, is the rising number of mothers working outside the home. Working mothers of preschool children in particular rose from 12 percent in 1950 to 40 percent by the mid-seventies. Who, we may wonder, is taking care of these children? Still, Bane finds no evidence that children are less well cared for now than they ever were. Even though fewer children today live with both parents than in the past, more children live with at least one parent than previously—children are less likely to be orphaned or abandoned than they once were.

And the prediction is that the increase in one-parent families will continue.

The crucial issue would seem to be the working mother—of young children. Bane assumes that with complete economic equality and an increase in "the bargaining power of women within the family,"[33] it would be a tossup which partner in a marriage "should give up his or her income to assume family responsibilities."[34] (Most committed egalitarians assume that all kinds of differences between individuals are artificially imposed and that if the barriers were removed everyone would be pretty much alike and want more or less the same things. They seem to find it difficult to entertain the possibility that partners in a marriage could consider their roles equally important although different. Equal does not mean equally valuable to them, but the same.) In this less than perfect world, however, Bane finds some women opt for being childless rather than giving up their work, others choose to stay home to care for their children, and still others "choose work over child care, though not over maternity." They decide to have children but hire someone else to care for them. Progressive women may thus succeed in returning to the practices of two hundred years ago, when every respectable woman who could afford it hired a wet nurse.

When "vigorous enforcement of equal pay and equal opportunity legislation" finally results "in substantially equal economic status for women . . ." as well as "equal status within the family," Bane thinks it possible that a number (unspecified) of men may prefer to stay home and take care of the children while their wives go out to work for pay.[35] It's an interesting possibility, but there lurks the suspicion that mothering, even if culturally reinforced, can't be entirely without a biological basis. Social scientists tend to talk as though "cultural" meant "arbitrary," when in fact culture, like the heart, has its reasons.

Oddly enough, not all women want to work rather than care for home and children. Most who do so probably have little choice; they are poor or they are unmarried, widowed, separated, or divorced. A few who work have lots of money—and jobs open to them that do

not represent realistic choices for most women. Yet feminists assume
that any woman who had the opportunity would choose to be employed.[36] Bane dismisses housework as "a wretched job."[37] Compared to what? To factory work on an assembly line? To clerking in
an office? To a high-level position in a policy-making organization,
perhaps. But not every woman, for whatever reasons of nature or nurture, wants that particular life. Even some well-educated women
enjoy cultivating the arts of domesticity, and technology has made
housework a matter of relative ease and convenience. The picture
of the average American housewife's life painted by militant feminists is as distorted as their view of the average working woman's
world is romanticized.

Is pregnancy a "disability" to be dealt with by legislation covering
leaves and insurance? Should fathers also be entitled to child-care
leaves? Is the care of children once they are born a public responsibility? The answers to these questions will depend on whether one agrees
with Bane's view of sexual equality (a matter not of equal value but
of "fairness," meaning sameness in all things) as an overriding social
goal and with her statement that while only pregnant women can
have babies (there are some manifestly unfair things social policy
makers have not yet been able to influence), "child care, however,
can be done by anyone." Most of this book is concerned with disprov-
ing that statement.

Even Mary Jo Bane suspects, in her heart of hearts, that men and
women may be somewhat recalcitrant about accepting the new
roles a socioeconomic order of perfect equality might require of
them. But she reassures herself and us that "there may be legisla-
tive and legal actions that can stimulate questioning and perhaps
change behavior. The extension of the Fourteenth Amendment
into family law or the adoption of the Equal Rights Amendment
may generate such action."[38] Meanwhile, there are stopgap measures on the way to ultimate equality, such as a guaranteed maintenance allowance for single-parent families. There are, she admits,
"some problems." Cost, for one—in the double-digit billions, even
as she wrote in the early seventies, and with single-parent families

expected, partly as a result of present social policies, to continue to increase. "Society" must be prepared to pay the bill.

Bane admits that "family life is incompatible with some aspects of equality among citizens. As long as children are raised even partially by families, their opportunities can never be equal; however much resources are equalized, affection, interest, and care remain idiosyncratically centered in families."[39]

She stops short of specifying, in her chilling phrase, "mechanisms for articulating" the equality that may conflict with family rights and family privacy. But others are less hesitant to do so.

Politics and Parenthood

A troubling view of the causes and cures of the American family's condition was provided in the late seventies by the Carnegie Council on Children in a radically slanted and respectfully received critique of our society.[40] In *All Our Children: The American Family Under Pressure*,[41] Chairman Kenneth Keniston and the members of the Carnegie Council maintain that parents are not responsible for their family life or their children's fates. Ignoring the historical testimony of the multitudes in generations past who sustained a rich family life despite economic hardship and, in spite of poverty and prejudice, educated children who were able to enter the mainstream of the society and both benefit from and contribute to it, the members of the Council caution parents not to "define their family problems as somehow rooted in themselves." It is society that is to blame. Parents are making a mistake when they ask "what they themselves are doing wrong, not how the society is pressuring them."[42] They are society's victim, and it is wrong to blame the victim.

Instead of thinking in terms of individual responsibility for how one lives one's life and raises one's family, we must ask "how to make distribution of rewards in our society more just, how to limit the risk of technology." The answer, of course, is through the agency of the federal government, which will redistribute income by means of taxation and provide a panoply of social services to relieve the family of the "pressures" that interfere with child rearing.

The sources of those pressures are technology and laissez-faire capitalism; the solution is regulation by the state, which will "extend public vigilance through old and new agencies of government."[43] Any program that makes individual parents and individual families the focus of change stands in the way of reshaping society.

The idea that the formation of character is a function of government policy, that not the legislation of equal opportunity but the legislated equalization of rewards should be the basis of our political system, is bound to have some adherents—including those who would plan and run such a system. However, it is more probable that a number of people would be willing to benefit from such an effort-free and risk-free way of life than that many would be willing to pay for it. In any case, the idea that the government, and not the individual family, must be responsible for the welfare of the child, has certain consequences.

What the Council proposes is "that the nation develop a family policy as comprehensive as its defense policy." One can only guess at the actual extent of the "government initiative, action, and regulation"[44] that would be required in order for "government to organize, provide, and pay for services"[45] that would change society, or the real effect such government involvement would have on individual lives and individual behavior.

If the history of our time has shown us anything it has been the price paid for total control of society, no matter how great the good it was originally intended to serve, and the degree to which men and women will succeed in circumventing it regardless of statutes and in the face of whatever force.

Arguing for income redistribution, Keniston et al. tell us that since the existing state of things is "patently unjust" it must be changed in order to bring "American social practice into line with American ideals."[46] This is at the very least a debatable interpretation of what those ideals have been, are, or should be.

Is every need of every individual at every moment someone else's responsibility? Will "measures to modify economic and social factors . . . and the degree of social justice in the nation"[47] contribute to the development of character in our citizens of the future? Do "children need advocates in politics"[48] or do they need appropriate parenting in healthy families, and other advocates only when parents have been unable to assume, or persuaded to abdicate, the responsibilities that should be theirs?

Is this really what we should be talking about, this network of comprehensive social legislation and enforcement, if what concerns us is what makes life better for the child in the family? Is income, earned and unearned, really what determines parents' ability to raise children who care for others, who can learn from the past and apply its lessons to the future, and who take pride in themselves and their work? Generations of the offspring of poor families would be very surprised to hear so, just as most Americans would be surprised to hear that we no longer live in a time when a family can be "assumed to be self-sufficient and able to care for its own."[49]

In order to grope toward ways of answering the many questions about the child's place in the family and society that have been raised so far, we have to turn from the big picture to the small one—the child—and ask what we know about children's needs as they grow from infancy toward adulthood.

2

The Child

Introduction

While all babies are different from birth, and all lives are lived and experienced in unique ways, there is a general pattern to the growth process by which the helpless newborn develops into a competently functioning adult. Human development proceeds through a series of related stages in each of which certain challenges are met, certain tasks accomplished that build on what has gone before and prepare for what will come later.

The newborn must adjust to life outside the womb while having his physiological needs satisfied by someone who thus becomes important enough to him to be recognizable. The baby must then gradually separate himself as a psychological entity from that all-important caretaking figure and feel secure enough to venture out into a gradually expanding world on his own, exploring and experimenting little by little as he touches, tries, moves away, comes back, tries again, and gradually achieves control over his body and his feelings in ways that make it possible for him to feel like a self, to connect with others, to form a realistic picture of the world around him—to love and to learn.

The Child

He will go to school, his world will widen to include relatives and friends, he will move further into understanding and achievement, his body—and with it his mind—will change from that of a child to that of a youth and he will decide who he is going to be as an emerging adult.

What he is like, what kind of life he chooses to live, who he decides to live it with, and what kind of work he will want to do, will be the outcomes of a process begun before his physiological birth, partly determined by genetic factors and constitutional givens, and continued through the experience of interacting with his environment. The process is never the progress of a straight line, never without problems, setbacks, conflicts. In fact, it is the resolution of those conflicts encountered in the interaction with his environment that makes of him a person. In the earliest years of life that environment is the family, in the earliest weeks and months, his mother (or whoever mothers him).

Up close, there are no clear demarcations between the stages of life. One is not an infant one day, a toddler the next. But standing back and taking a broader perspective, it is possible to see consecutive stages that, while they do not occur at specific ages that are the same for everyone, do follow each other in an order that is pretty much the same for everyone. The sequence, not the timing, is what is the same, and is what we can talk about knowing it will apply to all children. Certain potentials, then, exist for the biological and psychological development of the human being, although that development will be different for males and females, will be affected by other inborn characteristics as well, and is capable of enormous variation in response to conditions met with in the environment from the moment of leaving the mother's body and proceeding through their mutual experience as it prepares him to meet the rest of the family and eventually the rest of the world.

When we talk about the process of human development we are talking about the development of character, the sum of all those things that make us uniquely human and uniquely our individual selves. The most convenient way to chart its course seems to be in terms of those recognizable stages of psychobiological growth, mind and body being closely related throughout life and inextricably intertwined at its beginning. Understanding what happens as the child progresses from one set of capacities to a greater one—how growing up proceeds in general—should give parents an idea of what kinds of difference they can make in their children's lives and how.

The general outlines of maturation are programmed into the genetic code. Most of what we see grownups capable of as we move around our world will take place anyway—they learn to walk, and talk, and feed themselves, and at some point have left their mothers and fathers behind. They've gone to school, they've learned some kind of work, they have children of their own. It is not necessary to be aware of the subtleties of human development in order to be a child or raise one without disastrous results. It is *optimal* development that is at issue here—what *kind* of self we want our children to develop.

Even assuming a shared set of values that includes independent thought and affection for others, the ability to wait and plan for desirable goals, to enjoy achievement and withstand disappointment, we can say it will be created to a gratifying degree in the average expectable situation of most families in the late twentieth-century middle-class American culture in which this book is being written and will be read.

Raising children doesn't require a great degree of special knowledge or baptism in the waters of theoretical science. The reason for making available to mothers and fathers a description and an explanation of what goes on in the early life of their sons and daughters is that parents are being assured it doesn't matter who cares for their children, that women are being told there are more significant means to self-realization, more durable sources of pride in oneself than taking a hand in shaping babies into the boys and girls who will become adults both like and unlike their parents.

The reason for choosing to view young children's growth from a psychological perspective is that psychological factors are those over which we have a crucial influence as parents in determining the form our children's natures take, and emotional growth has a determining influence on other aspects of development—aspects that actually require less of a direct contribution from parental presence and therefore are not the ones most in need of being called attention to at a time when parents are being told their presence in their children's lives is somehow superfluous.

Physical maturation, as charted in developmental studies like those of Gesell,[1] and cognitive development, as described and analyzed by Piaget,[2] will come about in the normal course of things as long as a child's emotional growth is not interfered with. When children are hungry—for food or stimulation—it's obvious. They tell us. And as long as we feed them and answer their questions appropriately they'll grow in size and intelligence as long as there's no obstruction introduced via their not always equally obvious emotional needs.

These are best met in the ongoing process by which a sense of separate selfhood gradually replaces a strong bond with a caring mother. The process involves both the establishment of a clear identification with the parent of the same sex and the internalization of both parents' rules of behavior, and adds up to what we mean when we speak of a person's character.

Of course, it is in feeding and teaching (which means teaching things like toileting as well as things like talking) that much of the relating between parents and children takes place. But other things are going on during that relating that make it not at all a matter of indifference who gives the daily bread or the nightly milk, who reads the story, fixes the toy, explains six "whys" in a row with patience—and even who gets moderately impatient sometimes, so that not a terror of being abandoned but a mild disquiet at one's behavior (but not one's self) being disapproved of bothers one. It is this feeling that leads to the need to make the rules of those one loves and needs—the givers of milk and stories, of help and hugs—one's own rules, so as to be surer of them. This is surely not a process to be left to the efforts of just anyone.

And yet the received wisdom of the day seems to be that having given birth to children, we can safely leave their development in the hands of others, that Utopia will have arrived when every woman has a job in an office and a day-care center looks after her child.

We cannot say that group child rearing is an unequivocal evil. Compared to what? Some children of our urban slums are better off at home with their own mothers taking care of them than they would be in any alternative setup, and to provide aid for these dependent children would seem to be in the interests of society as a whole. It depends on the mothers and the children. Others, there is no doubt, are at risk for their emotional if not their physical health, and might better be cared for by neutral strangers than demented kin. Most ordinary middle-class couples can give their infants and young children more of what they need at home in a family than anyone else can provide for them anywhere else. Yet there are voices raised on every side demanding "alternative" arrangements to the traditional family, not for those who cannot afford child care, economically or emotionally, but for those who can.

It depends, of course, on what you want—what kind of life, what kind of children.[3] Capturing the next generation has always been the most obvious way of changing the world. It has been tried with varying degrees of success, depending on how Draconian the measures one is prepared to adopt. A totalitarian system has the best chance of success. And even in a democracy, those who have no faith in the ability of the system to balance and to regulate itself have the best chance of doing away with all perceivable distinctions and imposing uniformity of outcome throughout the society if they can succeed in removing children from the traditional family as early as possible. For there is no doubt that in the traditional nuclear family—a masculine man and a feminine woman (of course, he can be a dancer and she can be a corporation counsel—what matters is how they feel about their own sexuality and each other's and not what kind of jobs they do) who have combined their lives to their mutual satisfaction and want to raise children who will be much like them and live much as they do—there is a deep attachment between child and parents that breeds rivalries and conflicts, desires and ambitions, and it is in the reconciliation of these that an autonomous self is forged.[4] That self can care for others and plan for the future, is not afraid of trying to understand and tame nature, values independent thought and action. In short, old-fashioned. The virtues, we have been told, associated with capitalism and with the bourgeoisie. Yes, middle class. Virtues to be given a long, hard look before we discard them in the name either of greater self-fulfillment or greater altruism.

The media today routinely present us with all the latest ideas in alternative methods of arranging children's lives, from lesbian-couple parenthood to parents and children sharing the same bed.[5] For the many mothers and fathers—actual, past, or to-be—who ask themselves, does this really make any sense, what are the changes that have value for our lives as families, what should I take seriously as a mother or a father, this book suggests some things to think about as they think about being parents.

Before Birth: Nature and Choice

Even before birth, parents begin to make decisions that will affect their first encounter with their child: where to give birth, in what setting and with what kind of assistance, by what method and followed by what kind of arrangements. Faced with alternatives ranging from birth at home with the rest of the family looking on, to unconscious passivity in a machinery-filled operating room; with choosing between care at the hands of an obstetrician—and of which sex?—and a midwife; between a hospital that is close to home and one that encourages the presence and participation of fathers during labor and delivery; between a doctor affiliated with a prestigious medical center and one on the staff of a hospital that arranges for babies to room in with their mothers, how is a young couple to decide?

These are the first of many dilemmas parents will face in a world that has changed fast enough to offer them an array of choices, a feast of possibilities, and changed too fast for them to have inherited a tradition for deciding, a context in which to choose automatically. Their best help will lie in understanding something of the nature of the various alternatives—how did they come about and how do they work?—and putting that together with their understanding of themselves. What wishes and what fears do they bring to the situation, and what kinds of places and people do they feel most comfortable with?

Childbirth is one of the many human experiences that has had its history rewritten in recent years to suit a political agenda. Militant feminists have argued in books and articles that a male-dominated medical establishment has robbed women of the joy of giving birth by defining it as a medical event requiring drugs and surgical interventions that preclude a woman's active participation and reduce her to a passive object of their authoritarian ministrations. It is a somewhat jaundiced view of what has actually taken place over the centuries and what it has meant and can mean to birthing women and their husbands.[6]

Even a cursory review of the history of childbirth practices shows a striking improvement in the prospects for women and their babies. The fact is that until the last century in Western industrialized societies—as still today in numerous less developed parts of the world—most women had good reason to fear dying in childbirth and even more reason to fear that even if their babies were born alive they would have at best only an even chance of surviving infancy.

Medical science and technology have changed all that. As a gradual understanding of female anatomy and of the birth process itself replaced medieval religious strictures against observing or examining women's bodies, surgery replaced sorcery at the bedside as science began to replace superstition generally.

Nature, for all its seeming care for the race, can be notoriously careless of the individual. It can afford to win a few and lose a few. In approximately one out of five labors and deliveries some kind of complication occurs. Until about four hundred years ago most of these, in the absence of either the understanding or the tools to deal with them, were fatal, either to mother or infant. In the sixteenth century, the development of techniques for dealing with abnormal fetal positions made it possible for the first time to remove a living child from a living mother in such situations. With the invention of the obstetrical forceps and the development of Caesarean surgery, even more mothers and infants were guaranteed survival.

The professionalization of medicine meant requirements for training and the imposition of standards for midwives, male and female, as well as physicians and surgeons, but many women continued to die of puerperal fever, the infection commonly known as childbed fever. Until a little more than a hundred years ago, no woman giving birth, no man who loved her and whose child she carried, was free from the haunting specter of sudden death after giving birth.

Pasteur's discovery of the cause of bacterial infections and Lister's establishment of the principle of antisepsis in surgery around 1880 led to the identification and control of the fatal microbe. Medical science had changed women's lives forever by freeing them from the danger of dying in childbirth. Its next contribution was to free them from the necessity of suffering in childbirth. Anesthesia was welcomed in the nineteenth century as the greatest blessing women had ever enjoyed. Not until a century later was it described as a curse.

What had happened in the intervening century to make this difference? As with all changes in the way we perceive the world and our place in it, more had been learned and changes in technology and in economic and social patterns had brought new ways of putting that learning to use. Increasingly special skills and sophisticated equipment dealing with the frequent and inevitable complications of labor and delivery had resulted in moving birth from the home to the hospital, where most women were only too glad to be relieved of the effort and pain involved in having babies. But as pediatrics began to develop in tandem with obstetrics, it became increasingly clear to doctors and nurses dealing with newborns that babies who were born to medicated mothers were themselves affected. Heavily sedated mothers gave birth to drugged babies.

Except in occasional and extreme cases, these effects were reversible, and sometimes, in complicated and difficult births, sedation was the lesser of evils, making it possible to employ surgical techniques that meant survival. By and large, though, neonatologists, the pediatric subspecialists dealing with newborns, brought the news to obstetricians and their birthing patients that babies were better off, more alert and responsive, when they were born to mothers who had not been given analgesics or anesthetics that crossed the placental barrier and entered the babies' bloodstream. One result was the development of techniques for blocking only local areas of the mother's body by means of regional anesthetics. While still relieving her of pain, this left a woman conscious, although still something less than a full participant, some felt, in the birth process.

The movement for a return to what was perhaps misleadingly called "natural" childbirth began in England in the 1930s under the banner of a crusading obstetrician named Grantly Dick-Read, who held that most of the pain experienced by women in childbirth was the result of tension caused by fear and ignorance. By teaching them how to breathe and relax during labor he thought he would alleviate the fear-tension-pain syndrome.

His inspirational books[7] attracted many women, but unfortunately his ideas and techniques did not work for many of them. Either some of the pain experienced in childbirth is a physical inevitability or some women were not relieved of their fears by Dick-Read's methods. It remained for a Frenchman, Dr. Fernand Lamaze, to develop a method whereby a kind of mind control could take the place of pharmaceutical supports for many laboring women. A system of conditioned-reflex techniques, the Lamaze method consists mainly of breathing exercises which focus the woman's concentration elsewhere during labor contractions (a kind of mind-over-mater technique) and also involve the husband as a participant, as a sort of coach to his wife's strenuous efforts, thus not so incidentally providing her with the further psychological support of companionship and encouragement.

Today the Lamaze method of psychoprophylactic pain relief is widely used in American hospitals, with some flexibility as to how, and until what point, it remains the method of choice. It is always possible to provide pharmacological relief for the woman who decides she wants it at any stage. It is that flexibility that probably is the method's greatest asset and accounts for its popularity. It does alleviate anxiety, it can help many women, but—and this is the essential thing—no one technique for dealing with any experience in life can be successful, or even appropriate, for everyone. And particularly is this so in the case of such an enormously meaningful, emotionally charged experience as the events surrounding birth.

Every woman will bring to the way she experiences those events her own fantasies, the buried wishes and fears of her unique mental life, shaped by all her years up to now. For some women the important thing will be to feel in control, to participate as fully and to be as aware as possible in every moment of the birthing process. For others, anxieties may be so overwhelming as to interfere with the physiological processes and beyond being affected by techniques that may work for another woman. Still other women's muscles, or their pelvic structures, may have as much influence as another's principles or fears. And, while some men may want very much to be part of the birth experience and to share their wives' feelings and relieve their discomforts, others may be repelled by the sights and sounds and smells of the delivery room or perceive the request for their participation in the experience as a reproachful demand that they assume their share of the agony.

What matters as much as the choice that is made is the reason for making it, the feelings that surround it. And the trouble with so much of the "natural childbirth" propaganda is that it ignores the natural differences between people.

It also falsifies reality, romanticizing the idea of nature as though everything that happens without human interference is benign, as though tornadoes, cancers, and birth anomalies were not natural. The fantasy is of a lost past of innocence and ease in which everything came about with no effort on our part, and all was bliss. Even infancy is not quite like that—only the fantasy of infancy that underlies utopias and according to which if we would only throw out all the machines and go back to preindustrial ways of arranging our lives, our address would be Arcadia, our landscape that of the Garden of Eden before the fall.

After all, what is more "natural" about man's vulnerability to myriad forms of suffering and disaster than about his capacity to improve his lot, the species-specific ability to make life a little better in every succeeding age? A good deal of the bedrock of human nature, as of all nature, is wild and potentially dangerous, so, yes, we still have wars and poverty and injustice; but we also have peace and plenty and justice. It depends on whether you see the cup as half-full or half-empty. "Natural" seems a pretty neutral term, applying as it does to aggression and sacrifice, greed and generosity, ugliness and beauty. It just means what's there, and if we limit what we find acceptable to what was there before man began to tame himself and his world, we would surely throw out a good deal of what makes life pleasurable, meaningful, even bearable, to most of us. Used as it is by the antitechnology forces, it means nothing at all, except "what I like."

The problem is to resist the dehumanizing effects that technological means and political ends can have on our lives without at the same time depriving ourselves and our children of the ways in which man's scientific imagination and the achievements of his invention have conquered disease, prolonged life, and made it possible to live in ways that even our great-grandparents could only dream of.

A nice example is the fetal heart monitor, a device that, by means of wires attached to electric sensors placed on a laboring woman's abdomen, transmits electrical impulses to a screen and records them, making it possible to keep track of both the woman's uterine contractions and her unborn baby's heartbeat. Monitoring the relationship between changing patterns of contractions and fetal heart rate makes it possible to pick up signs of impending distress and to take appropriate measures in time to save the baby from damage or even death.

This seems like a miraculous gift when we remember the frequency with which the umbilical cord becomes tangled around the fetus and how many babies deprived of oxygen were stillborn in the past because there was often no way to tell what was happening *in utero* until it was too late. Our technology makes possible both prediction and intervention, ways of spotting trouble and doing something about it that can mean the difference between a stillbirth and a live one, a brain-damaged baby and a healthy one.

Yet vociferous critics of hospital childbirth charge the use of machines in the birth process is "dehumanizing," "demoralizing if not demeaning," only "an extra bit of insurance that is unnecessary in normal birth,"[8] ignoring the fact that we cannot tell ahead of time which births will be normal. There are always some cases of unforeseen complications, events that occur suddenly in the natural birth process that could not be predicted. To most women and men, the important thing is to have a healthy baby, and whatever contributes to that end is what is most truly human.

In the past a woman expected to bear many children, some of whom would live and some of whom would die, as she might herself in giving birth to them. Today, most couples have babies by intention rather than by chance, they have fewer of them, and we have very high expectations for the survival and health of our offspring. It seems a poor trade-off to forgo the safety a hospital can provide, not only by means of monitoring but because of the proximity of many other kinds of equipment and the availability of people trained to use it, in those instances when something does go wrong.

There is a built-in tendency in hospitals and among some doctors to intervene and to offer help, not only to avert clear physical danger but to prevent it. This is understandable; it's what medical people know how to do—to improve, prevent, control the possibilities, dangers, outcomes they've been trained to assess. Sometimes they even overdo it, are too quick to administer anesthesia or perform surgery on a woman who may be willing and able to cope with the stress, in which case the intervention is unnecessary and in some cases may even be harmful. But obstetricians are increasingly aware of women's emotional needs in childbirth as well as their physical ones, and it is no longer impossible or even difficult for expectant parents to involve themselves in the decision making about their baby's birth, to expect to be consulted, enlightened, and heeded by their doctor. But this implies a responsibility as well as an expectation. Mothers- and fathers-to-be will need to inform themselves intelligently if they are to evaluate the recommendations of the medical professional sensibly. Only then can they, parents and professionals, proceed together.

Deciding to have a baby at home, as urged by some members of the now-vanishing counterculture or some feminists who want birth to be "a woman's event," is taking unnecessary risks, and taking them not for oneself but for one's child.

Within the context of hospital delivery, there are many possible choices, which should depend on a woman's—or a couple's, if that is the nature of their relationship—sense of her own needs and desires. Some people care more about their judgment of a specialist's skills as testified to by his position or reputation; others more about the personality at their bedside (always assuming, of course, a certain level of professional competence). As long as the doctor is affiliated with a reputable, accredited maternity department, a woman should follow her own intuitions in choosing. She should not be inhibited about asking whatever questions will make it clear whether parents and physician can talk comfortably about the pregnancy and have similar expectations of the arrangements for labor and delivery. A certain flexibility is probably the best touchstone to look for at first. No one, however expert, can reasonably advocate the same regimen for every individual, and since an obstetrician is neither psychiatrist nor lover he can't count on a particularly deep understanding of each woman, what she wants and what she needs, but only on his willingness to adapt to these as they reveal themselves in the months before and then in the heat of battle.

And it is a battle, for both mother and child, this wild expulsion of a part of oneself and this rude exposure to new elements, which is why it's so important to arrange it in ways that suit the individual—despite whatever it is the latest issues of the women's magazines are recommending.

Increasing numbers of hospitals and maternity clinics are providing midwife services with backup by physicians. Many also encourage husbands to stay with their wives during labor and some allow them in the delivery room as well. If that is what a couple wants—both of them, not just one—it's worth holding out for, but no one should be made to feel inadequate, a failure, that something unique and irrevocable has been missed, for not having labored without any medication, been wide awake during delivery, had her husband beside her while giving birth, or handled the infant immediately following birth. Each of these can be an exciting experience for some women and some men—but not all. The trouble is that too often the inspirational rhetoric with which a new trend is presented in the media—and sometimes even in the professional literature—makes it seem as though there is only one way to do things authentically.

The most recent of these trends is "bonding," the idea that a unique attachment is formed between a mother and an infant (father, too, if he's in on it) who have body-to-body contact immediately after birth, the baby being placed on the mother's abdomen while the umbilical cord is cut and before being taken away to be cleaned up and weighed and measured.

There is no doubt that some women (and men) have found this moment, in the phrase most often quoted, "a high." In the exhilaration of the moment, the first sight and feel of one's child may produce an even greater surge of joy than if that first sight and feel takes place a few hours later. There's really no way to tell. What is certain, however, is that this moment does not, as some enthusiasts would have us believe, influence the nature of the mother-child relationship forever. The analogy with attachment behavior in certain species of animals that must "imprint" to their mothers at certain critical moments or be rejected, abandoned to a fate in which they are not loved or taught, is totally unjustified.

In the studies of "maternal-infant bonding,"[9] the impoverished and emotionally immature mothers considered at risk for maternal attachment who did well by their babies after being permitted to "bond" with them in the moments after birth, might, for all we know, have been responding to the first empathic attention they themselves had ever received. Figures of authority had sent them a kind of valentine, a message that told them their babies—and they themselves—were important enough to be paid attention to. There may even be other factors influencing the researchers' results, such as their strong interest in what those results should be.

In any case, human beings are not birds or cats. They have a vastly wider repertoire of responses, and many chances to form attachments, to learn to love, to learn to learn, before all is lost. Many times in the early weeks, months, and even years of life, there will be opportunities for bonds to be forged between parent and child. Many of them will be missed, inevitably. Many more of them will be fulfilled, in the various, differing, eccentric ways that human beings have of connecting with each other. To say that any one moment, even of such heightened intensity as having just given birth, is irreplaceable, is to do parents and their children a great disservice.

A woman doesn't become a certain kind of mother because of any one experience but because of the kind of woman she is. We spend a lifetime practicing to be parents, so that we can begin to help our children become people in their own right, and, eventually, parents themselves. We have a great effect on what they will be like, and for most of us throughout history, it's our crack at creativity as well as immortality. Raising children is probably the most effective form of social action in which most of us will ever engage, and understanding how they grow and learn and become individuals, and what we contribute to that process and in what ways, should make us proud and ambitious, for ourselves and for them. Very little that most men and women do in the work force, or even in the arts, is as satisfying or makes as much difference.

Parenthood and the family are in bad repute these days, but those who say they are not still the organizing experience of most lives do not understand most men and women. Those who talk about "freeing" men and women from each other and from their children can offer little that is not sterile as an alternative, although there is a great deal in life that can be enjoyed *in addition.*

Assuming, then, that having babies is not a doctrinal affair, undertaken and carried out so as to prove something, but a choice made in full understanding that we will have to do some hard things, make some sacrifices, give up some dreams we may not even know we've had until they are disappointed, and somehow end up with a full harvest of remembered pleasure and pain—which is what it is to be alive—it's clear that thinking as parents begins long before the birth of a child. The arrangements made grow out of your character, reflect your tastes and values, express your hopes. So will being parents.

If one doctor seems too impersonal, one hospital unnecessarily regimented and routinized, look for another. Where you first meet your child, and how you're feeling at the time, will not necessarily set the tone of the rest of your life together, but it can make it more pleasant, at the time and in memory, and every increase in joy in life that's not paid too much for should be welcome. By the same token, when friends or experts tell you one way is best, don't believe them. Ask them, best for whom?

With a little self-understanding, a little common sense, and a little luck, you'll have chosen a way of having your baby—with an obstetrician or a midwife, in a medical center or a maternity clinic, medicated or awake, rooming in or resting up—that suited you. If so, it will probably have suited the baby, too, because in the days and weeks following birth the human infant is relatively insulated from the outside world, aware at first, as far as we can tell, only of an inner state of comfort or discomfort, satisfaction or need. He cries to indicate his disequilibrium, until his needs are taken care of from an outside he cannot clearly distinguish from what's inside of him. The mediator between his sensations and the outside world, the gratifier of needs, the assuager of hunger, cold, and nameless discomfort, is a mother. It sometimes has to be—and certainly can without disastrous results be—someone other than a baby's biological mother. It can even be several people. But there are many reasons why the optimal situation is usually one loving person, and most often the mother. The reasons why this is so will become clear as we look at how the baby develops from the somnolent creature carried home from the hospital to the active toddler and eventually the confident individual ready to go off to school for part of the day.

IN DEFENSE OF THE FAMILY

The Newborn: Attachment and Awareness

Psychoanalysis has made up for its sins of omission on the subject of adolescence, leading us to believe that the *only* course of development through those years was one of turbulence and active rebellion, disorder and early sorrow, *Sturm und Drang,* by telling us more than we have learned from any other source about infant development. This has been largely because the psychoanalytic view of adolescence was derived from observation of a patient population, neurotics observed in treatment, while in the last several decades a number of thoughtful and sensitive observers have studied normal babies and young children, watching to see how they behave in order to put together the likeliest story of how they feel, begin to think, and meet the problems they face in the ways that eventually define their characters.

There have been a number of theoreticians carrying on the radical revision of our understanding of human nature and human development begun by Freud, and if what they have provided are myths, because they are unprovable—we can no more see the id, the ego, and the superego than we can see Perseus, the Medusa, or Persephone—they haunt our thinking and prove viable because they enrich our understanding and lead to new ways of seeing what we find around us and even to finding things we didn't know were there. These myths tell us more that we can make use of than all of the factor analysis of statistical studies of what can be reduced to numbers in order to be measured. But they don't help us very much in providing rules for actions with regard to our daily lives with our children. They are of an order of truth so general as to be symbolic rather than descriptive in terms of everyday life.

Witness the confusions they have been used to justify, the contradictions they have spawned, the warring schools that all claim them as their foundation. This is not because the theories of psychoanalysis are not true, but because they are complicated, and they have been preempted and distorted by those who want clarity and simplicity more than anything else. Despite Freud's tragic view of the inevitability with which we must pay for what we value most in civilization with what we long for most in the life of our instincts, despite the fact that if psychoanalysis says anything it says that all mental life is based on conflict, psychoanalysis has been used to justify a permissive child rearing in which frustration is avoided as much as possible, and a progressive education in which imposing standards and making demands are avoided as much as possible.[10] We have seen the results in recent years of the popularization of these programs, as children who could not respect their parents grew into grownups who could not respect themselves but thought the rest of the world should do so anyway.

But if distortions of psychoanalytic theory have a lot to answer for, the discipline itself has given us, both from within its ranks and from among those it has informed in other fields, a way of seeing what happens in the early years of life between children and their parents that explains much of what those children will start life like.

It is the nature of scientific creativity, unlike the legendary loneliness of the artist, to begin where others are and go on from there. One builds on what is already there, the work of those who were there before. In choosing to describe the vicissitudes of the first three years of life in the scheme developed by a particular observer, Margaret S. Mahler, and her colleagues, it has to be made clear that their work[11] seems to be the best synthesis of everything we have learned up to now, seen and organized in ways that are fresh and original, but that it builds on the works of many others and therefore includes them, if for no other reason than that they showed where to look, and often where to dig, for the buried treasure that has come to light in the last half-century of psychoanalytically-informed observational studies of children.[12]

Many theorists began by looking at abnormality—at infants in institutions whose basic physical needs were met but who failed to thrive and eventually died; at children who were locked in a private prison of autism the walls of which could not be penetrated and from which they could not be rescued—and found that asking what was missing suggested what it was that was present in the average expectable environment. Others started out by observing children in normal settings and gradually putting together a sketch, if not a blueprint, of the structuring of the individual character.

Observing babies—in hospitals, at home, in nurseries—watching, listening, feeling empathically; comparing and contrasting what has been observed and what has been made of it; neither ignoring nor relying too much on abstract research tools like rating scales and tests, a pattern has emerged. The pattern has grown out of the observations, has not been imposed from the outside or dictated by theoretical considerations. Where facts do not fit theory, theory has to be abandoned or revised.[13]

The pattern is, briefly, one of a gradual process of change from undifferentiated union with the mother who feeds and cares for the baby, to a sense of individuation—a separate identity for the child that becomes the basis for an independent life. What parents do in the normal course of family life is to gradually facilitate the utterly dependent child's separation and individuation, not just physical but psychological. It is this process, the gradual acquisition of a separate sense of self, that Mahler refers to as the second or psychological birth of the infant. How that self is defined, how the little boy or girl thinks of himself or herself, is the basis of character and sets a style of feeling and thinking that persists, with some modifications, through life.

The newborn baby seems hardly to know he has left the inside of his mother's body. He remains asleep most of the time, waking for gradually longer and longer periods but at first only when some discomfort—he is hungry, he is cold, he is wet—rouses him. When his tension has been relieved—he has been fed, warmed, changed—he falls asleep again. Perhaps because his pleasurable relief is associated with being held and touched, such physical comfort and stimulation gradually becomes one of his desires, which at this age is the same as one of his needs. He cries when he needs something. It is the only language he has for signaling his distress, and how soon and how effectively his cries are responded to and his needs met is his first indication of what the world is like. His global feelings do not yet distinguish between himself, the mother who soothes him, and everything beyond, and he/all is either good and warm and pleasant or awful and uncomfortable. It is this general feeling at this early stage of undifferentiated awareness that according to Erikson[14] lays the basis for a sense of trust or of mistrust later in life. The baby seems to be protected from too much stimulation from the outside by his drowsy state and from too much stimulation from the inside—strong feelings of hunger or pain—by the ministrations of his mother.

Several things follow from this state of things. For one, his cries are the only way he has of reaching out for help, so totally helpless is the human infant at first. They are signals of need and should be met fairly promptly and effectively. No young infant can be "spoiled" by being picked up, rocked, fed, wrapped when he cries. He is not just exercising his will any more than he is just exercising his lungs, and he is incapable of conceiving or concluding who is "boss." What he needs at this stage is not training but satisfaction of his primitive needs and reassurance that he will not be overwhelmed by sensations beyond his control.

Now, it is not always clear to even the most sensitive parent just what the newborn's cry is *for.* Can he be wet already, hungry again, is he wanting release from some vague pain that disappears when he is touched or held? Until he is able to tell her himself, only experience can tell a mother what a baby wants, a question that has been raised as frequently as that more familiar query of our day about what it is a woman wants. As Freud well knew when he made his rueful little joke, never dreaming the trouble it would cause his more literal followers, the answer can only be another question: Which one? When? The only way to guess what someone wants when they can't tell us is to extrapolate from whatever it is we do know about them, to think of what has gone before, to read the language of their gestures, to put ourselves in their place. This is what a mother does with her baby, and eventually she gets to understand his language, know his cries, distinguish his needs—not all the time, but a lot of the time. The baby is giving her cues, and she is responding to them and cuing him back by doing so, letting him know the world is a good place. Your cries get answered, help comes. Pleasure, on the whole, outweighs displeasure.

Because a newborn baby is clearly unable to differentiate one comforting person, one soothing voice, one set of helping hands from another, it can be said with a certain justice that it doesn't matter who takes care of him at this point, as long as the care is given appropriately. It must also be said, though, that it is by practicing the care she takes of him that a mother gets to know her baby, understand his cues, and establish the mutuality that will enable her to meet his needs now and also form the basis for their following encounters.

So while these earliest weeks are a time when a mother can have someone else stand in for her if she travels, works, or turns her attention to other aspects of her life and leaves the infant's care in other hands, without affecting the baby to the degree that her absence from his daily life will have at other times in the next two or three years, it does deprive them both of the earliest opportunity to start the give-and-take, the ongoing conversation that will define their relationship, the mutual equilibrium in which the shaping of the baby's self begins.

In the early weeks the long periods of dim awareness are punctuated by fleeting states of alertness[15] in which the baby begins to respond to sights and sounds around him—particularly the face and voice of his mother as she holds and soothes and feeds him. At around two months she will notice his first smile.[16] And sometime around four or five months he begins to smile specifically at the sound of her voice and the sight of her face—his first social interaction, and his first rudimentary distinction between what is out there and what is inside him. As a delighted mother bobs her head and coos at the smiling infant, she is starting the processes that will someday lead to language learning and even to falling in love—but they are still a way off. It's enough to say at this point that vestiges of this mutuality between mother and infant that Mahler calls the symbiotic phase will persist throughout the life cycle.

The baby's "mother smile," the specific sign that he has differentiated one face, one voice, from everything else, is the sign that a bond

has been established between them. The baby has been kept free
enough from tension—comfortable enough inside—so that his available energy does not have to be used to insulate himself from the
outside world but is free to pay attention to the things around him—
his mother's eyes as she feeds him, a wisp of her hair his fingers have
found and become tangled in, the feel of a blanket, the color of a
stuffed animal, the sound of a rattle. As he spends more time in a
state of alert awareness, he finds more to notice and respond to, to
stroke, push, pull, kick away. He will eventually become aware of the
effect his actions have on things out there, and begin to construct
a sense of separate self.

Awareness at this stage is sensorimotor; neither thoughts nor feelings are capable yet of being distinguished from what the little body
does, how it acts and is acted upon. His experience of life now is
shaped by how his mother holds him, the way he snuggles up to her,
her style of soothing him. The way he experiences pleasure now is
taken over and incorporated into later modes of pleasure seeking—
whether through contact with others or through autoerotic activity,
for instance. Patterns are being laid down for the infant who is comforted by being held and for the one who is left to cry and eventually
learns to comfort himself by rocking or finds other internal means
for shutting out the unfriendly outside world.

There is also a strong constitutional factor at work that predisposes
different infants to different degrees and kinds of comforting. Some
babies are harder to soothe than others, more irritable, slower to calm
down. Some like being sung to and others like being rocked. Some
eat more or sleep less than others, or show the usual sequence of developmental events at different times than others. Many of these differences are genetic in origin, which is one reason, in addition to the
different characters of mothers, why no one can prescribe a specific
regimen for all babies. Only care that is responsive to a baby's
own needs, his own nature, will lead to the optimal development
of his capacities. Anyone can feed him and he will survive. Various
hands can cope with him in scattershot ways and he may even
do pretty well. But for him to thrive, to become everything he can

be, he will need the environment created by responsive mothering.

What this means, of course, is not necessarily always a baby's biological mother. Some women, for reasons of temperament or necessity, are unable to care for their very young children on a daily basis. Ideally, they will look for and be able to find a substitute who will provide empathic and consistent care in their place. In cases where a woman's emotional makeup or life circumstances make it undesirable or impossible for her to care for her own baby, we all know this would be the best alternative. We also know how difficult it is to achieve in reality. And if it's asking a lot to find a good mother substitute, how much more unlikely is it that any institution, private or public, nursery or day-care center, can provide the kind of consistently sensitive care young children need for their best development?

Group arrangements and "professional" care (whatever that can possibly mean in the most intimate of human relationships) may be preferable to a child's fate at the hands of a parent so immature that, never having had her own infantile needs met, she is unable to meet those of her child. Unfortunately, the physical capacity to conceive and bear children is not always accompanied by the emotional capacity to nurture them. Looking for what they still long for themselves, some parents deeply resent the demands an infant makes and may turn on it or away from it.[17]

Abusive or neglectful parents are the only ones whose children are really better off in other hands and other homes, for the very reason that most of us should hesitate to relinquish their care in their earliest years: It is in the shaping that takes place in those years that we influence our children's characters. This process of becoming himself by means of how he accepts and rejects what he perceives of his parents through their daily care of him is already well under way by the time a baby first smiles at his own mother and father (about whom, more later).

The Child

The First Three Years: The Awakening Self

By around the middle of his first year the baby is engaged in exploring his own body and the faces and objects around him, beginning to distinguish the familiar from the unfamiliar. He studies his fingers, grabs for his mother's necklace, laughs at the face that appears and disappears above him in a game of peek-a-boo.[18] He begins to prefer one special object that can stand in for his mother when she is not there, a blanket or a toy that seems to comfort him when she cannot.[19] For, of course, no mother can be there every single moment, nor can any mother provide constant and complete satisfaction, an expectation that is not only unrealistic but not even desirable. Little disappointments and minor frustrations are as much a part of experience as pleasure and fulfillment.

They shouldn't be sought out on principle or used to rationalize arrangements clearly not to a baby's advantage when they're avoidable, though, because nature and necessity do a good enough job of providing them for us. They are inevitable, and it is in coping with those that are givens in the human condition that we become most human and most our individual selves. Propping a bottle, constantly giving a baby an inanimate object for company in place of oneself, putting him in front of the moving and distracting images on a television screen, are ways of depriving him of what he needs most— stimulation and soothing, when he needs them, in a human context. Letting him find his own means of comfort—usually he chooses a cuddly object that gives him tactile pleasure—that makes him feel less alone, serves as a stay against the confusion of feelings that seem to threaten him when mother is gone—has a different meaning. A use of the imagination to meet the inevitable can be a step toward becoming a person. Accepting what is thrust on one to make up for an avoidable deprivation is not.

Much of what the baby sees and responds to in those early months is connected with the act of feeding, the child's main activity during

51

the time he spends awake and alert. While many mothers and their babies find breast-feeding a uniquely gratifying experience, the significant factor is really the contact between mother and child. And this can take place just as satisfactorily with bottle feeding, providing the baby is held and talked to, feels his mother's encircling arms, and sees her responsive face. No woman should be made to feel inadequate because she does not or cannot breast-feed her infant, as long as the feeding situation itself is one of mutual pleasure.

From being a student of his mother's face, the baby goes on to a perusal of the others who move in and out of his orbit and, some time around eight or nine months (as always, with great individual variations in timing and intensity), the curiosity with which he undertakes this inspection leads to a distinct apprehension in the presence of unfamiliar people. This "stranger anxiety" is a sign that he recognizes his mother as a uniquely important person, she who gives pleasures and relieves pains; he has made a cognitive distinction as well as an emotional one.

Again, there is no prescription for how to "handle" or respond to this phenomenon beyond a tolerance based on an understanding that it is developmentally appropriate. In general, babies whose experience has been more happy than not up to now in the emotional climate created by their interaction with their mothers, will find their curiosity and confidence gradually overtake their apprehension. Letting it happen seems to be all a parent can do in these early stages of life—facilitating growth, not interfering with unfolding capacities.

This precludes extremes of indulgence as much as of frustration. The mother who regards her infant as part of herself and keeps him close to her body despite signs that he would like to begin to move away is no more responding to a reading of the child's own needs than one who fails to come when he cries. At the most extreme, these behaviors lead to pathology, in the one case to a child who fails to establish a separate sexual identity from that of the body from which he hasn't had a chance to differentiate his own;[20] in the other to a child who may shut out completely the outside world that has proved so unresponsive.[21]

The Child

The implication here is not that every moment is fraught with danger for the developing infant but that a mother who uses common sense in applying a general understanding of how a child's development proceeds from one phase to another, growing out of and leading into past solutions and new opportunities, will, more often than not, hit on what works for her and for her child. Most mothers do so, and even without benefit of experts to tell them how. The great danger—aside from those tragic but infrequent extremes that create pathology no one can prevent by precept because it grows out of existing pathology until the chain is broken somehow—is that women stop listening to the voice of their own reason and what Bruno Bettelheim calls "the informed heart" and listen instead to the voices that assure them there is something more important than caring for their own children in the earliest months and years when the bedrock of character is formed and ways of feeling about oneself and others, of seeing the world and moving in it, are given shape in the relationship between the child and who he perceives as taking care of him.

Is there? Is there really much that most women find to do in the work force that is worth giving up shaping the next generation for? Some women have to work; their life circumstances dictate the necessity. That fact is bound to make some difference in how their children perceive their absence as well as how they themselves feel about it. They may regret it but will not be defensive or overcompensate by giving objects in place of themselves—offering candy and toys and, later, expensive schools and camps instead of the minutiae of daily care they are not there to provide.

Women who have to work are not making a choice to leave their children to others' hands, and both they and their children know the difference. Later we will talk about some of the kinds of arrangements they can make. Here we will just say that to seek out another individual to take your place in the life of your child may be necessary and sad, or it may be unnecessary and therefore even sadder, but to leave the job to the staff of a day-care center, in any conceivable meaning that phrase may have in reality, is besotted. Looking at the process of growth in the earliest years should make it clearer why.[22]

Having formed a bond with one special person and a clear idea of her as distinct from others and from himself, the baby now begins the process of gradual separation from her. Around the end of his first year he is beginning to be able to move away physically by creeping and crawling, and she lets him go, although she remains in the background for the moment when he will need to look back and see she is still there. She neither pushes him off before he is ready to go nor holds him back, and she remains within reach while he practices his new-found ability to go off on his own and investigate the terrain, and reassures himself that he can end these brief separations when he has had enough. The important thing is that he is leaving, not being left. Six feet away from Mother he is an adventurer, an explorer. But it's a precarious business at best, and even a sudden loud noise may remind him all at once of how small he is, and how far out in alien territory. As long as reinforcements are there, in a mother who is physically present and emotionally available to him, he will refuel and return to the fray—if not right then, soon.

Still inseparably psychobiological, his motor skills and his emotional functions intertwined, he is practicing moving his arms and legs, hands and eyes, at the same time that he is practicing moving away from his mother. And it seems that the more certain he feels that his mother will be there when he remembers and needs to return to her as a home base for emotional refueling,[23] the further and the more often he will be able to venture away from her.

Like all their babies, all mothers are different. And different women have themselves had different experiences, in childhood and all through their lives up to now, that have predisposed them to differing styles of mothering. Some women find the care of the youngest infants tedious, and can't wait for the smiles, the sitting up, the moving away that indicate a growing responsiveness and independence. Others are highly gratified by the sense of oneness with a cuddly infant but become anxious when he seems to move away, afraid he will hurt himself, that he will feel frightened as they themselves do.

We have to start somewhere, and that somewhere is always with the next generation. That means our given is ourselves, as we exist when our children are born, with all our faults and virtues, strengths and weaknesses, talents and understandings as well as the sorrows and envies that intrude themselves into our wishes, our expectations, and our behavior. We cannot change the longings and perspectives that make us uniquely ourselves; in many cases we are not even aware of them. But we can summon from somewhere in our informed hearts the understanding that we are now the adults, responsible for doing the best that we can for our children, which will not always be the easiest thing to do.

We have to cultivate the sympathetic imagination that enables us to adapt to our children's different needs at different stages of their lives, to change from the all-important center of their world who provides all nourishment and comfort to the more peripheral presence who can sit back, while keeping a watchful eye, and encourage those first steps away from us. It's a stance that—not to be confused with abandoning them or ourselves, with not knowing or saying what we want for them and from them—will stand us in good stead in the years to come.

In this first year of life, a mother begins the gradual shift from holding to letting go, as the baby begins the gradual move from her side, transfers his explorations of the world outside him from her person to the objects she provides and then to those he finds for himself. By some invisible and indescribable means he will be aware of her attitudes: whether she is pleased or irritated by what he does, whether she shares his pride in his body or suggests, in her subtle fears for his safety, that there is indeed a lot to be afraid of out there.

LOVING AND DISCOVERING

It seems built into the species that given half a chance we should feel proud of our children and bask in the glow of their accomplishments. Perhaps it is the buried memory of our own "love affair with the world"[24] that makes children so irresistible around the first half of the second year, when they begin to walk and are so full of delight with themselves, their bodies, their growing repertoire of accomplishments. They seem intoxicated with the sheer joy of discovering what they can find and do and make happen.

We intuitively play with their new capacities—the age-old games of peek-a-boo, of swooping them up in our arms as they laughingly try to run away, or hunkering down and holding out our arms for them to run to. Standing upright and walking changes everything. The world takes on new perspective. The little boy discovers not only the horizons beyond but the parameters of himself. He discovers his penis from a new perspective and the pleasurable sensations it affords him. Little girls, less apt to be awed by the sight of their less conspicuous genitals, react differently. But they, too, discover ways of giving themselves pleasure, and masturbation is common in both sexes at this age. It's another manifestation of the urge to explore—in this case, oneself.

Adjustments always have to be made in terms of a mother's character. She is, after all, as human as her child. If knowing that he needs to feel emotionally and not just physically free to move away from her can help her overcome her anxieties, the good of both is served. He is launched on a road he'll need to follow for the rest of his life, increasingly independent in the security that he can cope with what's ahead. And she is less likely to suffer the legacy of regrets that cumulative failure to clear a developmental hurdle causes by making it harder to meet the next one.

But life is not always that simple and if an anxious mother reads that it's important to be there when her child begins to walk she may hover in the background like a cloud of doubt. If she is really made too uncomfortable by his precarious posture and his inclination to knock things over or bump into them, she might do better to bring in a ringer for a time, perhaps another mother to join her as their toddlers bumble about together. In extremis, she might find a substitute for herself in the person of someone almost as familiar to the child—father, grandparent, older sibling, housekeeper. There'll be other stages where she will find herself less threatened and more useful to them both.

Now is when many fathers begin to play a new part in the lives

56

The Child

of their young sons and daughters. Usually more comfortable than mothers with rough-and-tumble play, more easily able to deal with aggression, they begin to be perceived by the young child in a special way, complementary to Mother. The soft and the tough will both become part of the child's nature, and in identifying with two different parents the little girl or boy has a chance to develop more fully the different facets of his or her own nature. Greater intimacy with fathers early in life may also contribute to the affection that has to accompany respect if identification is to follow and take hold.

Moving and thinking are the means by which the toddler "hatches" into a separate individual. In learning to talk and playing games he first makes use of symbolic intelligence, learns how one thing can stand for another and that what he cannot see at the moment has not disappeared forever—his toes in the blanket, his toy over the side of the highchair, his mother in the next room. He wants to know where things are, his mother in particular. He needs to bring her everything he finds, show her everything he can do, be reassured that she still finds him irresistible even though he may prefer now, at around two, to see her, to talk with her, to play with her, but not to be held or carried by her—even out of what may seem to her like harm's way. It's a moment that calls for great maternal tact—which it's worth summoning up for the occasion. The child who makes it successfully through what Mahler calls the "rapprochement" phase of the separation-individuation process, with the help of a mother who understands both his need to be close and his need to move away from her, has laid the groundwork for an independent self relatively free of the ambivalence about dependency that haunts so many grownups' lives.

A mother may feel she is living with a secret agent as her toddler watches her every move, follows her around, then suddenly darts away, only to reappear and resume his surveillance. As he has ventured further and tried more, he has begun to experience obstacles as well as achievements, frustration as well as the exhilaration attending mastery. He is often too short to reach, too weak to push, too small to grasp what he wants. It is easy to understand his discouragement, the irritability that leads him to lie down on the floor and stamp his feet when they refuse to go into his rubbers, to use "no" more than any one of the other words he has learned now that so many things seem to be saying no to him.

He's a pretty miserable character some of the time. And his one overriding fear—worse than not being able to reach or have or do, because if she's still there none of that matters—is that his mother will no longer love him. He knows he can't help expressing his frustration; he doesn't know he'll grow out of it fairly soon, with a little help from his friends. Now it is not her presence but her love he cannot bear to be without. And while it is not always easy to love a monster, she must be able to see that he is more frightened of his own monsterlike behavior than she is, and with more reason. What he needs is not to be taught or trained or disciplined at this point, but to be protected from his own excesses of passion and violence by a calm hand, and then reassured that he is still good and still loved, that the monster and the angel are one and the same and not two different beings, and that all aspects of that undeniably sometimes-frightful sometimes-gentle self of his are acceptable in her eyes.

He is gradually realizing that he is not as omnipotent as he thought when he first stood up and looked around, that those big people out there who mean so much to him have interests of their own that are not necessarily the same as his. He can easily feel defeated, a feeling he fights against and a situation he tests even as he provokes his mother and father, against all the odds.

This is a critical moment for all of them. If their annoyance is extreme, he will try to deny the aggressive part of himself, to his lasting detriment, inventing devices for closing off a part of himself that can only do away with what is potentially creative as well as what is potentially destructive. If no attempt, or not enough, is made to curb his aggressive behavior, he will conclude that the grownups are paper tigers who must be as afraid of him as he is of himself, and that he must have good reason both to fear himself and feel disappointment in them. Actual physical punishment will seem so unjust—given his limited capacity to understand what is happening—as to lead him to a rage he fears may overwhelm him and all the world with him.

Fortunately and obviously, most parents do not turn their backs on their two-year-olds, or let them run wild without curbing them, or beat them up. Some, of course, do—the ones who were never helped to solve their own childhood conflicts—but most of us who are reasonably healthy and happy with ourselves have a realistic picture of our children's power relative to ours coupled with a deep affection for them. We realize that while they need help accepting the nature and limits of reality, they are more to be pitied than censured, and they are even touching and a little funny in their maniacal attempts to rule the roost when they can hardly even reach it. While sensible parents will not let him hurt himself or anything else, and while at moments he may be just too much not to evoke an all-too-human shout or smack, by and large their attitude to him will be one of tolerance, respect for his plight, and shared amusement at the devious means he invents for circumventing it.

There is lots of playing and pretending, by means of which, given their cooperation, he begins to imitate and identify with his parents.

LANGUAGE, PLAY, AND GENDER

The beginnings of language make it possible for the child to substitute words for actions. They are the basis not only for logical thought and abstract reasoning but for self-control—the ability to delay the satisfaction of some urge and substitute for it some idea or some other kind of action. Now the child can begin to organize mental events in a way that makes clear their connections and consequences. Symbolic thinking is what makes it possible to deal with our instincts rather than to be completely ruled by them, to discharge aggression in games and fantasy play or vicariously through stories heard or read. But language is not only the key to mastery of the self. It is in imitating the verbal proscriptions, denials, and cautions of his parents—no, no, don't do that—that we first see the child incorporating their rules and making them his own.

A child this age needs to use his time for playing, in what Mahler calls "symbolic reenactment of his own reality." For the infant, the basic primary experience of self is of the body, and the three-year-old expresses his fears about his body—of loss of one's penis, of one's feces, of the warm feeling of one's mother's body—in his play. He may become very interested in things that get broken or things that get lost, in fixing and in finding. He may feed his toy animals or rock them to sleep. It's not a parent's place to join him at play or to comment on his play (except to answer his questions) but to make sure he has occasion for it. Without the repeated opportunity to confront his preoccupations in disguises of his own invention, and then to alter them himself, many things do not take place that help him find ways to translate infant sorrows and infant longings into feelings he can make use of as a grownup.

It's easy for parents to be seduced by the apparently well-intentioned surrogate on the screen and the quiet, smiling child in front of it, but every moment a little child spends alone in front of a television set robs him of an opportunity to play. He may be obstreperous, a nuisance, hard to handle when the set is not on, but he may need to be that way, if only to learn that someone can stop him and then that he can stop himself.

He is learning language now and, some way into his third year, becoming more of a social creature—mirroring the behavior of others, noticing other children as well as adults and wanting to have what they have or to do what they do. The still precarious sense of self is very much physical self—"me" is my body. Boy and girl toddlers discover the anatomical difference between themselves which girls inevitably, despite the demurrals of feminists who wish it wasn't so, are observed to react to as something others have and they do not. (What is made of that observation will vary in the mental life of different little girls.) Little boys often wonder in the face of the evidence whether it is not possible to lose theirs.

In some children these observations and the fantasies that accompany them lead to what looks like mild depression in girls, anxiety in boys—a sense of loss and a fear of loss, respectively, that may be transient or may leave some temperamental coloring. In any case, only extreme naiveté or doctrinal blindness can lead anyone who has observed children this age to deny their awareness of sexual differences or the importance they attach to the phenomenon.[25] The sensations of pleasure connected with the genitals even at this age, the level of excitement aroused in touching and handling, assures that those parts of the body are felt to be very special, not just another part like toes or elbows, not just a difference like having brown hair or blond. Despite propagandistic or moralistic efforts to deny the special importance to small children of their own genitals and the differences they perceive between their own and those belonging to others—the awesome organs of the full-grown as well as the different kinds belonging to children of the opposite sex—it does exist, along with a general sense of the integrity of one's own body and its products as belonging to oneself.

Around this age, children of both sexes, but especially boys, resist being held or hugged or made to hold still while being dressed, want to do things for themselves, and, in general, resist enforced passivity. Toileting, usually begun some time around the last months of the second year or early in the third, can easily become a battleground for possession of the child's body. He is small and can easily be routed by a determined opponent, but it is a matter of real importance for him to have a sense of autonomy, of being in control of his own body, the feeling that it belongs to him and not his large and powerful parent.[26] If the reciprocity has been good up to now, he or she will want to please the parents, and using the toilet will be a gift to them. If it is freely given, in a desire to be like them and be liked by them, it represents a real achievement on the child's part, and for his parents. It's no achievement, on the other hand, to force a child to submit to a stronger will, and nothing is learned by it except the worst uses of power. Learning to use the toilet is one of the ways the child imitates the grownups to their mutual satisfaction and identifies with the parent of the same sex who uses it in the same way.

Toward the end of their second year most children are physically capable of beginning to regulate their sphincter muscles and postponing urination and defecation, but they are also at a stage where they're busy practicing regulating their autonomous wills. They can be recalcitrant about interrupting some activity they've chosen, to pursue one they haven't. Adamantly applying too much pressure to perform in this situation now often extracts a price that will be payable later in difficulties about elimination or more subtle derivatives of the situation, such as a fearful neatness, an exaggerated avoidance of anything suggesting dirt, or a stubborn negativism.

Toilet training can be a step in establishing the self when what it means to the child is control over his own body and a decision to use that capacity for control to be like those he admires. It takes a certain amount of tact and patience to introduce him to the experience at the time and in the way that will make it possible for him to accomplish the process with pride, but a wise parent will avoid battles or contests of will in this particular situation. No one can win them. The child can only lose, even when he seems to win. He can hold on defiantly to the treasures of his own body, for so they seem to him. Or he can be overwhelmed, defeated, and shamed. Only if he volunteers the gift of his cooperation in this arrangement that makes no apparent sense to him beyond the fact that it pleases his parents is it really an achievement that contributes to his growth and not just to his cleanliness.

The last thing he needs now is an enemy. He has enough trouble dealing with the warring parts of himself. Nor does he need a playmate no more purposeful than himself. What he needs is direction from a tolerant but sure authority confident enough to forgo impatient escalation of demands in favor of calm repetition of what's meant, what's wanted, what's expected. It can be a tedious business, but if we want our children to develop mastery over their powerfully tugging urges we'd better be able to show them—not just tell them— how it's done. In the end, the way we influence our children is by being there for them to see what we are like ourselves. It's in the thousands of interactions we have with them—feeding, cleaning, comforting, listening, answering, reading, explaining—in their first couple of thousand days that we educate them. What they learn is to be like us.

Only a gradual education that allows time for new structures to replace the old, and puts something in their place along the way, builds character that has firm roots in the autonomous self. Training can be done impatiently—through force and fear—or it can be left to nature and the child, avoiding any struggle for him at all, but in both cases the integrated self that is the aim of education will never appear.

The helping parent is the one whose need for the superficial proofs of affection doesn't interfere with giving love in the form the child needs it most—help in overcoming the need to discharge all his aggression, satisfy all his appetites, fulfill all his desires immediately. The paradox is that only a parent who has gratified an infant's instincts enough—but not too much—in the first three years of life can begin to require the renunciation of those instincts later and expect the child to make the effort to control himself rather than submit to or resist control from outside. By then, the child not only has the mental and motoric capacities but the emotional capacity to do so.

Only a child who knows that his parents wholeheartedly approve of some behaviors—for instance, defecating in the toilet rather than in his clothes—has any reason to curb his powerful urges and begin to accept substitute pleasures—the sandbox; a hammer-and-peg toy; later a game of make-believe, a bedtime story—for those he relinquishes.

Moving into the outside world away from mother, the first person the child encounters is his father. The father has always been there, but usually not a real part of that mother-baby dyad from which the child is hatching. Father's importance, in addition to his obvious attractions in his own right—helpful, imposing, playful—is that he is important to Mother. It is in what he feels about how they feel about each other that the child begins to grasp the meaning of being a man or a woman.

Certainly fathers have always begun to assume a special place in children's lives when they begin to move around more freely and join more easily in the kind of roughhouse play that has always been a father's specialty. Even in the days when fathers kept out of the nursery and had little to do with their small children until they became toddlers and talkers, these large and strong and noisy creatures were peculiarly beguiling, to follow around or be swept up in the air by, to admit one to manly companionship on a stroll together or add a new note to the admiration of some newly acquired skill.

In this age of increased participation by fathers in the daily lives of their infants and small children, sometimes feeding or changing them, carrying them around in backpacks or on their bicycle seats, fathers have become not only more visible but more accessible to their young children. Among other benefits of the greater involvement of fathers in child care—greater understanding of their children, readier identification on both sides—is the widening of possible behaviors a child is exposed to in himself and others. Father is different, and he elicits different responses than Mother. Father and Mother, just because they are two different people, have different ways of doing little things, different capacities for tolerating a child's various inevitable idiosyncrasies. The child's world is widened to the extent that fathers spend more time with their children.

This is not to say that fathers should become indistinguishable from mothers, though. No child needs two mothers, any more than he or she needs two fathers. It is the addition, not the replication, of functions that enriches, and children need a structuring figure as much as they do a nurturing one. Of course there is always some overlap, and an individual of either sex can be what we have traditionally called "motherly" or "fatherly," but for both cultural and psychological reasons it is usually the male who is more comfortable setting the limits that define the uses of aggression and teach the child how to control it for adaptive purposes.

This is the process that makes possible the self-discipline a child will need in order to learn and be creative, the way of channeling his aggression that will make him able to express his thoughts and feelings coherently, pursue goals, and tolerate competition. Some adult in the family has to exemplify these traits and while it is usually the father who establishes expectations of performance and makes clear the consequences that follow from how one meets them, many a woman has had to assume the task herself. The pioneer mothers of history and literature are exemplars.

While most men have always enjoyed this function and seemed to perform it naturally, mothers and fathers can exchange these roles when one is more psychologically suited to the task, as long as *somebody* in the family is providing structure and setting standards. Strong and gentle should both be part of the parental picture, although sometimes a particular parent will shift from one tendency to the other. Who performs what function in the parental-children matrix is less important than that discipline be provided by someone in a consistent way.

It is not just from observing who does what in the family that children learn what it is to be a mother or a father, a woman or a man, but in observing what these all-important figures seem to feel about themselves and about each other. And about him.

Since self begins as body, how the child feels, what attitude he learns from his parents, about his body parts, especially the genitals which arouse such pleasant feelings in him and the products that come from his own body-self, will determine how he feels about himself as a person—good and valuable, or disgusting and worthless. He takes his cue for this, as for so many things, from his parents' attitude, and he is not easily fooled. Again, not what is explicitly said so much as what is felt is what counts, and that is expressed in how they treat and handle him on the thousand daily occasions of bathing, dressing, toileting. If he feels that the way he is made, the way his body works, disappoints or repels them, he will be disappointed in his own self, his own sex, and wish to be other than he is.

Gender identity[27] is at the very core of the sense of self that begins with the child's first separation of inside from outside, of his own body from that of his mother, of the sensations of his own body and what he perceives it to be like into what he learns to call by the word "I." Observing the differences and similarities between his body and others, the concept that takes form in his developing mind with its new capacity for language and thought is "I am a boy made like Father" or "I am a girl made like Mother."[28]

In Defense of the Family

Without going into the question of the relative weight of biologically and socially determined, genetic or cultural factors, it is possible to state the fact that little boys and little girls begin quite early in life, as young toddlers, to exhibit observable differences in their development. That they do so, and not why this is so, is what concerns us here, since this book is not concerned with changing what is but with describing it in order to illuminate the role parents play in the childhood of this culture rather than how they might operate through their children to radically change it. It seems enough of a challenge to raise men and women who can learn, love, and work well in this world as it is.

There are infinite permutations of the various combinations of endowment, mothering, and chance events in life that give to every child's personality its particular style, and every individual varies in some ways from every other. In general, however, little boys are more aggressive. They show more tendency to be active, to move away from their mothers, more curiosity and a greater tendency to explore, while little girls begin to talk earlier and develop greater verbal facility, and tend to remain more closely involved with their mothers, although they often show considerable ambivalence—alternately negativistic and clinging—around the time they first make note of the differences between their bodies and those of little boys. This is not an invention of the slavish followers of Freudian theory but a conclusion drawn from what many careful, sensitive observers have noted occurring again and again in children in the same order and at roughly the same age.

The greater aggressivity of males has its basis in the level of sex hormones,[29] although the direction it takes is culturally shaped. Some males are more or less aggressive than others. Some females are more aggressive than other females or even than some of the less aggressive males. And obviously some families, and some societies, will be more or less tolerant than others of individuality in this regard as in others. But unless one is guided by a political agenda requiring a society in which as few distinctions as possible remain between individuals or groups, it is hard to deny that sex-linked biological predispositions exist.[30] In other words, sexual stereotypes have some biological basis in reality.

These tendencies elicit different responses from parents, depending on their own concepts of what is appropriately male and female behavior, and an interaction takes place in which parents both guide the choices of their small children in such matters as how they act and what they play with and respond to the children's natural preferences. Little boys usually do show a greater interest in moving objects and like to push toy cars and trucks around; little girls are more likely to sit still and cuddle something like a doll in the way they once molded to their own mothers' bodies, an experience they often seem not quite as eager to give up as boys.

But here as elsewhere with very young children, response is the key. A sensitive parent lets a young child find his own routes to the outside world of experience; he doesn't close off any but really dangerous avenues. There is no reason why a boy toddler shouldn't play with a doll if he wants to; perhaps he needs that cuddling experience or is working out some problem in being a separate person that a parent neither could nor should try to intrude on. A little girl might of course prefer blocks or a car to a doll. Neither of them will for this reason alone become a sexual deviant, any more than they will be "liberated" from their natures by a parent's attempts to influence them by foisting doll play on the little boy who's not feeling paternal or pushing a reluctant little girl into being the train conductor if she prefers to be a passenger on the trip.[31] Sexual identity is not a matter of what one wants to play with but of who one feels one wants to be like.

A little boy may very well have the fantasy of having a baby when he plays with a doll, or a little girl a wish to have a penis when she puts a shovel or a bat between her legs. The best chance of the child's coming to terms with the pressures that arise from these wishes lies in the freedom to act them out in play, without any adult intervention, interpretation, or judgment. As long as the child is not forced to become explicitly aware of these feelings he can deal with them in his own way and they need not disturb him and interfere with a budding sense of identity. Every means a child finds to sublimate an instinctual wish that cannot be gratified in reality is a contribution to the growth of his personality.

In a family where a mother and a father are happy with themselves and each other and where a child's first couple of years have gone well—he has enjoyed a closeness with his mother followed by a gradual separation that she has tolerated and even gently encouraged—by the time he is three he will have a rudimentary sense of himself as an individual, at the core of which is a sense of being one sex or the other. This gender identity is subtly fostered by his relationship with both parents, the one of the same sex and the one of the opposite sex. Little boys find it easier to give up their closeness and dependency on Mother when they can become closer to Father; they find an ally in his encouragement of their natural desires to assert themselves and they try to be like him, a process that is encouraged by both parents.

Little girls, on the other hand, find a different kind of response as they move toward their fathers. Males treat females in a certain way; that's one of the ways you know you're female. This has been true since the beginning of time and is not necessarily the stuff of which exploitation or a sense of inferiority is made. The self-confidence throughout life that Freud predicted for the little boy who is the undisputed favorite of his mother is matched only by that felt by the little girl who is her father's undisputed favorite.

How a father treats his daughter, his image of what is attractive in a female, like a mother's of what is desirable in a male, is a great influence, along with the child's imitation of the parent of the same sex, in shaping masculine or feminine behavior. To both boys and girls, Mother is primary at the start of life. To both of them, Father becomes important not just because he is there when they begin to move away, but because they sense his importance to her and hers to him. A child of three with two affectionate and encouraging parents will have acquired in the normal course of things a sense of himself as separate from his parents and as of the same sex as one of them or the other.

The Child

TIES AND UNTYING: PARENTS WITHIN
AND THE WORLD WITHOUT

All this sounds very smooth put this way. But as inevitable as the process is, so are the problems that crop up along the way and the variety of ways different children find to meet them. It is not the complications, whether they are created by a child's endowment, the nature of a parent's response, or chance circumstances, that make the difference; it is how they are met. And since each solution builds on the one before it, the earliest remain the most fateful. The specific way we each come to terms with the universal fears of childhood—of being left, of being unloved, of being hurt—have such resonant effects on later life that it seems well worth a parent's while to be there having as much influence as possible on all this potentiality and all this vulnerability.

For instance, at around a year and a half, children are often upset when their mother is gone. They seem to worry about where she is and not be quite certain whether she will return. This is not the best time for a trip, a job, an operation, a new baby. When choice isn't possible, special understanding and patience are in order for the toddler who's sad or the one who's overactive.

Any separation is experienced by the very young child as an abandonment. Unless the mother has avoided any intimacy from the beginning, when she is not there—for whatever reasons—she has left him. Of course, he has to learn to deal with separation, to realize that when his mother goes away she does not disappear forever, that she comes back. But this takes time, and a mental readiness coupled with emotional security.

As they get a little older, children find it easier to cope with Mother's absence. They make friends with another adult, or invent games in which things disappear and then reappear again, or become like their mothers themselves, taking care of dolls or teddy bears.

The child of two can use words to name things and can express his desires through language and through play, in which he acts out his wishes and overcomes his fears symbolically.

But there is still a lot of ambivalence in the average child this age caught between the wish to be separate from Mother and the wish to be one with her, to push her away and to cling to her. He needs her tolerance if he is to integrate these incongruous desires that continually beset him. If she holds him too close for too long, he may give up the struggle to be himself. If she pushes him away too soon, he may collapse in retreat. He can be very irritating, but patience with his ludicrous attempts to tie his own shoes or butter his own bread now will have positive effects reaching into a time when no one will be able to remember what the hurry was then. And being glad to see him back is a better idea than being resentful because he turned away from you. Children have enough ambivalence of their own to master without having to deal with that of their parents.

What really matters in a child's life is not so much what happens to him but what he makes of it—and how he responds to that. At every stage, the meaning events take on for him and his ability to cope with them are colored by his history up to now—mainly his relationship with his mother, which is not a matter of effusive kisses, expensive toys, or empty words of praise but a sense of her good will fairly consistently expressed in the minutiae of her care of him.

If he is too afraid of losing her (because she actually leaves him or withdraws emotionally too often when he needs her) or losing her love (because she shouts at him or hits him too often), he cannot afford to take those difficult little steps that will begin to separate him from her and inaugurate his individual existence.

If she has gratified his every whim, anticipated his every desire, and never allowed the possibility that she might disagree with or disapprove of him, he is not much better off.

In order to define himself in his parents' image, he must see them as capable of providing both pleasure and moderate frustration and be able to face the fact that it is the same parent who gives and, when necessary, denies. He has to face some frustration; usually enough of it comes with the territory of being human—small and weak and full of contradictory longings that have to be somehow appeased or renounced—and parents hardly have to go out of their way to construct more in an attempt to provide lessons for a child. But the pleasures and satisfactions should, on balance, outweigh the denials and restraints life sets up for him and both should come from the same source rather than being split between indulging and punishing adults. This is what makes it possible for him to deal with his contradictory feelings and sort them out satisfactorily, rather than keeping love split off from responsibility, what feels good from what needs to be done, looking for fun from doing a job. If he is to develop the kind of character we want in our children, it must be based on a closeness with parents he both loves and respects and has no reason to fear gradually distancing himself from, because he has taken into himself many of their essential qualities as the basis of a separate autonomous self.

By the time he is three, if he has had flexible and understanding mothering and fathering, he has confidence in his parents and in himself. He has gradually acquired a sense of himself as separate from his parents and of being able to imagine them and love them even when they are not there, not just, as earlier, while they were fulfilling some need of his. He has had some experience of their disapproval when he has not behaved as they wanted him to, but that disapproval has not been too harsh.

Feeling positively about them and knowing what they expect of him, in order not to lose their love he has internalized his parents' demands, making them his own. This is the beginning of conscience. He has made his image of his parents—both giving and sometimes denying—into part of himself.

And with a stable image of his mother fixed in his mind he can afford to be more engrossed in play and learning. He doesn't have to worry about her actual physical presence every moment.

This is about the age when most children are ready for nursery school, can tolerate separation from their mother and enjoy the company of other children.

The three-year-old has a sense of how things extend over time and in space, noticed at first in terms of his mother's comings and goings and the regularity with which events—mealtime, playtime, naptime—recur in his days. He is beginning to be able to wait for things to occur or to come back. He can use his imagination, in which things happen by magic because he wishes them,[32] but he knows he is playing, and he has an increasing grasp of the reality that's out there beyond his control as well as of the effects he can produce by means of his own efforts.

All of this structuring of reality—noticing, testing, deciding, defining—takes place in the context of a life that is fairly predictable. For the child whose days and nights are formless or chaotic—in which different people come and go and there is no way of predicting events and therefore of coming to terms with them—there is not much possibility of forming strong attachments[33] and not much impetus to make sense of things.

ISSUES: DAY CARE AND NIGHT THOUGHTS

Some practical implications for parents follow from this view of the first three years of life. Because every child and every parent and every situation are different, they are general and not specific, suggestions and not scenarios. And because we have looked at the first years in such detail in the preceding pages, we can deal with these implications in a much more summary way, assuming they will be understood in the context of what we have seen about the nature and needs of children from birth to about three.

We know that the most significant aspects of human development—of character, intellect, and personality—depend on the establishment of ties to parents who both gratify (mostly) and frustrate (somewhat), with whom the child identifies and in order to secure whose love he internalizes a set of rules that become his conscience. Basically optimistic about the world they have surrounded him with, he explores and experiments with his maturing capacities and develops a sense of himself as a separate individual of a specific sex and of a degree of competence that enables him to let his mother go for increasing periods of time.

It follows that under normal circumstances, it's best if a mother can take care of her child as much as possible during his first three years, the years in which her style of mothering will have such influence on how he faces the world when he is ready to leave her. The better things have gone between them up to then, the smoother that transition will be. A mother who has a choice—who is emotionally and economically able to do so—is laying the foundation for her child's future life by caring for him herself. When he goes off to nursery school is the best time for her to resume or begin working part time. Few jobs and even few professions can offer a woman who is also a mother anything that will turn out to be more important to her in the years to come than what can be accomplished in her interaction with her child in the earliest years of life.

This speaks, of course, to the situation of the woman who is ambivalent—whose natural desire to be with her baby may give way to the social pressure to "be somebody" in a society that is increasingly telling women that what counts is achievement, however trivial, outside the home, just so it is outside the home and apart from child rearing. No woman is really free unless she can follow her nature in defining her life; the point about liberation is having options. But feminism, like some other sociopolitical movements of our day, attempts to substitute one form of tyranny for another. Separating mothers from the daily life of their infants, when preventable, does a disservice to both of them.

And what about the cases where it's unpreventable? Obviously, the best alternative to one source of individual responsive mothering is another responsive individual. Mothers who have to work, and there are increasing numbers of them as the divorce rate rises and so does the birth rate, would ideally provide their child with someone—some *one*—who can meet his needs at the different stages of his growth in such a way as to foster first security and then independence. Despite the undeniable justice and necessity of equal work for equal pay, of equal opportunity (although not necessarily of outcome) for every individual in every sphere of life, the women's movement propagandists tamper with basics they barely seem to comprehend when they encourage attitudes and even legislation that would separate women from their children's early life.[34]

Public mothering is a contradiction in terms. Those who clamor for facilities where working mothers can leave babies and children too young for nursery school are ignoring their real needs as mothers and those of their infants.[35]

Women who could afford to do so have traditionally brought substitute mothers into their homes when they have been occupied elsewhere; common sense has usually led them to seek someone whose maternal capacities—quality of judgment and degree of empathy for the child—seemed to be in proportion to the extent to which they would be taking a mother's place. Women unable to afford the luxury of chosen paid mother substitutes have turned to arrangements with relatives, friends, neighbors—the more stable and lasting, the better for everyone concerned.

Of course, for women in dire poverty, group care facilities can have another meaning altogether. And there are women whose own resources, emotional as well as financial, may limit their capacity for flexible mothering. If you have not been well cared for by your own parents, it is very hard to feel like a loving parent yourself. The immature, the defeated, the hostile ought to be given the option of placing their children somewhere where a better beginning than they can offer might help to break the cycle of diminished lives.

But these are not the mothers to whom this is addressed. No woman whose interests may clearly be different from her child's should be forced to care for him. It's the many women whose interests are inseparable from those of their infants—who stand to gain along with their children by contributing to their growth, but who are told they are wasting their valuable time and energies, squandering the years in which they could be realizing themselves—who might benefit from being reminded of the old-fashioned idea that sometimes you find yourself through another self, particularly in the process of helping to create one.

The idea that anyone can be as affectionate, responsive to, and concerned about a baby as its own mother—and that therefore it doesn't much matter who cares for infants—is a peculiarly political one: It focuses on institutional arrangements with no considerations of the complexities that motivate the behavior of real men and women and children. Even more absurd is the assumption that there is a great number of warm, devoted, patient women somewhere waiting to be put in charge of other people's babies for pleasure and profit, and who can discharge that responsibility effectively.

Effectively, we have to ask, compared to what? It makes a difference whether the alternative is care by an inadequate parent, by an indifferent or abusive parent, by a parent who really has no choice but to be absent from a child's life because of illness or economic necessity, or whether it is an average woman with normal emotional resources, predisposed to be attached to her child and to appreciate him, who has no real need to turn him over to anyone else until they both are ready. Let's not pretend we need to construct day-care centers in the interest of this woman or her child.

Having taken the unfashionable position that mothers should when possible stay home and care for their babies and young children until they've mastered the critical developmental tasks of the first three years of life, we can now state an equally obvious corollary. Children should have two parents, and they should be unequivocally of opposite sexes.

Young children learn what it is to be male or female by identifying with a parent of one sex or the other.

The first discovery by a young child that there are other kinds of bodies different from his or her own body—the basic "given" of his or her existence—is inevitably experienced with surprise and dismay. What a child sees, no matter how it is explained, is that something is missing on one that is present on another, and it follows that someone must have removed it.[36] Most children overcome the fears and fantasies that accompany this primitive view of things. They do so with the help of parents who reassure them, not only by giving explanations but by not being threatening. Most of all, though, they come to realize that they have always been as they are, that they began life that way and that it's a good way to be, because they are like their mother or their father. They are made the same way as a parent they admire. Here, in the feelings one has toward the parent of the same sex—and not in statements made or in information given, now or later—is the basis for pride in one's own sex: in being a male like Father or a female like Mother.

Children learn what value to place on their sex and how to feel about the other sex from how it seems to them their parents feel about themselves and toward each other—whether a mother seems to enjoy being a woman and to prize her husband, and whether her husband is confident in his maleness and devoted to and proud of his wife. If this is what the child perceives, he will want to be like one of them someday and have someone of his own who is like the other. It doesn't matter much what he is told at this age; what matters is what he perceives and what he makes of it in his own mind.

He hasn't yet developed logical thought, a clear idea of cause and effect, a dependable understanding of how things work in reality. Things seem to him to happen by magic, to come and go for reasons that elude him and in ways that are not clear, and he invents his own explanations. They are fantasies that will be gradually relinquished as his opportunities to test reality and his capacity to do so increase.

At this stage, a dark room may be filled with terrible devouring monsters; a noise in the night may be one of them coming to eat him; if he is angry at Mommy she may disappear forever; if he has a bad dream he cannot be sure it wasn't real. And not only does he have a hard time with what he dreams up; he often misunderstands what he actually sees.

A young child who sees adults in sexual intercourse can easily interpret what he sees as a violent assault, what he hears as cries of pain. A woman in childbirth may seem to him about to be rent apart. For children to share their parents' room, let alone the parental bed, or to be present at a sibling's birth, may be "natural," but like much of what can be found in primitive patterns of behavior these experiences have been found to work against what we value most in civilizations—the freeing of the mind from primitive fears and the ritualistic thinking that defends against them.

A child does not learn that bodies are natural and sex is matter-of-fact from exposure to parental nudity and adult sexual intimacy. He learns to defend himself against the excitement he cannot discharge and the fears he cannot handle.

Birth, death, and copulation are not experiences with which a young child can cope; they are all terrifying to him, no matter what grownups may intend or explain in exposing him to them. They touch his own fears of being hurt because he is so small and weak and helpless, and they interfere with his own attempts to consolidate his image of his own body, still a precarious one. He may not appear perturbed to the casual observer, but the two-year-old who "isn't even paying attention" is often preoccupied with shutting out what cannot be assimilated yet, denying what would be too threatening if admitted to awareness.

In the time roughly between two and four years of age, children are particularly vulnerable to the effects of overstimulation—experiences that rouse too much of their sexual or aggressive feelings. How much is too much will vary, of course, from child to child, depending on a complex interaction between his own biological constitution and the patterns of physical care given by his parents. Those patterns in turn are influenced by the parents' own psychological makeup and their relationships with each other and with the rest of the family.

If a child feels too much unsatisfied longing or rage, if he is angry because he feels those he loves most are not giving him enough affection, attention, or care—whether it's because his mother is ill, or depressed, or drinks, or goes away on a trip, or has another baby, or is upset because her marriage is on the rocks, whether it's because his older siblings beat him up, or his father beats his mother, or his father and mother shout a lot, or yell at him, or hit him—he is trapped by his own aggression. He wants something he can't ask for, perhaps can't even verbalize. It might be a wish something like, If you really loved me, Mommy, you would get rid of Daddy, or you would feed me the bottle the way you do the new baby, or hold me the way you hold her, or you would let me bite her or you'd give her back and just take care of me. These are perfectly natural wishes in a small child, but like so much else in nature, they have to be channeled. Normally nurturing parents will be sensitive to the young child's vulnerability and do their best to create for him a setting in which he knows that although there are things they won't let him do, he is special to them and they will not stop taking care of him.

But parents can't always control their lives or their fates. Other children are born, illnesses occur, even loving mothers have bad days, sad hours, quarrels with their husbands. And these things can seem cataclysmic to the small child, who only knows he is not getting what he wants and needs. He's disappointed, hurt, enraged. But at whom? He doesn't know whose fault it is, who to be angry at—Mother, Father, Sister, Brother. In any case, he can't act on his murderous impulses. He's too little, and who would take care of him? He's a prisoner of his own feelings—he can't discharge them and he can't get rid of them, either. They're too strong and too pervasive. What he does to rid himself of the burden—and two- and three-year-olds do a lot of it—is decide these angry feelings are not his at all but somebody else's. It is not quite like his making up an imaginary playmate or a puppy who spills the milk or breaks the dish, leaving him free of any blame for those regrettable deeds, but a much more pervasive conviction that leads him to attribute his furious and destructive urges to others. Unable to cope with the feelings within him, he projects them outward, onto the adults around him. It is *they* who are angry. They are angry at him. They know he's a bad boy (or girl), with bad thoughts, and *they* would like to get rid of *him*. He thinks they see him not necessarily as they see him in reality but as he feels he is. And, full of anger at his father, he will have the image of an angry father in his mind.

More often than not, this fairly common situation has a benign outcome. The difficult circumstances improve—Mother comes back from her trip; Father spends more time playing with the child, who realizes there are advantages to being the older one and not just the baby; it becomes clear as time passes that he is not going to be abandoned in favor of the newcomer; parents make up and calm is reestablished.

The Child

But sometimes a child remains trapped in his rage, caught between his resentments and the part of himself that reproaches him and threatens him with the harm he wishes he could inflict on others. The only solution for him will be the construction of a fantasy world, and later perhaps a style of life, that reassures him that he is not as weak and helpless, as bad and guilty as he feels. Revenge of some sort—against other boys or girls; later, against other men or women; later still, perhaps against children of his own—dominates his imagination and, in subtle or overt ways, his relationships. The mental mechanisms that compensate him for feelings of powerlessness and reassure him that he can get for himself what has been withheld by others shape his fantasies of omnipotence in childhood and are translated in adolescence into impulsive behavior, delinquency, and more serious crime.

And no amount of social engineering—from getting rid of toy weapons in the nursery to passing laws that are attempts to assure everyone a fair share of the community's benefits—will eradicate the resentment that originates in infantile longings and infantile rage, in internal conflicts never resolved. The prisoner of his own past can never be freed by changing society. This kind of criminal does not kill because he is in danger or steal because he is hungry. The danger and the hunger he feels are the danger and the hunger of infantile fantasies unfulfilled. Ungratified in childhood, they can neither be appeased or restructured now.

While limits must be set for children, and while it is not the inevitable existence of conflict in their lives but how it is met that matters, feeding and toileting are two areas in which it's best to avoid confrontations between parent and child. Because the developing ego starts from the sense of "me" that is "my body," the child's most basic identity rests on his belief that he is in control of his own body, that he regulates what is put into it and what comes out of it. The small child can easily be overwhelmed, forced, defeated, shamed in these areas, but although he may become "a good eater" who cleans his plate of everything that's put in front of him or a child who is spotlessly trained at the age of a year, he will not be a child who feels sure of himself or grows into an adult whose sense of mastery is all it might have been.

In other areas of behavior, it's less a matter of avoiding conflict than of resolving conflict in ways that help the child learn self-control. There are events that cannot be prevented. Another child may be born just when the first is beginning to move away from the mother, and he may react with daytime clinging and nighttime fears. Unavoidable surgery may stimulate terrors that cause bad dreams, a death in the family may require a mother's absence, and while she is gone a child who's been weaned may want his bottle back again.

One cannot always postpone another child's birth until a child is old enough to understand what is happening to him, or even always hold a marriage together. What one can do is be aware of the process by which an infant becomes a child, his early attachment to and, later, partial separation from his parents as he defines himself and identifies with them, and help the child respond to the problem he faces in a way that's most appropriate to his stage of development and most likely to be of help in growing up.

Sometimes that means letting him remain a baby for a bit longer. When a new baby has just arrived is not a good time to send him off to start nursery school; when his mother has to be away for a while is no time to ask him to give up the bottle; when he is beginning to be more independent is no time to get into a struggle about toilet training.

These are times, though, when the presence and understanding of a father can make all the difference. He can be someone to turn to when Mother is not available, physically or emotionally, a companionable presence as well as a bulwark against uncertainty in the young child's life.

When a child has an accident or illness he'll need special reassurance that nothing terrible is being done to punish him, that he is not in danger of losing some part of himself and has in no way brought this misfortune about by thinking harmful thoughts or doing naughty things. If his father leaves his mother, he'll need not only reassurance that it's not his fault, that she will not leave him, too, and that his father still loves him and will be with him when he can, but other people in his life as well. Not to take his father's place in his affections but to provide others to turn to and identify with, so he doesn't feel there is now no one in the world but Mother, that he can't afford to ever have angry feelings against her and had better remain a good, quiet, passive little child if he knows what's good for him.

In each case, as in every kind of fate or fortune life throws in our paths, there is no reason for the child to be traumatized forever. Individuals have met every kind of disaster—even the loss of a parent—without necessarily being doomed. The crucial thing is how the event is met, and whether it becomes an opportunity for the child to feel some new sense of mastery and some better understanding of himself and others.

The best way we have to help this come about is by giving children the opportunity to tell us what they think and fear, wonder about and anticipate, and then to tell them the truth as we understand it.

Being honest with a child doesn't only mean not lying to him; it means telling him what we really believe in terms he can understand at his stage of mental and emotional development. A scientific explanation is of little use to a child who has not yet grasped the concepts of time, space, or causation. Letting a three-year-old think the sun comes up in the morning to tell him it's time to get up and start the day will not impair his cognitive functioning forever. He won't continue to think that's so when he's six (although he still won't be able to understand the niceties of the laws of the physical universe). He'll ask the same questions over and over again through childhood and probably go on asking some of them in different form until old age.

So although one would like to postpone events that are hard on a child—the birth of a sibling in some cases, an operation in others—or prevent still others altogether—the end of a marriage, the death of a parent—it isn't always possible to do so, and while one wouldn't exactly order pain for the purpose of building character, still, the painful situations that inevitably arise in every life can be the occasions for helping a child to strengthen himself and become more, not less.

It's a matter of how we help him meet them. One tries to be understanding of his feelings, to take them seriously and never ridicule even his most farfetched ideas. He's not only learning how things work in the real world, he's learning how people act toward each other. Respect for others, after all, is the basis of morality.

One aims also not to leave him trapped alone with a head full of fears he'll have to lock off parts of his mind to defend himself against, but to help him tame them in the light of day. He has to describe them to us, however, in order for us to bring the right equipment to the job, not a machine gun when what's wanted is a fly swatter. It's easy to be wrong about what's going on in a child's mind, and the best way to find out is to invite him, not just in words but by a responsive and encouraging attitude, to tell us. Only when he does so do we have the right to intrude our notions into his view of things, although we always have the right, as parents, to expect certain behavior of him. We let him see that we have certain expectations of him. If they are realistic ones for his age and his individual capacities, the respect we show him in our confidence that he can handle things is a great contributor to his self-respect, his own confidence.

Every child is frustrated, feels desires that could not possibly be gratified, wishes for things he can never have. If not every child becomes a violent or more subtly destructive man or woman, it is not because no conflict was experienced but because there was appropriate help in finding ways to shift one's desires to the possible, find alternative satisfactions in accomplishment and affection. The best kind of help we know of in this process comes from parents who provide both enough affection and enough clearly structured limits for their child.

How much is enough? That can only be answered in terms of each individually endowed child and his particular family circumstances, and the only one in a position to be familiar with both are his parents. The only one who can help them figure it out is him. Not necessarily by what he explicitly says, even after he can talk, but by how they read his real needs, with the understanding that these will be what contributes to a mind not disabled by basic uncertainties about the self—Do I want to be a boy or a girl? Am I loved or not? Is it better to be fed or feed myself?—and eager to meet the world on its own terms.

From Three to Six: Becoming a Person

With the beginnings of love and attachment come the beginnings of a sense of self; together they create the possibility for that discipline which becomes self-discipline and sets the stage for a more abstract and formal kind of learning.

SEX, EDUCATION, AND THE OEDIPUS COMPLEX

Having separated his image of himself from that of others and defined himself as this boy called David, or this girl named Martha, having acquired the rudiments of language and of abstract thought, seen a bit of the world beyond his room, his home—and of other people who are not Mother and Father, sisters and brothers—the child of three to six finds himself full of questions about what things are, how they are made, how they work, and where they come from. And nothing anywhere is of more urgent interest in these respects than his own self. He is a creature of insatiable curiosity: experimenter, theorizer, framer of hypotheses and questioner par excellence. How his curiosity is met—with what attitude, not with what information—will influence his attitude toward learning and the thrust of his efforts to understand the world and himself in it, throughout his life.

A little girl or boy who is made to feel that it is best not to ask questions, not to try to figure things out, because questions and experiments lead to embarrassment and shame, anger and reprimand, often gives up trying. The kind of interest and attitude that grows into curiosity about how genes combine, how light reaches earth from the farthest galaxy, what is the best way to construct a building or cure a disease, and the conviction that it is worthwhile trying to find out the answers, has its earliest beginnings in such questions as, Where did I come from? How did I get there? and How did I get out?

Because children of four and five, who universally ask these things, do not yet have the mental capacity to understand much about cause and effect in the real world,[37] and because their emotional capacity is similarly limited, the most significant thing is really not the exact nature of the information given. Children will distort much of what they are told or hear at this age in any case, and it will go through many transformations before they make sense of and come to terms with the fundamentals of procreation, birth, growth, and death.

What makes a lasting impression at this age is parental attitude. Is it all right to ask questions—about anything at all, even what daddies and mommies *do* that makes babies? Are attempts to find out for oneself what things are like—perhaps with the willing cooperation of a playmate equally interested in a close inspection of how other selves are made—tolerated? And beyond these questions is the most basic one of all: Is there anything to worry about, to be afraid of, in all this?

Parents who give neat and informative lectures on anatomy and reproduction to small children may not be responding to their real needs, their unspoken questions at all. Those who worry too much about what the neighbors or the grandparents think about masturbation, or are uncomfortable dealing with questions they would rather not have been asked, are sending a message. And all children, whatever else they are good at, however else they differ, are highly sensitive receivers of attitudes toward themselves, their bodies, and their behaviors.

The information given by an earnest and enlightened parent will often be beyond the small child's understanding; it will find its way, diluted and distorted, given shape by his particular imaginative style, into a fantasy scheme that will slowly be outgrown and abandoned

The Child

for ways of seeing things that work better. The stork that brings the baby, the cabbage in which the baby is found, the seed the daddy plants in the mommy, the sperm that finds its way to the uterus to fertilize the ovum, are equally mysterious to the young child, and equally likely to be heard and remembered in some way of his own that contributes to a temporary but highly idiosyncratic cosmology.

What the child inevitably gets right is the attitude of his parents. Anxiety (evidenced by too much eagerness as well as by too much reluctance to deal with these matters), a distaste for the body and what it does, dislike for oneself, hostility toward the other sex, its members, and their members, make an indelible impression, far stronger than what is actually said in words.

The best one can do is be pleased to answer questions without fuss but with no need to anticipate them. They will recur—again and again—at each stage of development through adolescence and there is no need nor even any possibility of getting it all straight at once. The thing to get straight for the preschooler is that his interests are neither unusual nor unappealing, and that if the answers are not clear now he is welcome to keep asking in the new ways that will inevitably occur to him.

Knowing that there are various stages of development does not mean simply enduring the passage of each while tolerating whatever behavior arises. It means understanding what a child is capable of at each stage and helping him to achieve it. It is the function of parents in the family to help children with the struggles out of which they fashion their social, intellectual, and moral selves.

It is not necessary to encourage or even tacitly to condone by ignoring it any behavior a child would be better off abandoning at his age. Normal infants play with themselves and later look at and touch each other. As children get a little older they can be told that they can find things out by asking questions, that masturbation is one of the activities we consider private—not dangerous or shameful or bad but intimate, that some things are not done publicly. One of the first ways a child learns to respect others is by respecting their privacy—their desire to be alone at certain times—and having them respect his. As long as he is free to ask anything and his questions are answered respectfully and patiently he is unquestionably better off having reasonable limits placed on his activity than if his curiosity becomes the occasion for secret excitement he can neither direct nor understand. For one thing, he is more likely to learn the more reason he has to verbalize his thoughts so they can be clarified and corrected.

The natural curiosity of the infant and toddler gradually finds more grown-up ways of being satisfied than looking and touching, and as long as a child is free to wonder and ask, to think and talk about his thoughts, he will not be learning shame but self-control. The guilt and anxiety a child feels is a function of his fantasies, not just what happens—what he does and sees—but what he imagines and feels about it. And anxiety and shame, we know now, accompany overstimulation as much as they do overrestriction.

The once-fashionable idea that parental nudity, allowing children to share the bed or bath with mother or father, would satisfy their curiosity in healthy ways and prevent neurosis, was a ludicrous misinterpretation of what we know about the vicissitudes of the instinctual life of children.

Children need to know they will be helped to avoid more arousal than they can handle, more desire than they can satisfy—and to learn to direct their curiosities and their energies into a whole repertoire of other kinds of satisfactions.

The child who cannot discharge every impulse at the moment it is felt is likely to find another way to use his energy. He plays games, makes up stories, and talks to those around him. A parent who is there when he asks a question about where babies come from or what it is grownups do to make one or how it gets out of the mother's body is in a position to start by asking the child what *he* thinks—he always has some theory—and answer the question the child is really asking, in the child's own terms, rather than talking at cross-purposes, leaving some misapprehension untouched, or giving the child different information or more information than he is really asking for, leaving him more confused than enlightened or

reassured. Most of the reassurance will come from tone and attitude anyway, and not from the scope or structure of the explanation.

Children do not make notes about their questions to bring up at
a more convenient time. They wonder about things according to the
rhythm of their inner life, and ask whoever is there at the moment.
Being there more often than not when he's constructing his view of
reality, his outlook on life, is a value to be seriously weighed against
the reasons any mother may have for not being there.

Sex education is not, in early childhood, so much a matter of instruction in the facts of life as it is of demonstration of what it is
to be male or female. Its object is not the acquisition of information
about the mechanics of anatomy or procreation but the acquisition
of an attitude toward the self—that it is a good thing to be a girl
like me or it is a good thing to be a boy like me.

This attitude, like so much else, is a function of the child's feelings
about his parents and what he thinks they feel toward him. A little
girl will be happy about being a girl and look forward to growing up
to be a woman not because she is lectured to about being proud of
her sex or instructed in how to avoid the exploitive traps laid for females, but because she feels she is like her mother and she sees that
her mother is satisfied with herself and happy with her life and cherished by her husband.

Her mother may be a housewife or an executive; that alone is not
what makes the difference. In either case, if she is miserable with
her sex and feels unfulfilled by her fate, her daughter has no reason
to want to grow up to be like her, even though she becomes a housewife like her or a professional like her. (And, of course—does it really
need to be said?—not every full-time mother is unfulfilled and not
every highly paid career woman is happy.) Similarly, whether she
stays home or goes out to work, if her son feels she scorns or humili-
ates the father he resembles, he is likely to grow up confused about
which sex he would prefer to be.

A common clinical finding has been that homosexual men have
grown up in families with a domineering and possessive mother and

a passive father; they have been unable to separate from their mothers or identify with their fathers. The engulfing, too intrusive mother who cannot seem to relinquish her control over her child's body and the father who fails to serve as an ideal for his child occur again and again in various forms in the literature on homosexuality.[38]

The outcome of a deviant course of development should not be persecuted, but it shouldn't be regarded simply as an "alternative life style" either. It is a deeply determined inner response of an individual to a parental situation that fails to encourage one kind of psychosexual development and fosters another in its place. The psychological defenses adopted to ward off a terror of devouring women—or women who seem so in the fantasies of a little boy—do not contribute to the character structure most of us would wish for our sons, if only because the homosexual life—and, of course, the same is true of heterosexual perversion—is an impoverished one.

Conflict never resolved in childhood leads to the closing off of potentially enriching experiences. For most people, these are found in the love of a member of the opposite sex and in parenthood. Despite current cant, the traditional family remains the best way to raise men who are proud of their manhood and able to love women, and women who take pleasure in being women and loving men, and this will probably continue to be the desire of most parents.

It helps for parents to be aware that their boys and girls of about three to five are playing out an age-old drama, struggling with hopeless rivalries, wishes impossible to fulfill, dreams that are bound to be disappointed. It does not help for them to say so to the child. He needs help in the form of affectionate support, reassurance that he is lovable most of the time and at the very least tolerable all of the time, and that he will never be physically deserted or emotionally abandoned. He needs to be reassured that he will eventually win his struggles to define himself and take his place in the world. But if his discomforts are interpreted for him, his lot is made harder. He could not accept the statement that he has rivalrous wishes toward one parent and would like to possess the other completely and forever. He would be terrified at the dangers inherent in such longings and espe-

The Child

cially at his vulnerability in the dangerous situation of their being known.

The best help lies not in meddling with his inner conflicts but in encouraging him to resolve them by giving up the useless old dream of merging with his first love and gradually taking more and more satisfaction instead in trying to be as much as possible like the parent of the same sex. The new dream then becomes, around the age of five or six, to grow up like Mother or Father and find a husband or wife of one's own.

It is more than a coincidence that this is the approximate age of starting school for most children. An emotional struggle has ended with a resolution that frees the psychic energy necessary to fuel the capacities that by now exist for learning. The child is calmer, is looking outward beyond the home, is secure enough in the love of family to connect with others, and is capable of manipulating symbols—of learning the language of words and that of numbers. These are the tools with which he will commence to find the answers to his questions and find his own place in the world, and the best parenting is that which has brought him to this stage with both his questioning and his capacity to look for answers intact.

How well he has managed to come to terms with his inevitable sexual feelings toward his parents—the so-called Oedipus complex—is a major factor in his ability to separate from them, the particular style with which he will do so, and the way in which he will begin to move beyond the world he has shared with them up to now. Just what is this universal reality with the mythical name?

The oedipal wish is to possess one's parents forever. The oedipal conflict is caused by the simultaneous but opposite wish to be free of them. The oedipal crisis is resolved and the child on the way to mature personhood when he is able to relinquish the wish that he and his parents should belong to each other completely and begins to separate himself from them. He accepts the necessity to go out into the world and seek his fortune—find a place for himself and someone of his own.

How well he is able to resign himself to this enticing but painful necessity depends on how much hope he can feel for himself—how much confidence he has in himself and how much trust in the world of others.

That is why, allowing for many subtle variations, the combination of a generally indulgent mother-in-infancy and a resident father whom the child comes to see as both strong in his own right and loved by his mother, is the most encouraging situation a child can have for moving from infancy to a separate childhood self and later, in adolescence, from childhood to an adult self. It is what most of us mean when we speak of a family.

We do not mean any group of people who choose to live together, of whatever sex and in whatever arrangement with whatever extent of commitment for whatever period of time. We mean an essentially nurturing woman and an essentially effective man who raise children in a situation of mutual devotion to each other and to their children.

Reality—in the form of illness, death, personal disappointment that shatters parents' commitment, or a thousand other imaginable circumstances—may change, distort, destroy that essential situation, and then we have to look for ways to make up for what is missing. But there is still no proven better way than the much-maligned traditional nuclear family to raise children who have an integrated self at the core of their being and emotional energy available for forming attachments, achieving goals in learning, and applying what they have learned to new situations in some kind of useful work.

The strong and loved father is not only worth pleasing but worth surpassing. His son wants to grow up to achieve as his father has done and to be loved by someone as his father is loved. The next step along the way from infancy in the journey toward selfhood that is growing up occurs when the child, sometime around the age of five or six, gives up his dream of getting rid of his siblings and taking his father's place and having his mother's love and attention all to himself. He realizes his father is too strong and too securely entrenched in his mother's affections to be supplanted, and he has begun to have a positive enough sense of himself to hope he'll grow up to be strong and effective like his idea of his father and find someone loving and caring of his own like his idea of his mother. And how he imagines them at this point will influence what he will look for the rest of his life, both for himself and in someone to love and be loved by.

The development of girls is complicated by the fact that in early infancy it is the mother who is the emotional center of life for all babies, male or female. Most little girls transfer a good deal of their positive emotion to their fathers around the time they first perceive the difference between the sexes. Then the little girl, too, must make her peace with growing up to be like her mother—instead of actually taking her place—and finding someone she will love and with whom she will have children of her own.

LEARNING AND MAKE-BELIEVE, TV AND TALE-TELLING

So you have seen to your child's emotional health and physical development as best you could by caring for him yourself in the earliest years of his life, not abandoning him to the indifferent care of others or allowing him to feel abandoned by even a subtle indifference of your own. You have indulged him appropriately as an infant and welcomed his first steps away from you as well as his returns, dealt with kindly understanding but a firm hand with his contretemps and gently guided him in the direction of greater independence, encouraging his explorations and on the whole standing as an ideal worthy of his affection and respect.

And now what? Does he stand there, a little paragon, a practically perfect person? No, of course not. He's a human being, and part of his charm, his ineffable distinction that separates him from you and from all others, what makes him an individual, is a peculiar mix of characteristics not every one of which—let's face it—you find adorable.

What these may be is a list so various as to defy any attempt at example or enumeration. After all, parents are human beings, too, with a history and a present that includes but is not bounded by their parenthood. You are a peculiar person too, an individual whose mental life gives a meaning quite your own to every encounter, even with your own child. Is he fatter than you think he should be, or less musical? Does she never sit still for a minute, spill things all the time, or scowl when you feel like having a nice chat with her?

Perhaps both of you have reached a new developmental stage, and what is being indicated is your readiness to move away a little more and let him practice being himself—he'll play many parts and discard most of them in the process before he settles on a way of being most comfortably himself—without feeling the hot breath of maternal solicitude at every turn. This does not mean adopting a laissez faire attitude when you are with him. He still needs to know you are aware of his doings and exercise judgment about them, have goals for him and expect him to do his best to fulfill them. It just means that perhaps you need not be physically with him so much of the time. Now, and not earlier, is when the quality of time together is more important than quantity. Now is the time to shift the focus of your attention—to younger children if you have them, to a job if you want one (part-time is preferable at first, for both of you), to anything you've been waiting to do or learn or try.

The child who's ready for school is not only ready to learn the alphabet and learn to count; he's ready to learn to get along with others on his own terms, the terms you've given him in all the time you've spent together but that he now has to practice using by himself. He doesn't need the constant presence of a full-time mother any more, and in fact the more he's had one up to now, available to him in the flexible ways he's needed, the less he's likely to need one now.

But wait. We started by saying you'd seen to his emotional development and physical care. How can he be ready for school if you haven't also seen to his cognitive faculties? Shouldn't you have been priming him for school, teaching him the things that will put him at the head of the class and pave his way for Harvard? Have we neglected early learning and preschool enrichment while worrying about empathy and independence?

Much research published in the early 1960s on the perceptual development of infants indicated that babies were more aware of sensations and more responsive to stimulation, almost from birth, than had been realized before. They could see and hear, paid selective attention to certain sights and sounds, "preferred" to look at a human face (meaning they spent more time looking at a face or a diagram of a face than other kinds of patterns presented to them, a trait that may have adaptive value for the species in facilitating social learning), and had a kind of stimulus hunger. The more they saw, the more they wanted to see. The more opportunities they had for looking, for visual exploration, the more they developed their capacities for seeing. Experience seemed to influence the genetic capacity for response.[39]

The idea that an increase in visual input would facilitate discrimination, recognition, and other prerequisites for cognitive development hung a mobile over every baby crib and bassinet in America. It also led to an alliance between the toy (or "plaything") industry, the academic world of grants for studies and experiments on early learning—how it takes place and what factors influence it—and the world of government institutes, which largely funded such research. The government was interested in interventions that might improve the learning capacities and raise the expectations for culturally deprived children, especially those of impoverished urban minorities; the manufacturers and publishers of learning hardware and software were interested in selling the materials with which to do so; and the departments of cognitive studies and developmental psychology at our great centers of learning and research were going to tell them how.[40] Many an alliance was forged between university professors and pretentiously-named toymakers, with the government picking up the tab for the projects that would establish how properly programmed materials in the home and in learning centers established for the purpose would raise the I.Q. and encourage the creativity of newborns, babies, crawlers, toddlers, nursery schoolers, and kindergartners.

American parents bought books on how to make their babies smarter, how to start them on the road to reading within hours after they had left the maternity ward, how to deal with them throughout infancy so that they would have an edge when they got to school.

They were sold transparent crib bumpers so a baby would miss no possible source of visual stimulation in the room that was now described as a learning environment. They were sold rattles for auditory stimulation and squeeze toys for tactile stimulation. Most of all, they were sold the idea that without their self-conscious efforts to provide the requisite kinds of stimulation, their babies and young children might never fully develop their innate capacities.

Naturally, parents want what's best for their children, as do societies as a whole, and a lot of toys and a lot of books and a lot of programmed learning materials were sold to parents and to the government for use in schools and centers for the preschool young. There are no available statistics on the results of what was purchased to provide the nation's children with stimulation. One thing that was undoubtedly stimulated was a good deal of anxiety in parents, and one can guess that it was transmitted in some form or other to their children.

The real question about the nature of early learning and the value of preschool enrichment programs from infancy on is, "For whom?" The fact is that most babies in ordinary families receive all the stimulation they need for optimal development of their gradually maturing capacities in the normal course of daily life with a "good enough" mother.[41]

Infants look at their mothers' faces as they are held to nurse or take the bottle; during the time they are awake and alert they look at whatever's in the room and listen to the sounds of the household. They explore their fingers and toes, feel their clothing or blanket. As they begin to reach for things, to crawl around, to stand up, to walk, they continue to explore their surroundings—looking, touching, listening, tasting, and gradually assembling and relating their impressions of the world of things.

What is most significant is that they do so in the context of a world of people. The most important thing about learning in the very young child is that it take place in relation to other human beings from whom he acquires the attitudes toward himself and others that have at least as much to do with the capacity for later learning as the practicing of visual discrimination. In the normal course of family life a child's capabilities will gradually unfold; it's a matter of increasing capacities with maturation. No extra little gimmicks need be purchased. As long as a child has responsive parenting, encouraging his spontaneous growth but not pushing it, he will continue to move ahead.

It is the child who does not have this kind of parenting, who is not attached to any particular person, whose parent is absent, whether away at work or physically present but depressed and withdrawn; the child to whom no one responds as a parent in the ways that elicit further kinds of reaching out, to whom no one talks, for whom the ongoing conversation between mother and child that begins in infancy does not take place, who needs "enrichment." Whether and how to provide it is a matter of public policy. But for most middle-class children, the nourishment of the senses that provides a baby with opportunities for sensorimotor exercise, perceptual practice, is built into the usual caretaking situation along with adequate food, warmth, comforting, and the later efforts of socialization—learning how to feed oneself, to use the toilet, to name things—parents provide.

The only instructions necessary for normal parents come from their babies, and those babies' education proceeds by means of how effectively they are able to communicate their needs to others. If this process is not disrupted but proceeds in the average expectable interaction between healthy infant and responsive parent, a child will learn everything he's capable of learning. If he's comfortable with his own body, confident of himself and in his parents, he will be curious and explorative. As his questions are answered he will think of new ones: What is that? How does it work? Where did it come from? What am I like? Where did I come from? What will happen if I do this or that? The pleasure he takes now in a sense of mastery and his desire to be like his parents are what influence his ability to learn, not special toys or structured "learning games." Everything is a learning game to the two- and three-year-old; what counts is who he plays it with.

In Defense of the Family

The best toys are the household items and personal effects—a saucepan, Daddy's hat, a bunch of keys, Mommy's shoes, a wooden spoon, a comb and brush—that foster identification with grownups through playing at being them and doing what they do. It's nice to have a doll, a truck, a puzzle, too, but no manufactured toy is really necessary to a child, and being given something that belongs to his mother or father or making something with them can be a more effective token of their love than something they've bought him.

In any case, the young child ought to be able to choose what he plays with and how he plays with it. It's in exercising his imagination that he plays out his wishes and fears and comes to terms with them. It's as limiting to push dolls and brooms on boys and trucks and doctor kits on girls as to do it the other way around. The point is not to push at all, but to allow the young child to choose according to his inner needs. An agenda that chooses for him with the intention of avoiding sexual stereotypes is as limiting to personal growth as one that says, This is what girls play with, or That's only for boys. Whether a little girl grows up wanting to be a doctor will have more to do with whether curiosity is allowed expression and competence encouraged and whether she is free of inner conflict—matters that get established in a thousand little interactions over bed and bath and dinner and story times—than whether she's told girls should be doctors or not.

If there are any rules at all about play and pastimes for young children, they follow from the fact that what promotes interaction and identification with parental behavior and parental values is what serves the child and the family best. Being told a story or being read aloud to is enriching; it gives the child food for his imagination in a way he can make use of, build on, and learn from. Television watching is a totally destructive activity. It robs the child of the opportunity to exercise his imagination by constructing his own images of what he hears read or is told or thinks of himself; it encourages intellectual passivity at the very least, and distortions of what human relations, human actions and their consequences are at its worst. Even the benign programs intended to amuse and teach young children are poor substitutes for a parent with a book and a lap; the child cannot ask questions, turn the page back to something he wants to go over again, share the delight his comments on the story cause the reader. Even watching the most clever televised demonstrations of the letters of the alphabet, the child is cut off from any truly human response.

It is the nature of television watching, and not the content of the programs, that is the real enemy of childhood.[42] It works against every important need of the young child: to be interacting with the members of his family, learning about them and himself; to practice skills not only in relating to people but in the active use of his own body and his own imagination; to learn to organize and express his own ideas verbally, first in thought and then in speech and writing; to create his own fantasies in order to work out solutions to his problems.

When a young child is stuck in front of a television set in order to be kept quiet or out of the way or to make it easier to pass the often irritable moments before meals, when television viewing is used as a pacifier or a babysitter, the child is being robbed of the opportunity to work out relationships in the give-and-take of life's many little difficulties and trying situations. He is being robbed of a chance to think up his own uses for his new skills and test his burgeoning capacities, the opportunity to use make-believe to come to terms with reality, to learn who he is and what he can do. Nothing he can possibly learn from television can make up for these losses, and nothing he can learn from television cannot be learned better in other ways, in the context of a responsive human relationship or in his own grapplings with real objects in space and time and his observations of their qualities and what effects his actions have on them.

Language skills show no lasting enhancement from the mere fact of children's being exposed to letters and numbers at an early age;[43] they depend on the human context in which a child learns to talk and listen, is read to and learns to read. The stuporous regression in which the child watches the progression of televised images passing before him does nothing to contribute to his own ability to use language to construct reality, organize feelings, or form connections with others.

What television teaches is mental and physical passivity, no matter what the subject matter of the programs. It consumes the time in which a child "doing nothing" would be daydreaming, drawing, making believe, talking, or even quarreling, filling in his inner landscape or, equally important, discovering what effect his words and actions have on other people. Taking in images he can't place in relation to a view of life he hasn't yet had a chance to form, he misses out on a chance to practice getting along with another child or to get a better idea of what makes Daddy tick. Daddy may watch television as a regression in the service of the ego; the small child's ego hasn't yet been formed.

Missed opportunities for self-discovery and the discovery of others, for independent activity that contributes to the realization of an identity of his own, are the price we pay for the peace and quiet in which the young child sits in front of the screen.

Avoiding quarrels with tired children at the end of the day is an evasion of a responsibility as well as a lost opportunity; it's in the resolution of quarrels, the settling of little daily differences, that children learn how to get along with others and that parents have a chance to make clear what they hope for and expect of their children.

The child needs to know when his parents will say no as well as yes—what they will not stand for as well as what they will permit—if he is to develop a self with inner rules that correspond to theirs. The use of television as a day-end tranquilizer, available without a prescription, may satisfy a child's desire to return to a state of blissful satiation of the senses; it does nothing to encourage him to learn to control himself or his environment, to provide satisfactions for himself or for others.

Is getting rid of television in the home the answer? Not really. The point is not to deprive ourselves of the benefits of our technology just because television is often misused. Instead, while doing what we can to influence its use in ways that are more life-enhancing than destructive of human values, we can exercise our own control over it in our own lives.

Anything, even television viewing, that's shared by child and parent has a meaning that derives from how it is experienced. A once-in-a-while hour spent watching in contact with a parent, sharing thoughts and making comments, not withdrawn into catatonic passivity, can't do much harm, although it's a poor substitute for time spent telling or reading stories together, making something that comes out a tower or a cake and seeing how one's real efforts add up to real pleasures, or just talking together.

And the television set can be an instructive presence. It's there for the grownups to use at certain times they decide on—election night, an old movie, the Superbowl. They have a life of their own full of different kinds of activities, and minds and wills to be understood and reckoned with. Why should a child want to be grown-up if it's the kids who have all the fun, if being grown-up isn't perceived as something special and desirable, a state of grace?[44]

Grownups make decisions about how they live. This is an important thing for children to realize, as is the truth that sometimes even loving parents have to say no to them. You can sometimes help a child more by denying him something—at the right time, in the right way—than by avoiding the occasion for the denial. How can parents bent on avoiding any occasion for disagreement, any denial of easy instant gratification, help a child learn self-control? How can children make parental values their own if they don't know what they are—not just how they are stated but how they determine behavior?

A child may learn from television to recognize letters and numbers at an early age, but that will not make a reader of him; it will only make him a television watcher. If we want to transmit to children our culture and our traditions, what matters to us in our past, and if we want them to make it theirs, they will need to read well and with pleasure. Ours has been a literate culture, and access to the works of reason and of the imagination depends on the ability to read with critical understanding and with sensitivity to the nuances of language, hardly abilities that abound in the population today, even among those who emerge from our institutions of higher learning.

The aim should not be to start a child reading early but to start him reading with pleasure, whether that begins at three or at six. Being read to is the commonest impetus to learning to read by oneself and the first key that unlocks the literature that enriches the self, as much for the little child who recognizes himself in Eeyore or Babar as the adult encountering Anna Karenina or Julien Sorel.

Sadness, danger, humor, risk, struggle, and happy endings are food for the child's imagination, but only when he is actively engaged in adding something of his own. This does not happen when all of his senses are bombarded by a barrage of sights and sounds that leave nothing for him to supply and no faculties unengaged enough to do so. It happens best through the medium of words, which leave the picturing to him.

Bruno Bettelheim has suggested[45] that fairy tales are the best food for the childish imagination, because in their traditional folk form they recapitulate the young hero's struggle to overcome adversities and emerge as a triumphant self, the process that occupies the child's life and his mind, and that they do so without preaching but by reflecting the unconscious conflicts of Everychild and reassuring him he can conquer the ogres within him, surmount the difficulties in the way of accomplishing the tasks assigned to him, and—but only after a valiant struggle to become both smart and strong—in the end one can live happily ever after with a king or queen of one's own.

Far from being unrealistic nonsense, fairy tales and the folk wisdom that has shaped them address the very real problems of the small child in a way he can respond to. The problems are not made explicit, for he would not recognize them in the form of rational statements. His own conflicts are not available to his awareness; in many cases he must deny or disguise them. But he recognizes them in the form of the fears, failures, worries, difficulties, that appear symbolically in fairy tales. Like all of the literature of the imagination, they restate the human condition as one of having to reconcile good and evil in the world and in oneself—the tolerance of ambiguities, the resolution of ambivalence that is at the core of character in real life as in real literature.

The little child, Bettelheim reminds us, must somehow win his struggle to relinquish his infantile dependency wishes; only by going out in the world can he ever find himself. Mulling over such stories in whatever way he chooses to make use of them, without being startled or offended by intrusive rational interpretations of his thoughts, helps a child cope with the problems of growing up and integrating his personality.[46]

The inexplicable delight children find in these stories is like finding themselves in a mirror, but here it is an unknown, secret self. The parent who leaves out the part about Babar's mother's death lest it make her child anxious misses the whole point. By meeting his secret fears and wishes, his deepest hopes and anxieties, in a form he can ponder and mull over, he finds a meaning for himself. Anything he accomplishes for himself is a step toward growing up and far more satisfactory than anything that can be done for him by someone else.

Telling the young child about the three little pigs or Sinbad the Sailor is providing him with an opportunity for inner growth. He draws his own conclusions about the value of effort or perseverance in the face of seemingly insurmountable difficulties and how this might apply to himself and his predicaments. Parents who pass up the literature of the fanciful for an exclusive diet of the more pragmatic stories written to acquaint the child with true life are overlooking the psychological truth that is a component of their subject matter and the style that disguises those truths in a way the child can accept and make use of.

Plenty of time to acquire a rational world view later. Childhood, the time Selma Fraiberg calls the magic years, is a time for beliefs that contribute to security, the best foundation for developing the attitude that, in Bettelheim's words, "life can be mastered in realistic ways",[47] that if one struggles he can succeed.

It can be an enriching experience for a parent, too, this going back to the country of childhood where we once lived like our children and spoke the language of magic like them. Something in the shared moment—like certain lines of poetry, like certain strains of music—is transforming. We experience a heightened sense of ourselves and a moving connection with our children. When experiencing literature is a joy shared with a child by a parent, the child is on the way to adopting it as a valued possession of his own. Schools cannot establish that sense of possession; they can only add to it. Like every real value, it grows out of an early identification.

DISCIPLINE AND CONSCIENCE

The aim of parenthood is to enable a child to grow up. The best way to accomplish this is to let him be babyish when young until he is secure enough and has matured enough to want to go off on his own, and then to encourage him. Pushing him off, like pulling him back, will make growing up harder.

There has to be enough satisfaction of his drives and at the same time enough ability to follow the rules of the world he lives in. Only when these can live together in harmony within the child, neither one winning out at too great a cost to the other, can the child find the kind of balance he needs.

The attempt to avoid any conflict, prevent all anxiety, keep peace at any price is a mistake. It's not in being spared frustration and anger that a child gains but in learning he can deal with them—in amounts that vary at every stage of his development—himself.

He doesn't know what makes things happen; he doesn't know much about the world outside himself. He is more aware of himself than of anything else and often thinks that *he* is what makes things happen. This magical thinking gradually gives way to more realistic ways of understanding the world, but while it holds sway over his mind he has many peculiar ideas and some frightening ones.

He needs some experience in bumping up against the limits of reality or he has no way of determining his own limits. The awful suspicion resides within him that he is omnipotent, and one of the first things he needs to learn is that he is not. It's very hard to trust people you can destroy with an angry wish, have confidence in a self that can wreak havoc or a world one can obliterate with one's rage. There have to be some occasions for learning one cannot destroy with anger and will not be destroyed by the anger of others.

He needs to see clearly that it is the same mother and the same father who give love and discipline, who give him food and comfort and who occasionally deprive or restrain him. If he splits his image of mother or father into an all-good and an all-bad, an all-giving and an all-depriving one—because the deprivation is so overwhelming or his fear of being abandoned so great that he cannot deal with his feelings and must preserve an image of a parent with whom he need not feel angry—then he can't put together his love and his pleasure with his renunciations and his controls. It is in the resolution of this ambivalence that his fate—in terms of his character—is determined.

What is determined is whether he will be able later in life to balance self-indulgence and self-discipline, freedom and responsibility, in his love and in his work, and whether he will be able to deal with authority without being either cowed into subservience or goaded into rebellion by the not remembered but never forgotten experiences of the childhood self.

Unless a child is strongly attached to someone, he has no reason to renounce anything that gives him pleasure. It is by reconciling his love for himself with his love for his parents—his desire to please them as well as himself—that the child begins to make their attitudes his own. In this way he can please them and himself at the same time. He need never be without their love if he can love himself in their place. So now he renounces on his own behalf those pleasures of which he knows they disapprove. Now he disapproves of those things himself, whether his parents are there or not.

He begins by attributing the prohibited behaviors and feeling to others, casting them out of himself. An imaginary animal has wet the bed, a monster has spilled the milk, someone *else* is angry at *him*. Emotions he would deny are his own are transferred to others outside himself, and the consequences of his failures to live up to what his parents expect of him and he expects of himself are attributed to others, too.

In Defense of the Family

These primitive defenses against self-reproach and the reproach of those he loves will fade away to the degree that he succeeds in reconciling opposing wishes—to please himself and to please others—and to find more and more alternative pleasures in the world. The search for substitutes for the desired-but-unacceptable is the basis for most of what we value in science and culture, the arts and the life of the mind.

You may know your four- or five-year-old is goading you into getting angry with him and putting a stop to his latest negative or naughty behavior, but that's no reason to tell him so. This is the time to stop him unequivocally but not unkindly, not to ask him why he's behaving this way. He doesn't know. All he can tell you, he already has—he wants to be stopped, to be reassured that you are in control, that you will not let him hurt himself or you but will not be angry enough to retaliate for his ill will with malevolence of your own.

Attempts to explore his psyche now, with or without his cooperation, can only bewilder and confuse him and reinforce his anxiety. A firm hand, a stern tone, and a sure stand are more reassuring to a distraught child in inner turmoil than attempts to interpret his feelings to him according to some psychologist's suggested script, and probably make it less likely he'll have to consult with any of the good doctor's colleagues later.

The sure parent has always known there was a time to send a child to his room, to say, No, I will not let you behave that way, You cannot impose on others in the family. We have been made unsure by too many experts who have misunderstood what their own discipline should have taught them—that it is in the resolution of conflicts, not the avoidance of conflicts, that character is formed.

Beginning with Dr. Spock's bible[48] we have had a liberal liturgy of child rearing that has told parents how they could make life easier for their children, not how they could make it better for them.[49] Under the new sun that rose on the postwar world in which Dr. Spock's *Baby and Child Care* was first published in the mid-forties, children were no longer seen as the dangerously driven little beasts to be tamed by physical restraints or as the malleable clay to be given shape by the behavioral training of earlier ages[50] but cheerful little creatures whose own appetites should indicate the correct response of parents, who should be guided by the child's preferences whenever possible.

Spock seemed to promise parents that if they did their best to allow their child to follow his own nature, avoiding the pressures and tensions that arise from imposing parental standards and insisting on parental authority, going along with the peer group and letting "other average children" be the arbiter of their child's conduct,[51] they would be rewarded with a friendly, well-adjusted, and self-confident youngster free of anxiety and able to get along with his peers in any situation. Freed from intensity, from the struggle for an identity separate from his parents, from any struggle with rivals or with his own nature, he would be independent—not of others, perhaps, but of his parents.

This happy hedonist may not necessarily be the character type "essential in an economy of abundance" required by the corporate structure of post industrial America, as a neo-Marxist analysis would have it.[52] The narcissistic character bent on self-indulgence and self-realization, with no deep attachments to others and no demanding goals for the self, seems just as consistent with a childhood that has not encouraged identification with parental figures and the attempt to renounce some degree of instinctual gratification for the sake of their approval and, later, one's own. But so does the pent-up rage of the reformer who would sort everyone else into groups and assign each whatever share he thinks is fair. And so does the groupie who must submerge himself in whatever secular religion or politicized faith in order to feel whole and a part of something.

Cause and effect is not so neat a matter in human affairs as in some other aspects of the natural world. There are many possible responses to every state of things, many kinds of character that develop in the meeting place between an individual's biogenetic endowment and a particular set of circumstances in the family or whatever agency of society undertakes to bring up children. The only thing that can be said with a fair chance of being on the right track is that recent history suggests that the restraints of parental authority and parental discipline cannot be so easily dismissed. Where discipline is concerned, less is not necessarily more. The impulses children don't learn, with the help of their parents, to control in childhood—to channel in acceptable and sometimes creative ways—can interfere with the possibility of a good life later.

Dr. Spock's mistake was to think that where there is no overt friction there will be no guilt. What is denied is the inner life, the forbidden wishes of every child that can never be fulfilled, the fantasies and feelings to which they inevitably give rise and the mental mechanisms that are brought into being to guard against the distress they cause and replace them with something else. Envy, guilt, shame, sorrow—like delight, pride, hope, love—are not simply imposed from without, and any doctor who thinks they can be avoided by parental forbearance is more of a doctor of social engineering—and a poor one at that, because his structures are likely to collapse—than of philosophy or medicine.

What parents cannot do is prevent feelings of envy, of rivalry, of sadness, guilt, or sorrow. These feelings are inevitable. They come with the human territory. What they *can* do is influence their outcome, help decide whether they are used to strengthen or weaken character. Introspection and self-judgment seem too great a price to pay for affability and popularity.

The sensible parent chooses both the occasion and the degree of discipline. A mild reproach, or simply disappointment, is about as far as one should go with very little children, and it would seem best to avoid making them feel guilty about wetting or dirtying themselves, handling their genitals, or other expressions of impulse behavior not yet brought under control lest we distort their reactions to instinctual satisfactions in ways that will have lasting effects. In the first couple of years of life it's best to encourage what's desired and, when necessary, control any dangerous behavior without frightening the child.

By three or four, when a child can clearly understand such rules, he should begin to feel guilty if he hits other children or takes their things away, as long as he also feels that by giving up such actions he can regain the love and approval of others and himself. Why else would he renounce killing and stealing as he grew up? How else would moral imperatives come about? Would there ever be enough policemen, enough prisons for a community in which all children were raised without any feelings of guilt?

Extreme punishment—inflicting physical pain, denying food, enforcing inactivity or isolation for long periods of time—is only an invitation to fantasies of retaliation and revenge. And while a swift spanking may clear the air, by the same token it leaves no residue of dissatisfaction with the self, no discomfort that would lead to the repudiation of the act. One's account is paid, and no further statement, from others or from oneself, will be presented. Behavior is affected externally—one may learn not to do something out of fear of punishment—but not internally. There is no contribution made to conscience, to self-discipline.

Empathy—the capacity to imagine oneself in another's place and to imagine another's feelings—is the basis of any true morality. It is achieved through the attachment to parents and the education given by them in the early years of life. It requires of the child the voluntary surrender of certain primitive pleasures but allows him to retain enough capacity for self-indulgence to enjoy life—what Freud meant by "regression in the service of the ego."

Withdrawal of love and approval, as long as it is temporary and clearly related to some behavior of the child's, not pervasive and long-lasting enough to create a feeling of complete and hopeless worthlessness, contributes to the creation of conscience and thus of character. It establishes the fact that the child is considered responsible for his actions and accorded the respect of being so treated.

Without the occasional criticism and disapproval of a loving and loved parent there is simply no chance of developing a conscience that does a realistic job of judging one's actions, controlling the basic human appetites enough to permit a person to live well in society. Such a conscience is neither a merciless tyrant forbidding all pleasures and indulgences nor an all-forgiving accomplice that permits whatever can be gotten away with. Parental love that is "unconditional"—no matter what you do, we will understand and comfort you—is as poor a preparation for adult life as the parental rejection that destroys all the possibility of love of self or others.

Parents have been made to feel guilty about their children's guilt feelings, but unless a child feels guilty about certain actions he has no reason not to repeat them when no one's looking. Of course, we don't want him to feel guilty about everything he does, but it is also crippling to grow up feeling guilty about nothing one does.

This is not a perfect world. Risk and pain are part of life, and how we encounter them is what makes us who we are. There are no perfect parents, no ideal fathers and mothers. There are only men and women who are the best they can be, do what they can, hope for the best. Oddly enough, most of them do quite well as parents.

The adequate father, like the "good enough mother" Winnicott describes,[53] is tolerant and flexible, sure enough of himself to allow a child's thoughts and aggressive, hostile wishes against him verbal expression while calmly limiting their physical expression in destructive acts. He gradually changes in response to his child's changing nature, more gentle with an infant and somewhat more distant and demanding of the child whose enlarging capacities enable him to do more things for himself. A boy needs a strong image of his father to live up to, to measure himself against, to strive to become like—someone it seems worthwhile trying to surpass someday. A girl needs to know she is respected by her father as well as cherished. Girls, like boys, know that their parents imagine their futures for them, and their own hopes, like their own despairs, have their origins in what they make of these parental imaginings. They need not be ineluctably binding, but they leave their mark.

The danger for most parents today lies not in following their intuitions; most of what their common sense tells them is what has worked since history began whenever affection was guided by individual life experience. The danger today is that an explosion of information, although not necessarily of wisdom, often pressures them to lay aside their own direction in favor of some agenda persuasively proposed by a special-interest group. Feminists, not content with removing barriers, supply schemes for directing children's thinking about the nature and roles of the sexes; never mind that the result, if any parent were foolish enough to follow their directions literally, would be more sexual confusion than sexual enlightenment. Others tout group day care to "free" the child from the family, use of the schools to teach "values" (theirs, of course). Still others urge early efforts to teach children, by means of their books, toys, programs, all of them expensive and most of them superfluous, skills the child will learn when he is ready in the normal course of family life. Most of these prescriptions for child rearing are of dubious value to the child or his parents; they are in the interests of those who prescribe them and profit by them.

The needs of a particular social philosophy or a specific industry are not necessarily those of the child or the child's family. Most people, using their own brains to guide their own hearts, will do fine as parents if they ignore most of what is said in the media and, where they have questions they feel they cannot answer for themselves, ask other parents about *their* experiences and think about how it might apply to themselves and their own children.

No one would suggest you have to spend every minute of the day and night with your child, but if you do not take care of him much of the time when he is very young you will not have a chance to establish that rapport that enables you to understand his needs and meet them in the way that both encourages identification and permits separation.

The real basis of independence is the capacity for self-control and children gradually learn to control themselves by borrowing the rules of parents they want to please—because they are aware they can displease them, too, but care for them enough to want to be like them and liked by them—and using these rules until they become their own. Some degree of anxiety about deserving his parents' love—and particularly his father's—is a requirement for the development of conscience and the kind of character—structured not around personal fulfillment or social adjustment but adherence to an integrated set of inner values—most of us want for our children.

It depends on what you want. Generations of a certain class of Englishmen have been given over to the care of over-stimulating nannies and then of brutalizing boarding schools. They grew up to love horses and each other and distinguish themselves in the foreign service or by writing novels, some of them quite wonderful. Who's to say that in removing the torments of their childhoods we would not have flattened their talents and deprived them of their glories as well?

And then there are the relativists all around us, reminding us that things are done differently in different cultures, and that primitive societies have a more natural approach to sex than ours.

But, after all, it is *this* culture and *this* society we live in. Civilization and the much-maligned technology that provides so many wonders in our lives and does away with the need to make slaves of each other do not go hand in hand with primitive life or primitive education for life.

For most of us, average middle-class Americans living during the end of the twentieth century, it is the traditional values of our existing society we want to foster, not subvert, and these are the values we want to transmit to our children, not because they have been perfectly realized, but because they have never been so well realized anywhere else. We can tolerate less than perfect justice for the sake of quite a lot of freedom, and plan patiently for things to become even better, although probably not by the day after tomorrow, because any kind of real achievement takes effort, and effort takes time. We are better off, most of us, than our grandparents, and we hope our grandchildren will be better off than we are. All we expect is that they have the opportunity open to them as individuals to go as far, and in whatever direction, as their endowment allows them to. Their birthright is a given capacity; their entitlement is the opportunity to develop that capacity to the fullest.

It is these traditional values of the middle class we are concerned to instill in our children, and we do not feel we need to apologize for this intention. We will give up a little at both ends of the spectrum—the finely honed sensitivity that may make an artist of a miserable man, the natural freedom of the primitive who tastes only what he grows and lives without the devices of machinery or the capabilities of architecture—for men and women who can befriend each other, plan for the future, extend our knowledge and control of natural forces, and more and more of whom gradually make life on earth fuller and richer for themselves and each other: men and women who have the discipline necessary to tolerate and contribute to life in a free society.

3

Family, Child, and the World Beyond

Introduction

The world a child enters around the age of five or six is what most of us have in mind when we talk of the world of childhood. These are the middle years of childhood, the stage usually referred to as the school years or the latency period.

The term "latency" is used in different ways. It sometimes defines an age, roughly the years from six to twelve, and sometimes a physiological state, from the loss of the first baby or "milk" teeth to the onset of puberty, during which time sexual drives seem to be relatively quiescent and there is a period of relative calm between the rapidly unfolding developmental changes of infancy and early childhood and the upheavals to come with the attainment of genital maturity.

In addition to these, it refers to a state of mind, a receptivity to all kinds of learning and a relative psychological calmness that makes it possible for this learning to go on. The child who has successfully negotiated the passage from close attachment to his parents and the establishment of a sense of self, an individual identity as this particular girl or boy, and who is able to relinquish the wish to go on forever belonging exclusively to father and mother, is ready to enter the latency period.

Another way of putting it is that the child who now realizes the futility of taking a parent's place and is ready to settle for being like the parent some day, becomes interested in learning all the things he'll have to know in order to do so. The desire to be a grownup is one spur to learning how to be one. Another, as any kindergarten teacher knows, is the sheer pleasure of accomplishment, of getting the pieces of the puzzle to fit together, of making things move, of getting them to go, of cleaning them, of putting a mark somewhere or taking one off. Gradually, the pleasure in doing is complemented by a pleasure in knowing, one component of which is a sublimation of sexual curiosity into more general curiosity—wanting to know how everything is made and how it works.

New cognitive capacities, the emerging mental structures that now make it possible to entertain abstract concepts, to understand ideas of time and space and deal with symbols in the language of words and number systems,[1] as well as physical maturation, the muscular development that with increasing size and strength makes new kinds of physical accomplishments possible,[2] must be accompanied by the psychological state we call latency if the child is to learn the skills he'll need in order to accomplish the tasks of adolescence and eventually do the work of an adult in our culture.

What is this state of mind, this apparent combination of psychological steadiness and readiness for learning, and why does it form a necessary bridge between the early childhood years and adolescence?[3]

Before we try to answer this question, it seems like a good idea to look at what the school-years child or, as one once described herself, the "middle-aged child"[4] is like. Boys' and girls' developmental patterns—and in fact their worlds—diverge so markedly during this period that we will look at them separately, to see how different forms of the same general psychological needs, desires, and defenses express themselves in the two sexes. When we have an idea of what school-children, "kids," are like and why they act the way they do, we can ask what follows for parents of children this age who are rapidly leaving them behind for the peer group—friends and *their* families—the school—the classroom with its teachers and the playground with its leaders—and the influence of other institutions of society, such as the increasingly pervasive media and, through the widespread funding of various kinds of educational programs, the government.

It is not always easy to tolerate their sometimes maddening idiosyncrasies and at the same time provide the desirable encouragement of kids' increasing independence without losing control over who is influencing them out there. And "out there" somewhere is where a boy this age is most often to be found. What is it he's up to out there?

School Days

On my block, when I was a kid, there was a lot of loose talk being carried on above our heads about how a father was supposed to be a pal to his boy. This was just another of those stupid things that grownups said. It was our theory that the grownup was the natural enemy of the child, and if any father had come around being a pal to us we would have figured he was either a little dotty or a spy. What we learned we learned from another kid . . . . When you were a little kid, you stood around while a covey of ancients of nine or ten played mumbly-peg, shifting from foot to foot and wiping your nose on your sleeve and hitching up your knickerbockers, saying, "Lemme do it, aw come on, lemme have a turn," until one of them struck you in a soft spot and you went home to sit under the porch by yourself or found a smaller kid to torture, or loused up your sister's rope-skipping, or made a collection of small round stones. The small round stones were not *for* anything, it was just to have a collection of small round stones.[5]

What boys do in the private world that now separates them from those older and younger than themselves is make rules. For secret languages, for choosing sides, for opening doors, and for closing them. They collect things. Stamps, shells, comic books, bubble-gum cards. They count things. Foreign cars, out-of-state license plates, joggers, red lights. They join things. Clubs for trading stamps (or shells, or comic books, or bubble-gum cards), teams for playing baseball (or football or stoopball), groups for biking (or hiking or setting up a lemonade stand—or just for belonging to—preferably with elaborate rules and ceremonies, secret oaths and passwords, and sometimes more officers than regular members). They make things. Models of planes or rockets. Cardboard-box shacks or packing-case houses. They are busy all the time, although preferably as far out of sight of parents and family as possible, and active all the time, with an apparent inability to sit still or even to remain at rest for any length of time except when asleep. They twist and squirm around themselves or the furniture while reading a book, and jab or punch each other while talking. While for many of them it becomes a point of honor to complain about school and pretend to dislike it, they are capable of mastering enormous amounts of new knowledge and are incorrigible learners, in and out of school. They try new things, keep at them obsessively for hours or days, then drop the interest completely for something new. They may neglect to wash unless firmly encouraged to do so on the grounds that the sight and smell of them has begun to give offense, and may be as disorganized and sloppy with their personal effects and their surroundings as they are ordered and compulsive with their collections and prizes. They seem preoccupied with injustice—especially toward themselves—and are often heard uttering the bitter and indignant watchwords of their age: "That's not fair!" They gripe about many things, not least the backwardness and lack of understanding that characterize those same parents toward whom they felt such awe and adoration only a short time ago. Such feelings are explained by them quite objectively on the basis that they alone of all their acquaintances of the same age are not allowed to stay up all night or watch horror movies on television or go downtown alone or have a sixty-dollar football helmet. In fact, they are kept in a state of abject poverty by the only stingy parents in a population of open-handed families. At the same time, and with complete equanimity, once outside of parental earshot they can be heard to boast about parental accomplishments and refer as the final authority to parental opinion. A similar inconsistency may characterize their behavior toward girls, who are traditionally maligned in the all-male packs and gangs and clubs in which boys swarm and in which they find their new identity, separate and unabashedly unequal, but they may enjoy the friendship and happily share the interests and activities of an individual girl—who is always declared to be an exception.

And what of her, the female counterpart of this collector-joiner-organizer? What is she up to as they go their largely separate ways through the culture of middle childhood?

> Your mother and my mother
> Were hanging out the clothes.
> My mother gave your mother
> A punch in the nose.
> How many punches did she get?
> One, two, three, four . . .[6]

Girls, too, collect (pictures of heroes or heroines of the entertainment or sports world, dolls, and, later, clothes—in addition to the things like leaves or matchbox covers they may share an interest in with boys), and join (although they have always seemed more likely than boys to be preoccupied with shifting alliances of friends and enemies and their secret clubs sometimes seem to exist mainly for the purpose of keeping others out, with any actual activity pursued in common only secondary), and team up (choosing sides to jump rope with the same ruthless abandonment of empathy with which boys let it be known who's worth picking for the ball team). They make lists (cities to be visited someday, favorite people, hated people) and draw clothes for paper dolls. Their need for large-muscle exercise and aggressive activity is less conspicuous than boys', and they are more likely to prefer formalized games like tennis and small-muscle skills like playing jacks to the rough-and-tumble of the boys' world. They are more likely now than they were a generation ago to be encouraged to play ball and participate in team sports but will still be eschewed as teammates by most boys on the grounds that they are smaller, weaker, and less skillful, even where this is manifestly not the case. Unlike boys, they take an interest in clothes and personal appearance. They like to take care of small things (although perhaps not their own younger sisters and brothers), and while they share an interest in dogs and cats (and especially puppies and kittens) with boys, they often, as they approach adolescence, go wild over horses. They have less difficulty than boys in sitting still, and may in fact spend hours talking on the phone. At the beginning of latency they are still much given to dramatic play, and like to dress up and play house, hospital, or, if both sexes are involved, office or store. The latter situation offers not only the role-playing aspect of all these games in which children pretend to be grownups doing grownups' work, but involves collecting and arranging a stock and counting out change, activities that are much enjoyed at this age.

There are always differences between individuals, even at this most conforming of ages, and there can even be more differences between two girls or two boys than between a particular girl and boy, but on the whole, looking at large groups of schoolchildren (which is how one is most likely to see them), boys and girls appear to persist, despite current efforts to equalize the experience of the two sexes in all things, in demonstrating different characteristics. Girls are generally more amenable in school, where they find it easier to behave appropriately; tend to be more interested than boys in language that describes feelings, as well as in feelings themselves and social relationships in general; and are more given to fantasy play than acting out of aggressive impulses. While there is a biological basis for these differences in the greater level of aggressivity in males[7] and the fact that in the middle years boys and girls mature at different rates, the

117

girls often towering over their male age-mates as they near puberty, much of it is clearly culturally determined, consisting of attitudes and patterns of behavior traditionally considered masculine or feminine.

Before we decide whether that fact should fill us with horror and whether we should rush to change this state of things, let us consider these characteristics of school-age girls and boys in terms of what meaning they may have in the context of what we understand to be the psychological tasks of the latency period. What do kids have to do during these years before puberty, and how does it get done?

WORK AND PLAY: PRACTICING AND PRETENDING

The start of the school years, around five or six, is the beginning of what Erikson calls the "age of industry," when "the child must turn from an exclusive, pregenital attachment to his parents to the slow process of becoming a parent, a carrier of tradition . . . . The inner stage seems all set for 'entrance into life,' except that life must first be school life . . . . The child must forget past hopes and wishes, while his exuberant imagination is tamed and harnessed to the laws of impersonal things—the three R's."[8] He must forget, and redirect, his wish to stay forever in the womb of his family; the repression of old desires and sublimation of instinctual energy are crucial during these years. Without an appropriate degree of this repression and sublimation of drives he cannot complete the business of these years, which is learning—applying himself to the acquisition of skills he will need to do the work of an adult in the culture, and to the understanding of the past, which will help him to continue to define himself by giving meaning to the world and his eventual place in it.

In a literate society, and a highly technological one, that means first of all learning to read and deal with numbers. A child this age who is overstimulated sexually or unable to leave his home and parents emotionally, cannot do the work of learning, master the skills he will need in order to go on in life in our society. It is not that the child this age has no capacity for sexual interest and sexual excitement, but that it must be deemphasized if he is to direct his energies toward learning and mastery. "Latency" does not mean that the child has no sexual drives—there are sexual desires and dreams at every stage of life[9]—but that he must be helped to detach himself from the inner preoccupations of another stage in order to be instructed in the culture he will inherit.[10] He must take emotional leave of the world of the home for the world of the school, and learn—through his play as well as through formal instruction—to enjoy work and take pride in what he makes, in what he produces and the process by which he does so; he must acquire a sense of competence and of responsibility for the consequences of what he undertakes.

Thus one of the requirements for acculturation is a period in which sexual gratification is inhibited—delayed until genital maturity. There are two paths of discharge open for the child's latent sexual drives: physical activity and fantasy.

There is less overt masturbation in early latency than among younger children or those already approaching adolescence, but much of the games and sports of these years has an obvious although disguised masturbatory quality.[11] Shifting the focus of their feelings from genital wishes to discharge them in real activities, children find games, competitive team sports, and athletic activities of all kinds a useful way to quiet the stirrings that would otherwise interfere with their ability to sit still and concentrate at least some of the time, to be studious and industrious when necessary. Boys, more physically aggressive because of a combination of hormonal, muscular, and cultural forces, biologically stronger and psychologically less fearful, tend to engage more in games and sports that involve movement of the whole body and even an element of violence and danger. Girls are apt to find pleasure in the genital stimulation involved in swings and teeter-totters or in horseback riding. Gym and recess are very important parts of the school day and the child who says his favorite subject is recess is not rejecting learning so much as acknowledging the necessity of periods of physical activity—as well as fantasy play—that make it possible for learning to go on.

This is a time of great activity, but the child also needs time for privacy and withdrawal into the world of his own fantasies and, increasingly, those of others—books, plays, works of art that can help shape the pretending by which he acts roles and expresses feelings. At the onset of latency, in the years from about five or six to eight or nine, there is a good deal of symbolic fantasy and imaginative play, of make-believe that moves from supernatural and magical to more and more realistic kinds of imitation of grownups until, during the years from about eight or nine to around twelve or whenever puberty occurs, the child gradually becomes ready to direct his feelings and wishes less to fantasy and more to other real people. Then fantasy changes to a form of planning for the future, games in which real-life situations in the adult world are acted out. Fantasies have more to do with the real world than they used to. While he is still afraid of the dark sometimes, the latency child no longer peoples it with the amorphous shapes of ghosts and monsters but with human forms like those of robbers and kidnappers.

Play can give the child the opportunity for control in fantasy of a world that still outruns and threatens to overwhelm him in reality, enable him to tolerate his real-life passivity by playing out an active role, like the child who after a visit to the doctor or surgery will enact over and over the events of the office visit or the hospitalization, giving injections and removing tonsils from afflicted teddy bears and dolls, reliving the occasion with himself in charge instead of simply having things done to him. Fantasy is also a way to work off unacceptable feelings of anger in pretended violence, being a bank robber or a soldier. And it also provides opportunities to identify with heroes and heroines, being a great pianist while one practices, or an astronaut while on the swing. Acting out his wishes in fantasy play is an outlet for the inevitable frustrations of the age; it enables the child to discharge some of the occasional rage and hostility he feels and remain at peace with his parents and teachers.[12]

Another kind of fantasy is not acted out but imagined, not played but thought, through words and stories, the legends and myths of the culture. Identifying with heroes, the child takes on some of their characteristics as part of himself.

Family, Child and the World Beyond

FEELINGS AND FOLLOWING, RULES AND READING

In the later part of latency, the years from about eight or nine to around twelve, or whenever puberty occurs, the child makes great strides in reality testing and thinking. He is more and more oriented to the outer world, aware of the approach of adolescence and already concerned about preparing for the future. Boys think a lot about body size and strength, about learning karate blows or excelling at team sports. The constant activity, the need to be always doing something, and doing it oneself, is a help in fighting off the fear of passivity, a reassurance that one will be able to assume the role of man or woman. Just as boys this age may feel anxiety about their masculinity, girls are often irritable with the most well-meaning of parents, and *"Please,* Mother! I can do it *myself!"* begins to replace "That's not fair!" as the most often-heard cry.

Whether they've heard about it from their parents or their peers, girls this age know about menstruation and await its onset as a decisive event in their lives. They wonder what it will feel like and when it will happen, they talk about it and pore over pictures of women's bodies, think about clothes and hairdos, and otherwise show a great interest in their changing bodies. Anxiety over changing body image and private fears and fantasies are not always amenable to common-sense explanations and rational information. Despite well-meant instruction, girls may be bothered by thoughts of dirtiness and messiness, fears of losing control of the products of their bodies, that refer back to early childhood experiences in being toilet trained and the fantasies surrounding those experiences. These emotions sometimes interfere with girls' capacity to concentrate on abstract problem solving, particularly those dealing with spatial concepts and mathematics.[13]

Unlike the sexual apparatus of the boy, which is clearly visible and familiar to him, the girl's is hidden and complicated, a mystery within.[14] A sensitive response to her questions and clearly presented answers are helpful, but her feminine identity is helped most by her

121

mother accepting her as a woman, being pleased by their growing similarities, not threatened or resentful or competitive, and by a father who is neither seductive nor withdrawn, neither excited nor repelled by her body changes and changing attitudes. No matter what she is told, a girl's first menstruation is always something of a surprise, and, again, attitude is at least as important as information in sex education, which we'll come to in more detail further on.

Puberty is a more gradual matter for the boy, whose first ejaculation is a private event and not the kind of milestone the first menstrual period is. It may be disturbing to a boy who is worried about his masculinity if it occurs in the context of a homosexual situation or homosexual fantasies, seeming to confirm a fear in the ambivalent or anxious child that he is abnormal. What he needs is reassurance, and how it might be given and by whom we'll also consider when we talk about schools and sex.

The schoolchild has to do a lot of things that are hard for him, and in order to keep trying he has to do some things that make him feel better while making no apparent sense to an outsider. He still has desires sometimes for what he knows must be given up—to be a baby again—and sometimes overreacts in order not to regress, swaggering and bullying to assure himself he's a "big guy." Sometimes he defends against the desire to masturbate openly by obsessional counting or compulsively following superstitious rules like hitting every fourth fence post he passes or only opening doors in a certain way, or ordering his collections of coins or stamps or rocks, all of which calm him, occupying his mind and giving him a sense of control over his world and himself. He may overeat, or bite his nails, or do a lot of scratching. Most of this behavior is usually transitory and will disappear with the need to fight off the discomforts peculiar to this age.

The rituals serve not only to keep the mind too busy and full to admit the unwanted thought or feeling, a kind of primitive charm, warding off internal dangers, but serve in their public forms, in chants and games, to connect the child with other children. The rites are known to everyone who belongs to the group, the rules are followed by everyone in his place. They are shared. To be a member is to belong.[15]

Another way to deal with the feelings of separateness and resist the desire to return to childhood dependency is finding a special friend, the intimate and confidante most girls find as they approach adolescence.

His budding conscience is a distinctive characteristic of the latency child, and a capacity he is also given to practicing in this period. Understanding and following the rules of the game becomes very important. By now he is aware of the rules of home and able to follow them even when he is not there and not being watched. He has internalized his parents' strictures and—at least most of the time—does not do the things they've taught him not to do, not just out of fear of being punished or shamed, but because he feels guilty if he does.

Now he is ready to learn the rules of school and playground, and he devotes himself to the niceties of what one is or is not supposed to do—and to how the rules can sometimes be circumvented—with a true legalistic bent. Rules are sometimes invented for games that are never played, the whole point having been the codification of the rules, the choosing of sides, the determination of a hierarchy of titular leadership. He is not just learning what to do, but learning to tell himself when to do what. You run around at recess, you sit still and pay attention—as much as you can—in the classroom, you daydream or masturbate only in the privacy of your own room.

Intellectually he has taken a giant leap, entering during this period upon the phase Piaget calls concrete operational thinking,[16] and he has conceptual memory organization as well. Abstract thinking and verbal memory open up the world of learning for him. He can learn and recall mentally now, not just through physical experience. He has gone from counting on his fingers to counting in his head, from physical to mental problem-solving techniques. This is what will make it possible for him to retain what he learns and apply it to new situations. He is developing a verbal repertoire of solutions that make it possible to deal with increasingly complicated problems, and he is developing realistic concepts of time (telling time is the great achievement of latency, like walking for the toddler) as well as of space and distance.

He is more receptive to new experience than he will ever be again in his life; his curiosity amounts to a great hunger for learning, made possible by the absence of other preoccupations—he is not in love, he does not have to earn a living—and the great contribution of parents to his well-being at this time of life is to provide him with the emotional freedom to pursue this bent. What does that mean in terms of the attitudes they take toward school, toward pastimes, and toward the media?

With his burgeoning capacity for both intellectual and social judgment, for making discriminations both in abstract problem solving and on moral issues, the latency child is spending a lot of time deciding between alternatives. Much of this decision making is on a daily basis, at home, in school, and out at play. But he is also thinking ahead, deciding between the alternatives that will eventually make him the kind of person he will go through life as. It can make all the difference how rich his range of choices is and where they come from. Traditionally, they have come not only from the real people he knows but from literature, the tales and stories, myths and legends, poems and novels that are the carriers of our culture and its values. Those that have lasted through time—the ones we have read to our children and our parents had read to us—are the shared myths that bind the generations.

The drama of all real literature is moral choice. Men and women choose between alternative ways of acting and being, and in identifying with characters in literature the child tries on a series of ways of living. This vicarious experience is enriching to the degree that the choices are subtle and complex and the characters fully realized. Books written to instruct children, like television programs, are pap compared to the classics—which include the *Odyssey* as well as *Winnie the Pooh*, *Alice's Adventures in Wonderland* as well as *The Sea Dog* and *Black Beauty*, and biographies of the men and women who are exemplars of the life well lived, whether in adventure, invention, art, or sport—as long as they are larger than life. This is not a stage of life for cynicism. Children need heroes. Out of how he pictures what they did the child constructs a system of ethics, taking a little here and there. He will identify with these figures of the past as he once did with his parents, pretend to be them, take on their characteristics, want to become like them.

The point hardly needs belaboring that a TV personality, a trendy teacher with an ax to grind, or a pop-music or film star is not a very satisfactory purveyor of alternative paths for the inner journey the child is setting off on. And reading about other lives is unique in permitting a choice of pace, a wandering of the mind, a remembering and looking back and thinking over, a picturing for oneself, that enriches the imagined life and makes it truly one's own. "Values," by which is meant what lives, what actions, what styles of thought our children will follow, has become a subject of instruction. Should it be? This is another question, like sex education, to consider when we turn to schools and their function.

To the developing self of childhood and adolescence, the world is always new. At each stage of life there are discoveries about the world around us and about ourselves. What the child sees, he applies to himself. Some of the heroes and images acquired now remain with him for a lifetime, reverberating however faintly in later experiences. The crudely depicted actions and the casual sadism of television and comics are regressive; they may do no harm except to waste time in the life of a child who has a lot else going on in his life, but they do nothing to enrich his breadth of vision or his sense of choice. Literature, on the other hand, whether fairy tale or novel, deals with choice—with the decisions between alternatives in life we call moral choices, questions like what is due oneself and others, how to pursue one's ambitions, what is the nature of love, what are some of the consequences of courses men and women have taken in their lives. Children are not bored by these questions; they are fascinated by them, because they mirror their own preoccupations both in the present reality and their imaginings of their future.

The "young people's book" and the well-meant classroom discussion of "values" may try to consider some of these questions, but they're a poor substitute, unlikely to inspire or to haunt a young mind for long. Flatness of language and absence of ambiguity and complexity of plot, of any sense of the depth and mystery of human character, are a mean trade-off, although easier of access, for what the best storytellers have left us.

Once children have been convinced to make the effort that might be called "the first hundred pages," to allow an author time to create a setting and characters of some complexity, they usually learn that the pleasure the ensuing adventures yield touches them in more ways and is remembered longer than the easily entered and shallow world of comics or "young people's books." If you can start a child reading *A High Wind in Jamaica* or *The Once and Future King* instead of the latest Judy Blume or other trendy book for preteens turned out by the commercial presses, you've made him a gift. He may not know it now; he'll thank you for it later.

He is interested in how his increasingly complicated self will manage in the grown-up world. Richer thoughts will be suggested to him by a book that has stood the test of time, because what it has to say and the way it has said it have touched one generation after another.

The function of reading is the widening of intellectual, aesthetic, and moral horizons and not merely the therapeutic recognition of one's own childish social problems in others and the exploitive assurance that as a child one is way ahead of the world of—for the most part—conventional and unimaginative grownups. This sort of thing has made a lot of "young people's writers" and their publishers rich while doing very little to enrich the lives of young readers. The new emphasis in these books on masturbation, on racial prejudice, on divorce, on teen-age pregnancy in the lives of young people is not honesty, because it's usually too simply conceived and expressed to contain any real human truth. It's simply fashionable. It mirrors the received wisdom of the segment of the population from which many writers and editors come, and it makes a lot of money for some of them and takes up a lot of space on shelves in schools and libraries.

What used to be on those shelves, in addition to the stories of imagined lives like those of David Copperfield and Jim Hawkins, Jo

Family, Child and the World Beyond

March and Sara Crewe, were stories of real men and women. Biographies of scientists, sports heroes, presidents, warriors, and adventurers of all kinds taught children about perseverance, fair play, dedication, courage. These are appropriate qualities for children to meet in a context of praise for the great achievers of the past and present, and such praise, even when straightforward and unsubtle, gives a young child more of what he needs than all the sophisticated, attractively packaged stories of kids just like him written in language just like his (no need to strain for meaning or cope with mystery) that are selling moral and cultural relativism and the joys of self-gratification and that stop short of offering any vision of how he might someday be more than he is now.

Where children once read stories, poring over books and their marvelous illustrations in their long hours of leisure on the porch or in the yard, in the neighborhood library or at home, the media have stepped in. There is no leisure for the minds of children anymore unless we make it for them, try to give them a ticket for a voyage at sea in a world peopled on every shore by creatures of their imagination, not imprisoned by the overwhelming barrier to imagining that is created by the sight and sound and now and pow of television, more exhausting than refreshing for the child.

But if there is no vacuum there is no place for the world of TV and exploitive movies, for the drug-and-rock-music culture. Children who are busy enough and happy enough at being busy, given books to read by people they love and admire, have a chance to talk about what they read with enthusiasm or dislike, feel themselves growing and enjoy the pleasure that growth gives to those around them, will participate in some of everything else that's around, too. That's natural at this age, when there's a need to move beyond home and participate in the world of other children. But they won't be as easily seduced by the world of the media. Hold off the influence of what you think is cheapening or destructive as long as you can. You may succeed in developing at least a partial immunity.

Only a very foolish and irresponsible parent would not take a great interest in what is directed at his child all day, whether from Harvard,

127

where activist professors of education, for the most part committed to restructuring society through the schools, formulate policy; from Washington, where funds are allocated to implement social experiments through school policy; or from Madison Avenue, which corners the attention of the child for the greater part of the time that he is not in school, delivering its messages directly into the home via the electronic tube.

A fact that should give anyone pause is that the main activity of American children is watching television. According to the report of the Surgeon General's Scientific Advisory Committee on Television and Social Behavior published in 1972,[17] and there is no reason to think things have improved in the decade since, more of the average child's waking time is spent in front of the television screen than in school. And about all that can be said for television as a diversion for children is that it beats public executions, which they often witnessed in seventeenth-century England and France, where other public amusements included bear baiting and dog fights to the death.

Even the much-advertised early advantage to vocabulary supposed to result in preschoolers who watch television is a chimera.[18] Whatever gain occurs is not maintained, if there is no practice in the usage of those words. Another problem with television language is that it is not the language of life—and not the language of literature, either. It has no richness, no strangeness, no power to evoke. What it does have is the capacity to displace reading, time together with friends and parents, talking, playing games, making plans, learning, getting to know each other. And ourselves.

When children do read, there are many reasons why they should be reading the classics, those books that have appealed to succeeding ages, rather than the realistic children's literature of the moment, by means of which adults attempt to manipulate them. What the books manufactured especially for children of school age by the publishing industry have always tended to do is teach the child a lesson. Whether it was yesterday's conformity to the group or is today's nonconformity to traditional values, it is still thin fare. It lacks the artistic ambiguities that stimulate thought rather than handing on opinion.[19]

Family, Child and the World Beyond

There is a good deal to be said for reading from the past; children get enough of the present all around them, in school and through the media. What has been preserved and inherited confers a longer perspective and serves to bind the generations; it has lasted precisely because of its appeal, whether the anonymous folk fairy tales or the creation of an artist like Lewis Carroll, to universal fantasies, conscious and unconscious. This is quite different from the fantasies manufactured by television or movie technocrats, with their packaged special effects that leave nothing to the child's imagination and their hard sell that makes it hard for him to escape from them. The magic, the dreams and the excitement in the fairy tales or the novel that has kept its hold on us are far more nourishing for the child than the earnest books designed to influence him about such matters as sex roles. And since you never really know what a child makes of any kind of reading, why not give him what provides the greatest possibilities of finding his own meanings, ways of seeing his own life?

Fiction gives us a chance to live other lives, for a time to wear the disguises of others' imagination and thereby enlarge our own. Fantasy, unlike acting out, permits a return to ourselves. It has that enlarging capacity the earliest dramatists understood of enabling us to see new aspects of human life and human characters. It doesn't just pass the moments, it changes us a little for always. If as a child you've never wept over the death of Abel Magwitch or mourned some other fallen character, you've had an impoverished life. But when will a child find time to read a long novel like *Great Expectations* if he's always in front of the TV screen?

The responsibility of parents and school is to see that he isn't. To offer better things to do, and to assign and expect homework. What if he complains that everyone else "watches?" He may grumble, but what does it mean to be the parent or the teacher if you don't indeed know better than he does—and have the grace to insist patiently, if not amiably? Amid the current talk of children's rights it should be made clear that just as babies have the right to be mothered, young children have the right to be educated, and that such rights are parents' responsibilities.

In Defense of the Family

THE PLACE OF PARENTS

What do school-age children need from their parents in order to maintain the equilibrium necessary to learn all the things they can in all the ways possible for them?

It seems fitting here, talking about these enthusiastic list makers, to make a list.

They need encouragement to learn and achieve, to master verbal expression and abstract thought, plan projects and carry them through. You show the child what you think is important not by hitting the ceiling about his shortcomings but by what you take seriously— schoolwork and, yes, grades, and not how popular he happens to be this term, or whether or not she should have a training bra like "all the other girls." Taking things seriously means just that—not making them unpalatable by being insistent or humorless or inflexible or punitive, but taking a calm yet obvious pride in those of his achievement you value without lecturing or hovering over him every moment. He needs to feel what he does is his choice and his achievement.

They need to define themselves as being of a separate generation and a particular gender, to have a sense of belonging, not only of loss, as they begin to move out of the parental nest, and to form the secure sexual identity that forms part of a stable personality.[20] The evidence is that what boys and girls learn about being men and women—and themselves—is learned not from what they are told, lectured about, or have preached to them, but what they come to feel observing their mothers and fathers in the context of daily family life.

Boys and girls going their largely separate ways at this age may be following self-made rules based on feelings appropriate to their stage of life. Pushing them together makes no more sense than keeping them apart. Whether they are actually aware of it or not, they are often avoiding precocious sexuality. This will not necessarily create either misogynists or shrinking violets, as long as they are free to associate at will on their own terms. And the spontaneous segregation of the sexes in middle childhood may make even more sense in today's overheated atmosphere than it did in generations past. Dating, "preproms" complete with little tuxedos and lipstick, is a travesty of what childhood is, what children need.

They need help in shoring up their wayward impulses. Overstimulation is the great enemy of latency, when the child's private fantasies must gradually take socially acceptable forms and he becomes acquainted with the legends and myths of the culture's past and makes the most of his newly developing capacity for abstract learning to acquire skills and knowledge. The ten-year-old who connects his own pride in his achievements in science class with his enjoyment of reading about Dr. Ehrlich's magic bullet or Thomas Edison's triumph in developing the incandescent light bulb is on the way to putting fantasy into the service of reality. But in order to do the experiment, read the book, he needs to be relatively free of troubling thoughts and the need to defend himself against them.

Parental cruelty and casual nudity—both sadistic and seductive behavior—are destructive, the one stimulating feelings of anger and rage, the other of sexual arousal, that interfere with the state of latency necessary for various kinds of learning to take place. The child's mind will be occupied with a personal fantasy life of revenge and/or gratification instead of developing more mature new ways of thinking and feeling. He has no outlet for these feelings except regressed fury and masturbatory fantasy. He may become hyperexcited and disruptive, have little attention span or ability to delay, and find it difficult to master language and other kinds of learning.

Such a child enters adolescence confused, with no clear goals, overwhelmed by sensation and unable to channel his excitement and fears. Without verbal outlets to make him feel better (reading, writing) or a belief in the future to tide him over present discomforts (preparing for goals chosen as worthwhile from among those presented in literature as well as life), he will look for easy ways to feel better and find regressive solutions like getting high on drugs or rock music or ersatz religion. Without a set of moral values and socially acceptable ambitions forged from his private fantasy world through experiences of achievement and reading, he remains a moral primitive dependent on the street-gang morality of shame (the voices of the crowd) rather than guilt (the voice within).

The questions children are always asking in different ways are, What am I like? What will become of me? As puberty approaches they are concerned about issues of masculine and feminine identity and need support in defining themselves in ways consistent with their biological development and emotional needs, not confusion about sexual roles and sexual behavior that suits some political philosophy. They need to be told—which is usually the case—that they are normal. They do not need to be told that everything people do is normal. It is not. And if *they* are not, they need help in finding out what the problem is and, if possible, solving it. The world will not be changed for the better by confusing issues of sexual development or blurring distinctions so that everything appears equally desirable if not actually the same. It is possible to teach children not to hate or hurt those who are different. We need not be so afraid of human nature that we can't trust them to recognize difference lest they persecute it.

They need unstructured time for play. In liberating our children from the dullness and drudgery of earlier days, have we deprived them of the exhilaration and release of play, of inventing games and making things of their own design from scavenged scraps instead of going from one lesson to another, having everything organized for them or bought in packaged kits for easy assembly?

Children this age can appreciate workmanship and like to make things they'll be able to use—to combine fantasy and accomplishment in reality by producing plays they write and for which they make the sets and costumes and print and sell the tickets. What makes this kind of activity most valuable is that it is their own, the spontaneous activity of a bunch of kids. As soon as it's the planned activity of a group of children—meaning some grownup is helping and supervising—it's not the same thing.

It's a real question whether children are better off feeling that they are bored unless they're being entertained—by grownups or by television—than they were when boredom was escaped by going off and doing things on their own, as in the world Robert Smith remembers.[21]

Passively entertained after school by television and provided with one prepackaged and quickly obsolete gimmick after another, there's little time to develop or test one's ingenuity, experience the satisfaction of inventing and regulating one's own play and eventually one's own work. Children need to realize for themselves that they can cope with a self-set challenge through their own efforts. Passing a test someone else has set for you can also be important, but it's a different sort of thing.

Games, too, are different from play. Games have rules; play is spontaneous, directed by the child's own imagination. Games have more to do with developing skills, play with creativity.[22] Girls and boys are more likely to join in each other's games (the girls playing ball, the boys trying jacks) and fantasy play (the boys playing house, the girls playing spaceship) than a generation ago, but this tends to apply mostly to children of parents who encourage them to do so, and they still tend to impose their own masculine or feminine styles on the activities. They still act out the same age-old dramas, in which the comparative inwardness of girls, given to the subtleties of relationships and to introspectiveness, and the thrust of boys' activities, pummeling, driving and hurtling against obstacles and through space, adapt themselves to different settings and different expectations, but remain visible and distinguishable. It is in their relationships and attitudes, not the content of their activities, that they express their preoccupations.[23]

The little boy described in a recent feminist tract[24] who refused to go to a summer camp because it advertised its "man-made lake" is not politically principled, he's trying to keep the love and win the respect of his author-mother, whose dismay is apparent ("although I've never stopped the action") when she walks into a room to find him playing "Bang, bang, you're dead," although he shoots with his finger, having never been allowed a toy gun. Little boys have strong aggressive impulses that have to be coped with and defended against (and particularly so, one might guess, with a mother who turns childhood into a political consciousness-raising event), and they will construct weapons with whatever comes to hand or is created by their imaginations. The weapons do not cause the aggression; it comes, inevitably, from within. They are devices for playing it out, relieving tension. Where once little boys pretended to shoot arrows, now they pretend to launch rockets. The impulse—and the need to discharge it—remain the same. With no toy, they'll zoom a hand through the air, or cock a finger at an imagined enemy. Eventually, they should learn to channel the impulse into organized sports and games and activities that use symbols—language and the other skills it leads to. But left to themselves in latency they will continue to perpetuate the conventions of traditional sex differences—because of the way these meet their emotional needs as they withdraw their primary attachment from the parent of the opposite sex, and help create the psychological state of calm required for attentiveness to learning. They will ape a political agenda if they're given one, but they will be meeting their parents' needs, not their own.

The same reasoning that applies to pressure to conform politically applies to pressure to perform intellectually. What the child needs is encouragement, and a clear message of what you consider important as his parents, a message that is better sent by example than by exhortation. If you read for pleasure, and read to him with pleasure when he is small, you will hardly find yourself needing to urge him to read as he grows older. What he needs is to feel directed by his own conscious choice, and anxiety about his learning to read in order to get off to the right start at school in order to do well later and so on usually backfires. Anxiety doesn't stimulate reading, it stimulates anxiety. Quiet expectations, a continuing interest in what he achieves are what you can contribute now. But here again we come up against the impossibility of making rules for parents, each of whom is an individual with a unique mental life expressed in the context of a particular family of other individuals.

If pressed for dicta on the subject, I would probably say, Don't join your children in their play. Allow it to them, a private activity carried on in a space somewhere between the invisible mind and the outside world—a place to manipulate meanings until they are grasped and ordered. I would also say not to hide from your children whatever comes up—which is not the same as looking for it—about the extremities of experience. The mysteries of birth and death, like those of sex, are filtered through your attitude, and if you seem to avoid them they will seem more threatening, since they frighten even *you* into avoidance.

Sounds good, right? And yet I know a sturdy fellow of five whose father gets down on the floor with him to play a game of pretending to be born, and whose mother always skips the part about the mother's death when she reads him *Babar the Elephant.* Despite these particular aberrations they are very caring parents, always there when he needs them and able to set realistic limits for him as he grows bigger, so that his basic trust in them and in himself is beginning to show in its extension to the world of the school he is just entering.

So the dicta are fine as illustrations and examples that make certain dynamics of behavior clear, but cannot be used as simple do's and don't's. It's not any particular actions—except for the extremes of abuse or seduction, violence or neglect—that influence development. There is a wide spectrum of attitudes toward children's reading, for instance, that has resulted in good readers. One mother's encouragement is another's pressure, one father's expectations another's demands. Consistency—of care, of day-to-day involvement that meets the general needs of his stage of development, of understanding his desires while maintaining your standards—is what counts. And it admits of many styles of conversation, many ways of organizing family rituals, many characteristic ways of expressing thoughts, as long as the child is able to identify with a mother and a father who are secure in their place in the family and help him to be secure in his and then to move out from it feeling he can do well on his own and also has a fixed point of return.

They need a family to come home to. The child of the electronic age, unlike the child of village or town whose life was bounded by family and school, meets the world of adult affairs early in life through the media on a global scale and in a sensational tone. Much of what he sees and hears he is not ready to understand, and his response is confusion and sometimes specific fears or diffuse anxieties. There is a vast world out there in which seemingly uncontrollable forces clash, threatening destruction in ways that mirror some of his most terrifying fantasies of losing control of himself and his own feelings.

Today's children hear so much, are exposed to so much, are stimulated so much, that they attain quite early a degree of verbal sophistication that is misleading. It is no indication at all of their capacity for real understanding. They can talk about many things that are completely beyond the grasp of their minds to relate to real experience.

The family is the child's refuge from the imagined terrors of the great world out there as well as from the inevitable insults of his own smaller world of school and friends. It is in the gathering together at mealtimes, taking care of things around the house, and going out together, that he feels secure knowing he is still part of a family whole.

It helps if he can feel himself to be part of as many kinds of life as possible, not just his peer group but, beyond the family, a member of a larger part of society—Catholic or Jewish, Irish or Italian—with its own identity conferred on him, its own history and rituals to learn and practice. The family itself can have its own rituals—birthdays, holiday dinners, and other celebrations that are remembered and looked forward to as year follows year—that help establish the child's sense of being both himself and part of something larger than himself.

Although it may look that way, the crowd of kids does not have all his attention. He is still listening at home, even when he seems to be putting up a fuss—although he might be the last to admit it—and he is reading, and enlarging his world of possibilities through vicarious experience. That's why it's important to think about what that experience is, and where it comes from. It's not just that the media and television in particular offer the equivalent of junk food to a growing mind that needs nourishment, or that they rob him of time he might spend practicing the use of his imagination or his muscles, but that they intersperse junk programming with commercial pressures to a precocity he's better off without.

It's too soon to know to what extent the material of television is replacing that ancient tribal lore of children, whether they're really all used up by what comes at them through the ubiquitous tube or whether *they* are using *it* to add to the secret heritage they transmit to each other. There are rumors of jump-rope rhymes that parody television commercials in devastating ways in some schoolyards. This would imply an encouraging backlash against commercially-induced conformism. Childhood sassiness endures, and in some of the same old rhythmic forms, once the kids get outdoors away from the set. Whether it will prevail remains to be seen, but it is encouraging to know that the assault on childhood—the push to precocity, the commercial pressures, the bombardment of sensationalism—has not done away with kids' humor, one of the outstanding characteristics of their age. As long as they still make the same old jokes, and add new ones in each generation, there is definitely hope for the human race.

Preserving the liveliness of childhood is one of the gifts parents can make to their young, and one of the ways to encourage it is to make home a place where comfort and good talk, interest, and warmth are always available when needed. And where self-respect is enhanced not only by what is given children but also by what is expected of them.

They need responsibility. Rather than be cast adrift on the voyage out from home, most kids will put up with a lot to feel they belong to the group, will settle for an unflattering nickname or an identity as a grind or a dummy rather than being ignored, having no identity at all. The important thing, until a more individual sense of self is forged, is to be one of the gang. This can lead to wanting to wear what everyone else wears, go where everyone else goes, and even to such seemingly strange complaints as that everyone *else's* parents are divorced—and *they* get taken on dates by Sunday fathers.

It may seem paradoxical that in his wish to be a separate self he seems to be trying to be just like everybody else, but belonging somewhere else is a first step in the process of no longer belonging exclusively in the family. The gang spirit recedes as accomplishment and experience provide other ways of knowing who one is and other pleasures. Meanwhile, parents do well to continue to maintain their standards while tolerating the child's many transitory deviations from them, and helping him to find satisfactions that do not necessarily depend on group support and group approval.

Nothing does a child this age more good than the feeling that he is really useful in his efforts to be grown-up and competent. Any real work—responsibilities given him where he can see his efforts make a difference, and for which he may even get paid—enhances his self-respect, whether the job is at home or on the outside. He may grumble, but whether it's setting and clearing the table, doing errands, or babysitting for the neighbors' children to earn pocket money, knowing he is counted on to be useful is a source of pride.

Helping out with younger children has traditionally been one of the most important ways children in a family took on responsibility and authority and practiced being like their own parents and the grownups they would themselves become. With smaller families there is less opportunity for this way of identifying with adult authority, just as there are fewer opportunities in urban living for a child to perform meaningful work around the house or outdoors, but babysitting remains a way to begin feeling some independence.

Helping around the house on a regular basis—taking care of one's own room, feeding and walking pets—is important, too, and not to be neglected just because it may not strictly speaking, in a middle-class household with machines of all kinds and sometimes even domestic help, be necessary. And certainly not just because children complain when asked to do things. It's necessary for them if not for the household, and one of the most helpful attitudes parents can have—and one of the hardest to maintain—is that it's all right to complain about doing something as long as you do it. The only thing that's harder is letting them make mistakes (of course, not ones that involve real dangers), try things you know are bound to fail, even when you've told them so, and not say, I told you so. At some point, experience is the best teacher even though father knows best. (And the thing about truisms is that the way they get to be such is by being true.)

They need encouragement to make individual choices whenever possible. The child needs to move away. He knows it and you know it, but it isn't always easy for either of you. As he moves away, sometimes he seems aggresively defiant, and unnecessarily so. After all, you are a reasonable parent, patient about telling him what you expect of him, affectionate and comforting when needed, and slow to lose your temper. Why, then, this attitude of truculence, this suggestion that his parents are enslavers from whom he must free himself? Why this pointless rebelliousness, this inability to deal with soap and water, to remember what time dinner is served, to hang up clothing or get to bed or, for that matter, get up in the morning?

To some extent, he is wrestling with the part of himself that wants to remain dependent, stay safe at home, give up the struggle. He's encouraging himself to break away.

The first experience of selfhood was of the body, and the first experiences of one's parents their provision of bodily care and comfort. And this is the very area in which many children choose to establish their separateness—the very basis of their earliest connection with their parents, the care of their physical self. They stop washing, dressing neatly, putting things away, as a kind of public manifesto, all the while they are sneakily conforming to parental values and parental expectations somewhere else.

The effort to be tolerant about table manners and clothes, hair and fingernails, hits most parents where they live. After all, these were, not long ago, *their* little bodies to care for and cleanse, dress and comb. And now all their habits seem to be forgotten. Well, not forgotten so much as temporarily rejected, inevitably to return. The amnesia for life's amenities is reversible. Now the child is saying by his sloppiness that the old basis for their relationship is superceded by his new independence, and never mind about telling him to wash or not to talk with a mouthful—listen to what he *did* to get so dirty, and listen to what he's talking *about.*

The trick—and whoever said it was easy, being a parent?—is to understand without capitulating, tolerate without joining. You have an idea why he acts this way, but you needn't share it with him. He doesn't need your interpretations. In fact, they are the last thing he needs. He needs you to remain your old self, without rejecting him. He may be reminded he has to come to the table clean, but he doesn't get sent away in disgrace. When he's washed, he's welcomed back. (And later, you can lie down with an ice pack on your head.)

This "biologically celibate soldier-dwarf"[25] knows, like his two-year-old self in an age gone by, and his fourteen-year-old self in an age to come, that he cannot be victorious fighting himself, that he must surrender some primitive pleasures and settle down to work. He should be welcomed, not humbled. Every child is a prodigal, to be feasted on his returns to the fold from his intermittent journeys into selfishness, in which he revisits infancy. If it's too hard to get back he may stop returning, and remain a grown-up child. How he manages now will set the style for adolescence—how he will use his drives, define himself, express his nature.

The more you can manage not to overreact to his occasional provocation, the better for both of you. You'll have less to regret and overcompensate for, and he'll realize he's not so rotten and hopeless as he may occasionally fear, since you don't seem to get too upset, although you do draw lines, set limits for what can be gotten away with. Sensing that you've seen it all before (a luxury afforded subsequent children more often than first-born, unless their parents grew up in large families) and view his troubles as transitory ones is vastly reassuring to him. He wants the approval of the group, worries what the others will think of him, but he still wants your approval—and your love. As long as you stay calm about it he won't be harmed by having to work a little harder to gain the former in the interests of keeping the latter. Be tolerant while maintaining your standards. He's listening, even though he seems to be a million miles away, scowling and scratching.

There's no need to overorganize his life, scheduling every moment for him. He needs to be busy, but he doesn't necessarily need you to keep him busy. He needs to begin to control his own life as long as he shows himself capable of following the rules. As much as possible, let him choose his own activities and get himself to and from them on his own or with his friends.

Of course, if you're going to let him go, you have to be able to trust the world he's going into. You owe it to yourself and to him to make sure of what he is meeting out there, who is influencing him and in what ways. He needs to know you support the school he goes to and back up his teachers and the professional staff, that he need not hide the ways of his friends and the households he visits from you, or be secretive for any reason but the natural desire to feel in charge of himself, about what he does, alone or with his friends.

But if you're to give him his independence and the school its authority, you need to know there's no basic inconsistency between what you believe and how you think he should behave and what they maintain and how they suggest living. Above all is this important in the matter of school. These are, after all, the school years. School is, or should be, the most important part of the child's world. What do you think he should be learning there?

What Are Schools For?

Having already taken two unfashionable positions about the lives of children—that they should be cared for by their mothers whenever possible during the earliest years and that they should not be discouraged from clearly defining themselves as boys or girls with separate patterns of male and female attributes—the time has come for a third.

Schools are for teaching children to read and write, to reason with words and numbers, to master the skills that are needed for understanding the past and operating in the future. That is their job. Everything else, like bringing about social change, teaching children how to get along with different kinds of people, diagnosing or treating children's individual emotional problems, is not their job. This does not mean these are not perfectly acceptable, even laudable aims. It only means they are not the real function of schooling and that they may even, if placed first, interfere with it.

141

What children need for learning may not always be what society—or some parts of it—thinks it needs for changing itself. For instance, the achievement of a particular racial balance in a school is not a factor that actually influences how much or how well children learn there.[26] Leaving aside the question of whether one person's justice can indeed be served by another's coercion, whether it is appropriate in social terms for the schools to be used in this way, it is simply irrelevant to the matter of learning basic skills and practicing them to a degree of refinement, which is what children—all children—need at this time of life.

They need to learn to read, to write, to do arithmetic and, eventually, more complicated mathematics. They need to learn to think—to apply intellectual experience to new situations—to understand and use what is read. A child doesn't learn well or badly because he goes to an integrated school, but because of what kind of school it is and what kind of pupil he is. Children have been well educated at schools that were all white, all black, or mixed, as long as teachers were knowledgeable and dedicated, discipline was maintained, and school and parents supported each other's high expectations for the children.

Evidence for this proposition is found not only in the facts reported by observers like Thomas Sowell (see note 26) but in the not surprising conclusions of the study by sociologist James S. Coleman on public and private schools.[27] What the Coleman study showed was not that private schools were better than public schools per se, but that they achieved more because more of them were able to impose high academic standards, require homework, and maintain a climate of order and discipline. It is these things, and not how many of the students are black or white, rich or poor, that make the difference.

Another way of using the school, to change not the larger society but the individual pupil, is also a misuse of the purpose of schooling, and one that is doomed to failure. Of course, children's skills can be improved, windows opened for them, opportunities provided, suggestions given, and all this is what schools are for. But schools cannot change the basic character of the children who come to them. They cannot make children perceive adults as worth pleasing and trying to live up to their expectations of them. Schools cannot create character—the ego strengths like motivation, ability to tolerate delay, capacity for concentration. Only families can do that.

The child comes to the school with certain capacities and certain attitudes that are developed in the attachments and experiences of his early years. They can continue to be developed in the school. They cannot be created there out of whole cloth. There is a great margin of difference that a school can make to any individual child in what it provides for him and what it expects of him. But it always starts with what comes through the classroom door—a particular child with a particular bent, partly constitutional and partly the result of earlier acculturation or lack of it.[28]

There has been a growing tendency for the elementary school to shift its emphasis from intellectual to social goals, from learning to deal with language and ideas to learning to deal with people. Neither is mutually exclusive; it's a question of relative emphasis. The unstructured, permissive school that lets children decide what they want to learn and do pretty much as they please as long as they don't actually assault each other, and sometimes permits even that, is not much of an improvement on the strictly regulated classroom where rote learning is enforced by physical punishment. Neither will help much to develop a creative intelligence, not just one that can "express itself" regardless of what is being expressed, and not just one that can repeat on command what it has passively taken in, but one that has learned to read critically, understanding what is being asked and how it is being answered, what the facts are and what theoretical assumptions may lie behind them, and how to write well, organizing thoughts and expressing them precisely and sometimes beautifully.

Such an intelligence depends on familiarity with the past, with what has been thought and said as well as what has taken place, with different ways of looking at human history, from different angles and with different emphases, but always with a clear sense of the value of what the human mind has produced in science, art, technology, that has transformed life for most people into something better than an animal existence and made that transformation a possibility for even more.

What such an intelligence requires is an education defined not simply in terms of instruction in basic skills or useful arts but comprising the whole moral nature of man and all of his capacities, what the Greeks meant by *paedia* and what used to be meant by a liberal education before that concept was debased by the lowering of standards that awards high school degrees to functional illiterates and college degrees to people who have never read a work of philosophy of any kind, whether of history, of religion or of science.

Part of the problem has been the creation of a class of professional educators who are not professors of any kind of real knowledge, any discipline but methods of teaching. *What* is taught is no longer the main thing. At the same time, education has increasingly been used to further the aims of government, as a means of social and economic planning—for instance, to achieve racial integration, or to remove teen-agers from the job market.

Part of the larger question of whether the power of taxation should be used to bring about social change is the particular question of the extent to which the public schools should be used to do so. In recent years, a kind of federal-academic complex has evolved in which the government funds research projects that justify the expenditure of government funds on programs as well as on further research, a self-perpetuating system with a vested interest as well as an ideological one in expanding the government's role in its citizens' lives. Its leaders are advocates for a radical philosophy of social change they seek to implement through a variety of social-service programs that they suggest should include the care of young children as well as the shaping of their values as they become older, from the infant day-care center to "family life and sex education" in the schools.

We must ask whether these programs will benefit children as much as they will benefit a new class of bureaucrats—planners, administrators, and lower-echelon personnel to carry them out.

Family, Child and the World Beyond

Education and Sex

The real question is not whether children should be given sex education but by whom and in what way. By their parents, of course. And by other caring adults, such as teachers, when they know the child well as an individual, when it is agreeable to the child's parents, and when the child seeks it. Whether it should be provided in courses planned by special-interest organizations and funded by the government, taught as part of the school curriculum, is debatable. Such courses are widely taught in schools throughout the country today, at lower and lower grade levels, and with a clear philosophical point of view about sexuality. The real question is whether that point of view is desirable and that age level appropriate.

A child needs honest information about sex—about what he feels now and what to expect in the future—*when* he feels the need for it, not necessarily when it's in the curriculum. He needs information about anatomy and physiology to the extent that he is curious about them, and this can be an aspect of biology taught in schools. He does not need propaganda for social goals that excites him by telling him more than he is really asking for, suggests that anything that feels good *is* good and no behaviors are really to be preferred to any others, that body pleasures exist in a self-contained vacuum rather than in a context of emotional and moral meanings, and subtly sends the message that since he is being told how all sorts of things are done he must be expected to be doing them. Whatever the professed aims of most curricula in "family life and sex education," this is often their effective agenda. One need only read the literature of the organizations most responsible for the teaching materials used in these courses to see this.

An example chosen at random from the library shelves of a New York City school is *Learning About Sex: The Contemporary Guide for Young Adults* by Gary F. Kelly, published in 1977 by Barron's Educational Series with an introduction by Mary S. Calderone of the Sex Information and Education Council of the United States

(SIECUS), who notes accurately enough that "a book such as this could not have been written ten years ago." One can only hope that a book like this will not be published ten years from now.

A perusal of the index finds in the chapter entitled "Different Strokes for Different Folks" the headings "same sex behavior, homosexuality and bisexuality; cross-dressing, transsexualism, prostitution, and other preferences." A reader who wonders what "other preferences" can possibly be left to present to the young in this "sensitive, intelligent book about human sexuality and responsible loving relationships for today's young people" will find, on turning to the chapter in question, that the high-school students for whom this book is provided are told "it is fairly common for some people to associate pain or violence with sex" and that "sado-masochism may be very acceptable to sexual partners who agree on what they want from each other." As for "some sort of sexual contact with an animal," the author tells today's young people "there are no indications that such animal contacts are harmful, except for the obvious dangers of poor hygiene . . ." Sado-masochism and bestiality are just "other preferences," with nothing at all said that might illuminate the origins of such choices or their possible consequences. Just "different strokes."

Even more positively presented are masturbation (its "positive benefits" include "help[ing] young people to understand and become better acquainted with their sexual feelings"), homosexuality ("Assume that a study is done which shows that 98% of fifteen-year-olds in the U.S. like pizza. Would that mean that the "abnormal" few who do not like pizza are sick?") and "heavy petting" ("being in the nude with another person is often intensely pleasurable" and "represents a very deep level of sexual sharing"). Another form of "sexual sharing" presented here is "to give each other massages." Mutual masturbation and anal sex are also explained, just to make sure no young person misses out on anything. In the chapter on "Problem Sex," the first "problem" considered is "guilt." The only thing the author and the SIECUS people really think is wrong or unhealthy is to feel guilty about any kind of sexual practice.

In the chapter on "Marriage and Other Partnerships" today's

young people learn about Homosexual Marriage (in which homosexual couples "have exchanged vows with each other in 'holy union' ceremonies . . . performed by ministers of gay churches") as well as Not Being Married (in which "many individuals live fulfilling, satisfying, happy lives"). Open Marriage and Swinging or mate-swapping are also explained. After all, "there is no general statement that can be made about the 'best' or 'healthiest' way to be." All that's necessary is to be clear about what you want and unhampered by those devils fear and guilt. There are no ethical standards, no moral strictures, and no need is perceived for them in the philosophy of Mary Calderone and her troops in the front line of the sexual revolution. Lest one think deciding to commit oneself to marriage might be necessary in the case of parenthood, the young are assured here that "unmarried couples and single people can be good, nurturing parents."

It is hard to believe that a large educational publisher puts out such claptrap or that it is not atypical of what teachers and librarians find acceptable today. Are there many grownups who think there is no difference between liking sado-masochism and liking pizza? Or do many parents simply not know what goes on in these books and the courses that use them?

A perusal of the multitude of curriculum materials developed for use in the schools—textbooks, study guides, films—much of it developed by organizations such as the Planned Parenthood Federation of America, SIECUS, the Sex Education Coalition, and much of it funded by grants from the United States Department of Health and Human Services,[29] makes it clear that the curriculum is intended to do far more than acquaint children with the biology and anatomy of sex and reproduction. It is intended to introduce them to "the varieties of sexual experience" in a "guilt-free atmosphere." Masturbation, mutual masturbation and homosexuality, for instance, are discussed in a context intended to promote what the Institute for Family Research and Education at Syracuse University calls "an appreciation for the wide range of sexuality, that sexual expression is not limited to heterosexual, genital intercourse,"[30] in a curriculum planned for kindergarten through the middle grades and on to high school, stressing "minors' rights" to information and access to contraceptives, and avoiding "moralistic presentations," which "seek to impose a personal point of view in a dogmatic way."[31]

It is hard to think of anything about which a "personal point of view" is more appropriate than ideas about sexual behavior and its place in human life. It is central to the concept of self and others, to how men and women arrange their lives and order their responsibilities to each other, and it involves both strong emotions and serious consequences. The idea that not parents but "health professionals" should be given the responsibility for interpreting these matters for children is hard to justify except, as with day care and certain other issues of the "liberal" agenda (the quotation marks are intended to emphasize how little this term has come to have to do with personal liberty as it assigns more and more functions to public regulation), where it may be a preferable alternative in the case of neglectful or abusive parents, parents too ignorant or too uncaring to provide their children with either necessary information or useful attitudes. We all know there are such parents, and that their children constitute the most difficult problem of our society, the "unattached."[32] But to extrapolate from their needs to those of most children in families that care for them is absurd, unless one accepts the proposition that "experts" know better than ordinary parents what their children need and how to give it to them.[33]

As a matter of fact, the last thing most children of school age need is to have their attention focused on sexual behavior, as distinct from an understanding of biology. "Have their attention focused" is the operative phrase here, because of course children should be encouraged to ask freely about whatever is on their minds. But the school curriculum in sex "education" today does more than educate; it stimulates and it proselytizes. It suggests to schoolchildren that they are expected to be indulging in those behaviors to which it gives so much attention, at a time when they are better off being neither sexually active nor sexually preoccupied, but using their mental and physical energies in the learning and practicing they need to accomplish before adolescence.

It is also designed to promote a particular point of view that is part of the baggage of modern relativistic social thought—that whatever feels good is good, and that to "clarify" values means simply to be clear about what one feels like and then to act on those feelings, not to be clear about what traditional values are, where they have come from, and how they might be applied to one's own life. This is what most thoughtful parents expect to pass on to their children—an understanding of their own past as a guide to their children's future—and when they say they are in favor of sex education in the schools they are usually thinking in terms of biology classes and information about the workings of the male and female reproductive systems, what the proponents of sex education in the schools today refer to scornfully as "the plumbing," and not the comprehensive view of how to act and how to think about sex that informs the programs planned and conducted by organizations like SIECUS and Planned Parenthood and implemented in the public schools with funding from state and federal health agencies.

There is very little real evidence on the effects of these courses, and no more reason to suppose that their tolerance for "increased sexual activity without guilt"[34] affects children one way or another, either actually increasing their sexual activity or serving to prevent early pregnancy and venereal disease by teaching children what sex-education professionals and lobbyists believe is "a healthy attitude" to sex from kindergarten on.

What is sure is that neither this emphasis nor this point of view are what the preadolescent child needs from school. What he needs there is to acquire the basic skills that are the tools of the culture, to learn to exchange and express ideas. To acquaint the child with the basics of language, mathematics, the sciences and the arts, their history and their present state, is a tall enough order in this complicated world. It is what parents have a right to ask schools to do their best to accomplish, while they, at home, transmit "values" and an understanding of the part sex plays in life, which is a matter of mystery, power, and awe, not just mechanics and self-gratification.

Children need to know about the biology of their own bodies. They also want desperately to understand their own feelings. What is it like to make love? How will I know the right person for me? Am I lovable? Am I normal? The problem is who they should turn to for answers to their questions.

Ideally, they are best answered intimately, in an emotionally appropriate atmosphere, when needed. This means a young person ought to be able to turn to an older and wiser friend, in a calm and private moment, and have the things on his or her mind answered frankly and warmly. Can understanding about sexual life be imparted by evangelizing gym teachers, or "professionals" in "health sciences," trained for the purpose, on schedule, in groups? Such teaching may be a better alternative to what is available to some children; most children are probably better off talking these things over with their own parents until they reach the stage of life where that may become awkward for some of them, and then turning to other adults they respect and feel care for them, in whom they choose to confide on their own terms.

The fact is, kids learn most of their attitude about sexual relations by extrapolating from the atmosphere of their parents' behavior toward each other; they can be taught the facts of anatomy, physiology, and the reproductive process in a biology class. There is some question whether they can learn anything else worth learning in such a setting. What they *can* learn there is something about the attitude of their instructor. And for reasons of self-selection and political expediency, that attitude has come to be fairly consistent. At the present time, those who are interested in planning courses in "family life and sex education," like those who are attracted to the "values clarification" curriculum, often share a particular political bias, a commitment to change in sexual mores and other aspects of traditional value systems.

In order for a child to respond best to what his school expects of him, he needs to know his parents support its aims and sanction its discipline. When parents cannot do that, they might do well to think about changing schools. A child's education is too important to be undermined by the shallow view of human nature and human

150

needs implied in the political agenda of various educational lobbying groups. In the preschool years it may seem like a harmless source of amusement that the progressive nursery school sometimes takes the child on trips when he wants to learn to read, when, as some parents in that situation feel, they would prefer to take him on trips and have the school teaching him to read instead of having him ask *them* to teach him at home. Still, he'll learn to read one way or the other, and it can be a pleasure learning and teaching together.

But now, in the school years, it's a question of what he does with that ability. Now is the time for reading, for thinking, for learning and practicing, and a certain emotional calm is required. Prepubescent children are capable of this degree of calm when not overstimulated by parental aggression or seduction, or not bombarded with stimulation through the media or in the classroom.

Does any sensible parent think what the child this age needs is to read books that tell him "all the activities in this chapter have nothing to do with 'should,' none of that 'I should be like this' or 'I should do things like that.' That kind of thinking can only get in the way of your exploring what kind of kid you really are"?[35] Or that children in fourth grade need to be told that "sex is a fun part of being a person" and masturbation is the "celebration of the body"?[36] There is nothing evil or immoral about these books, and one does not have to be a fundamentalist or a prig, intolerant or ignorant, to object to them. They are just terribly silly and simple-minded, and they pander to children instead of stretching the horizons of their intellect or their moral imagination. Better for a child this age to read a classic tale of adventure or a novel about how people once lived and what they did in that far country of the past that is preserved in the literary tradition than to be encouraged to stop where they are and "celebrate" themselves, exploring only what they "really are" now. There won't be much to know, much to celebrate, unless the child receives the lessons from the past that are the real gifts of education.

The question of what role sex education plays in adolescence, when the matter is no longer academic but involves real choices in living, not just "attitudes," engaging the mature body as well as the attention, properly belongs to a discussion of that stage of growth, and will be considered later. But even now children need not be sheltered from the truth that sex is more than "fun," that there is good reason for many of the rules that have evolved in civilized society for its regulation, that intimacy involves responsibility and that the intimacies of love-making are complex, touching on men's and women's deepest memories, dreams and desires, and one of the mysteries the young can look forward to unraveling in adulthood. Meanwhile, they have other things to do.

And it is those other things their teachers and their schools should be concerned with, leaving their private lives and personal feelings to them and their families. Sometimes a teacher becomes a helpful friend. It is more important, however, to be a good teacher.

Who Teaches Your Child?

A teacher should be someone who knows about something and is good at imparting that knowledge—of literature, of history, of physics, of mathematics. Knowing about teaching is meaningless unless you know about something to teach. A teacher should also be someone who will stand *in loco parentis* and not in an adversarial relationship to the child's family and its beliefs and values. Erikson says "good parents feel a need to make their children trust their teachers, and therefore to have teachers who can be trusted. For nothing less is at stake than the development and maintenance in children of a positive identification with those who know things and know how to do things. Again and again in interviews with especially gifted and inspired people, one is told spontaneously and with a special glow that *one* teacher can be credited with having kindled the flame of hidden talent."[37]

Someone in addition to you will be influencing your children during these years. Who will it be?

The ideal situation is to be able to give the school a free hand with the child, supporting its programs and its discipline, not letting the child become a battleground in a conflict between parental aims of education and those of the school. Many parents who are unhappy with the use of the schools as instruments of social change rather than transmitter of skills and culture, with teachers of the kind who are more at home with "values clarification" than great literature, have made sacrifices to find other schools to educate their children.

When that is not possible, there are some age-old "strategies" for keeping connected to one's children while giving them the freedom they need to take a distance from which to practice independence and, eventually, acquire it. One is to provide them with as many stand-ins for yourself as possible, adults they can spend time with, learn from, and confide in without being taught to distrust or despise what you believe in, prize, or expect or hope for in their lives. Aunts and uncles, family friends, teachers, secular and religious, have traditionally filled this need.

But most important is what goes on in the time you still spend together. There will be less of it as the child grows up and becomes busier and busier with a life lived outside of home, but there still needs to be a time you have together, parents and children, every day of his life. Usually, it's mealtimes.

It's important to get together at the family dinner table because mealtimes are the main opportunity for parents and children to be together during these active years, the chance to hear about his life as a boy, her life as a girl, and talk about your life as a man or woman—what you do, how you think about things, what interests or amuses you, your opinion of a friend's behavior or the world situation.

The child is constructing a picture of the adult world on the screen of his mind. Unlike the primitive child of preindustrial society or the rural child of a bygone age, he puts this together from much more than just what he sees around him in tribe or family or small cohesive community. There are the classroom, the playground, and books of all kinds, and there are television, movies, magazines. You cannot really isolate him from any of these aspects of the outside world without interfering with his need to learn to function away from home and beyond family. What you *can* do is make sure you are also being heard, also having an influence.

The main focus of the relationship between child and parents need no longer be his physical care, which can increasingly be turned over to himself. If he feels you consider it his body, not yours, and trust him to use judgment in caring for himself, he's more likely to take pleasure and pride in doing so than if it all becomes a battleground on which he has to prove his might. Although there is nothing sillier than treating a child as though he were capable of adult judgment based on adult experience—it doesn't fool him and only leads to a contempt for grownups who think so much of him and so little of themselves—he is beginning to be able to make judgments about the events in his life and should be encouraged to do so.

Hearing how his parents and their friends reason and behave, how they see the situations and choices that face them in everyday life and what they do about them, suggests patterns he applies to his own conduct, now and later. Talking about your life in his hearing, welcoming his questions and comments, and responding to them thoughtfully invites him to do the same. And when he puts his daily experiences before you, shyly at first, if he finds you take him seriously enough to tell him what you really think and not to patronize him, even if he seems to disagree at the time he will be impressed by the form as well as the content of your comments—by how you arrive at your opinions as well as what those opinions are.

And it is surely better for you to exercise this prerogative than to leave all of it to the crowd or to his teachers. He will be listening to them anyway; he should be listening to you, too. The "values clarification" that has become part of the school curriculum can become an arrogant abrogation of parental rights. You should give him the moral and social context in which to deal with life. If you do not, you leave a vacuum that others are eager to fill.

Family, Child and the World Beyond

Education and Values

It has been the fate of many of the world's great teachers to have attracted followers from whom they need as much protection as from their critics and detractors. Like Freud, Piaget[38] evolved a way of looking at aspects of human nature that has occasionally been adapted, oversimplified and distorted, and then exploited. An example of this misleading use of intellectual credentials for prestige and profit has been introduced into the schools over the last decade by graduates of the schools of education that turn out many teachers who know very little about anything except, presumably, how to teach. Unfortunately, they have little to use that knowledge on—much method but little matter. Among the pedagogic methods that has caught on is one for "clarifying" students' values or, in another form, contributing to their "cognitive moral development."

According to Piaget,[39] at the beginning of latency, around the age of seven, the "morality of restraint" (absolute obedience to the law as laid down by parental authority) gives way to the "morality of cooperation" (choice is made on the basis of distinctions between motivations as well as between actions). Moral judgment—the capacity to make ethical distinctions and choose one's behavior on the basis of them—becomes a function of maturation like language or rational thought: The potential develops at a certain stage of growth. Thus a child gradually develops a sense of rules, ideas of right and wrong, and the concept of being guided by a code of justice rather than merely acting so as to avoid punishment.

In the early sixties, psychologist Lawrence Kohlberg, applying Piaget's sequential stages of moral development based on levels of cognitive organization, came up with a scheme he claimed was universal, applying to all children everywhere. According to Kohlberg, the child's movement from obeying out of fear of punishment to following accepted rules in a spirit of cooperation was capped, in adolescence, by the ultimate stage of moral development—the acquisition of an unequivocal set of moral absolutes, universal and inflexible rules for conduct.[40]

It does not seem to have occurred to Kohlberg that the adolescent's strict and punitive moral code, judgmental and intolerant of those who see things differently, might be reaction formation. Adolescents often have problems dealing with the great upsurge of instinctual energy that accompanies hormonal changes at puberty and controlling their impulses. Some children let go and act out their impulsive urges, with varying degrees of destructiveness to themselves and others. Some manage to negotiate the conflicting demands of self and society by means of the ego strengths acquired during latency. Some others must call into play a superego that will not only control their own wayward thoughts and behavior, but that they would impose (as, indeed, they were encouraged to do in the sixties) on others. The observations and clinical experience of many analysts of adolescent behavior suggest that such an attitude is closer to pathology than normality,[41] that moral righteousness and the conviction that one holds the one truth for everyone may not be the ultimate stage of morality but a stage many adolescents pass through and some never transcend, and that the real maturity lies in a cooperative morality that may in time succeed it in the adult.

This does not mean equating every behavior or every value with every other ("it's all relative") but following the rule of law because it is the best way for most people to get on together, and having the patience to work at changing those laws that no longer seem to serve a broad enough social purpose. The adolescent visionary—revolutionary, uncompromising in the certainty of what is right and ready to impose his ideas on everyone else, by violence if necessary—had an appeal for many intellectuals in the sixties, but "moral certainty" has surely brought about less that has proved of durable value in human life than the "legalistic" social-contract approach. Carried to its extremes, and removed from the context of an established religion or culture with its accreted traditions, Kohlberg's morality makes every person the center of his own moral universe, his own judge and executioner. It may be a stage many—although hardly all—young

156

people go through. It is not necessarily where they should stay. If personal conscience is the only guide for the individual, there is no law at all; it is possible for each individual to feel that his law is *the* law.

This brings us to the subject—which is what it has come to be in many school curricula—of "values clarification." Building on the ideas of Kohlberg and some others it is not possible to take even as seriously, it is, like much of the sex-education curriculum, a way of using the schools to change traditional views of morality.

Kept at the ready on reserve in the libraries of most schools of education, where it is assigned reading in courses on the elementary curriculum, is the classic text in the field: *Values Clarification: A Handbook of Practical Strategies for Teachers and Students.* [42] It is indeed an instructive text. Its authors state at the outset that they are against "moralizing," which they define as "inculcation of the adult's values upon [sic] the young." They are against parents transferring what they consider desirable values, should's and should-not's,[43] and propose instead to teach children a process for selecting among various (presumably equal) value systems. They claim not to be concerned with the *content* of people's values, but the *process of valuing.* [44]

Their method proceeds by the use of a variety of "strategies" for "making choices between competing alternatives." One "strategy" involves rank-ordering some answers to such questions as: Which do you think more money should be spent on? (The possible answers: moon shots, slum clearance, cure for cancer.)[45] Another strategy is the Forced Choice Ladder, which asks children to rank their feelings about such individuals in society as a doctor who prescribes name-brand drugs of a company in which he has been given stock by the salesman, a national guardsman on duty at a college campus who is attacked by students and shoots them, a neighbor who calls the police because she suspects the teen-ager across the street is using pot.[46] Another strategy is Alternative Search, which asks students to search for alternatives in situations the first of which is "ways to personally stop polluting our environment."[47] Sensitivity Modules is a strategy intended to provide "something the student must do that will enable him to become more sensitive to issues and people in the world around him [and] . . . give substance to the students' developing values."[48] Some of the suggested "units of experience":

—Live for three days on the amount of money a typical welfare mother receives to feed a son or daughter closest to your own age.
—Hand out birth control pamphlets in an inner-city area. (Be aware that some Black people believe that birth control is a form of genocide.)
—Get on the morning train or bus that the Black domestics take to get to their housekeeping jobs in the suburbs.
—Go to the Goodwill Industries store downtown and see how many school clothes you can buy for a family of four children if you had $15 to spend.
—Read *Manchild in the Promised Land, Go Tell It on the Mountain, The Autobiography of Malcolm X,* or some other book which tells what it is like to grow up Black in America.[49]
—Walk four or five blocks in the inner-city at lunch hour. Buy a sandwich and a cup of coffee in a luncheonette where you are the only white person.
—Spend a weekend at workcamp run by the American Friends Service Committee . . .[50]

This is the absence of inculcation, of moralizing about what are to be considered desirable values? The tendency of question and example throughout, the unstated but clearly assumed values in this so-called "value free" approach adds up simply to making sure that the unquestioned values of those who thought up this simplistic program get a head start over those of the middle-class parents who might attempt to use their authority (horrible word!) to transmit their values, but who are hypocrites ("patriots who would deny freedom of speech to any dissenters whose concept of patriotism is different from theirs")[51] trying to be models for their children to emulate, a sneaky business at best.

The trouble, according to our values-clarification experts, is that there are too many models for the young person to choose from. (The tacit assumption is that they are all equally valid—with perhaps a slight edge given to *them.*) They do not help the young person "learn whether he wants to stick to the old moral and ethical standards or try new ones."[52] What young people need is to "build their own value system."

Out of what? Why, out of anything but what is taught at home in the family and those agencies the family chooses (the church or synagogue, for instance), and preferably out of the particular sociopolitical point of view of the values-clarification movement, as simpleminded as the propaganda of any fundamentalist sect, and as impoverished in providing insights into the complexities of human life.

Children could learn far more about moral issues by reading a great novel than by engaging in these classroom "strategies." They would be better off in the hands of any writer whose view of the human condition has stood the test of time than the teacher who has learned how to lead a classroom group discussion of some strategy in an education course.

What these courses do is, of course, create a new discipline, with its courses to be taught and its proliferation of books and articles, films, study guides and related materials for classroom use. But what is this discipline that is not part of all education, that does not come with reading and thinking about and discussing the great works of literature, history, philosophy?

Lawrence Kohlberg, the leading proponent of "cognitive moral development" programs in the schools, describes traditional education as indoctrination resting on authority.[53] Is "values education" any different?

Its proponents argue that the traditional school teaches conventional standards rather than promoting self-exploration. According to one of them, "As schools present such organizational values as order, routine, output, authority, and efficiency within the lives of young people, they compete with human values."[54]

Of course, it all depends on what you consider human values. The foregoing list sounds as good as any I can think of—while not exhausting the possibilities—of what young children should get from school. But according to the leading guru of values education, Sidney Simon, the schools must present students with the array of possible alternatives he provides because traditional values "have become meaningless platitudes or hypocritical meanderings." What he proposes to substitute for them is a nonjudgmental attitude, ethical neutrality, and a clear understanding of one's own likes and desires. Most of the "dilemmas" and "alternatives" proposed in the literature of values clarification have an unreal quality, and the alternatives presented are limited to say the least.

It is never even considered that one can be judgmental and tolerant at the same time, that it is possible to have a set of beliefs one holds clearly on the basis of thoughtful discrimination while still understanding that others believe differently. There is, as William J. Bennett has pointed out in commenting on the values education movement, no reason to assume that the only choices open to the individual are to conform to authoritarian standards or to self-created values.[55] There is a continuity of tradition in ethical thinking that did not suddenly become obsolete with the 1960s, where so much of the values-clarification movement not only began but seems to have gotten stuck.

Values-clarification "strategies" are intended to acquaint the student with himself, when what he most needs is to be acquainted with the thought and culture of the past, from which to fashion a self worth knowing. According to values-clarification dogma, there are no right or wrong answers to moral questions; what counts is being clear about what one likes and dislikes in a set of predetermined choices. One of Simon's oft-quoted "strategies" presents the following "dilemma":

> Your husband or wife is a very attractive person. Your best friend is very attracted to him or her. How would you want them to behave?
> a. Maintain a clandestine relationship so you wouldn't know about it.
> b. Be honest and accept the reality of the relationship.
> c. Proceed with a divorce.

This is an impoverished expression of human motivation to begin with, in its simple statement, and it is fascinating that the alternatives do not even include the possibility that one would expect the spouse and friend, by one definition of mature behavior, to consider something besides the gratification of their own feelings and perhaps choose to do nothing about their mutual attraction. It is assumed that they will satisfy their desires and no choice is offered that involves regard for others or respect for commitments, love, or faithfulness. Surely this is a strange and skewed view of "values." It is not a view I would value having presented to my children. It teaches that knowing what you want is all that matters, and this at an age when a young person can't have formed such knowledge on the basis of anything beyond impulse, having read little (the time for reading the best of what has been thought in the past being co-opted instead for these puny exercises in the least of what is being thought in schools of education today) and experienced less. Informed judgment is not one of the values of value education, with its limited options for conduct and its impoverished reasoning. As William J. Bennett and Edwin J. Delattre pointed out in a critique of the values-education movement,[56] "in the options offered, the student is treated as if his wants always conflicted with his obligations . . . it is never assumed that the student wants to be decent."

Ironically, Simon's own approach emphatically indoctrinates—by encouraging and even exhorting the student to narcissistic self-gratification. The moral superiority of Kohlberg's ultimate stage of moral reasoning is also arguable. In the book *Hypothetical Dilemmas for Use in Moral Discussions* distributed by the Moral Education and Research Foundation at Harvard, the most common type of dilemma encountered is sexual, and dilemmas dealing with homosexuality, spouse-swapping, extramarital sex and abortion are supplemented by examples focusing on My Lai and Mayor Daley, Daniel Berrigan and Daniel Ellsberg. Stuck in the sixties. The claims of individuals and groups are to be determined according to their "rights"— the chief of which, in the case of those whom Kohlberg has decided, or who consider themselves, to be "disadvantaged," and even in the "dilemmas" involving child and parent, is the right not to be imposed on by "authority," not to have to follow rules or be "indoctrinated" with traditional values.

These bleak narratives are hardly the stuff to enrich young minds, nourish a sense of the ambiguity and complexity of human life and stimulate an identification with those who have confronted the universal conflicts of humanity before us. What both Simon and Kohlberg oppose is not indoctrination per se but the indoctrination of traditional values, and what they offer instead in these programs is indoctrination in their own values—"the celebration of wants and desires, the exhortation to self-gratification, and a particular ideology of rights and 'special justice.' "[57]

In their respective limited views, there is no room for the special kind of love and responsibility that can prevail between the generations, only an adversary stance in which special interests driven by one's arbitrary passions—whether of the body or the mind—motivate relationships and behavior. In this antagonistic universe there is no room for what have always been understood to be aspects of the moral life—"friendship, love, fidelity, regard for work, care for home and family—which are, for the most part, not morally problematic"—and "no place for stories and lessons, for the passing on of knowledge and experience."[58]

Moral judgment should indeed come from within, but the moral man or woman is not simply one who is able to recognize an impulse when he has it. He must be able to distinguish subtle shades of meaning about behavior and his best preparation for doing so has been left behind by thinkers of the past—in volumes of fiction, poetry, philosophical reasoning and historical interpretation. It is those works, and not the classroom exercises of "educators" like a Kohlberg or a Simon, that parents should expect schools to be offering their children.

The empty self and the self-righteous judge that Simon and Kohlberg offer us can tell what's expedient, what feels good, what suits a particular unquestioned political agenda, but never do they reflect the truly moral man. It is hard to see anything of value in their games and setups, leading questions and simplistic answers, for the youngster moving into the large world in which there is so much to face, to learn, to come to terms with, to understand—especially as childhood begins to give way to youth.

Adolescence

In opening the subject of the stage of life we commonly refer to as adolescence, we have to begin with some distinctions. On the one hand there is puberty, a biological phenomenon. A spurt of growth at the end of childhood signals the oncoming development of secondary sexual characteristics (breasts, face and body hair) and genital maturity (menstruation, penile growth and ejaculation). This growth and development usually begin around the age of eleven or twelve, at the start of the teen years, although there is great variation among individuals. But neither biology nor chronology—puberty or teenage—serves to define adolescence, which is a social construct, a cultural artifact. Adolescence, as we define, expect, and experience it in our lives, is the creation of modern urban industrial life, which has greatly extended the period of education and training required for assuming an adult role in an advanced technological society.

Only a hundred years ago in our society—and still today in parts of the world outside the orbit of western industrialized countries—young people went to work soon after reaching puberty. Whether or not they left home, whether or not they were actually self-sufficient, they assumed an adult economic role, had a given place and set tasks of recognized importance to perform in their world. The contemporary extended moratorium during which the young person searches for his identity, defines himself through the process of formal education and in personal relationships, commits himself to a vocation and finally emerges to take his place in society only at the end of his second decade of life—and sometimes even later if he trains for one of the higher professions—is a relatively new phenomenon. And while we will discuss aspects of the anatomical and physiological changes that occur during the teen-age period, our main focus will be on the psychological consequences to young people and their families of the prolonged period of time modern life imposes between the attainment of biological maturity and the conferring of the privi-

163

leges and responsibilities of full social adulthood, the period that is adolescence in our society today.

In the early years of this century the developmental psychologist G. Stanley Hall called attention to adolescence as a unique period of life.[59] Harking back at least as far as Rousseau, he leaned heavily on the Romantic movement's idealization of youth and its wanderings, its travels and its inner journeys, in setting forth a picture of *Sturm und Drang*—storm and stress—that still remains the picture in the popular imagination of the years between childhood and adulthood.[60] The view of youth as inevitably a time of painful rebellion and drastic psychic upheaval was given widespread currency in our time by three disparate sources—psychoanalysis and psychiatry, the social sciences, and the media.

The classic psychoanalytic picture of adolescence was drawn at mid-century by Anna Freud, who declared that "adolescent upheaval" was not only inevitable but a sign of health—the external indication that crucial inner changes in personality structure necessary to accommodate an increased sexual drive are taking place, and that children who show no such outer evidence of inner unrest at puberty are in serious trouble, in need of therapeutic help.[61]

According to this view, "adolescence constitutes by definition an interruption of peaceful growth which resembles in appearance a variety of other emotional upsets";[62] in fact, adolescence resembles at times many kinds of mental illness. For instance, in the effort to give up his infantile ties to his parents, the adolescent may adopt a compulsive opposition to them, becoming a callous and indifferent boarder in his own home. His aggressive feelings may cause him such guilt and anxiety that his reaction shades over into paranoia and he perceives them as his oppressors and persecutors. Or, instead of projecting his hostility on them, he may turn it inward against himself, becoming depressed and even suicidal. He may simply turn away from home and family and replace them with a gang or substitute for his parents a friend, a group leader, a popular hero, or a cult figure. Other adolescents may take the ascetic path in warding off unacceptable instinctual urges, becoming unrelentingly high-minded and uncompromising in the principles they impose upon themselves and would impose upon others.

These examples are enough to give the idea of what Anna Freud had in mind in saying that "adolescence is by its nature an interruption of peaceful growth, and . . . the upholding of a steady equilibrium during the adolescent process is in itself abnormal. . . . that it is normal for an adolescent to behave for a considerable length of time in an inconsistent and unpredictable manner; to fight his impulses and to accept them . . . to love his parents and to hate them; to revolt against them and to be dependent on them . . ."[63] In fact, "it may be his parents who need help and guidance so as to be able to bear with him. There are few situations in life which are more difficult to cope with than an adolescent son or daughter during the attempt to liberate themselves."[64]

Now this description of adolescence as something like psychosis and of the plight of the beleaguered parent who must cope with it is insightful and even empathic as far as it goes. But how far does it really go? There are those who began to find a certain discrepancy between the undeniably apt picture of *some* of the young painted here and what could be observed of *most* young people most of the time in most places. Were all of them abnormal, failing somehow to accomplish the psychological tasks of that stage of life that would prepare them to assume the emotional tasks of adulthood? Or was it perhaps that those who sat for this portrait were a very select group—the population of patients seen by psychoanalysts in their consulting rooms? For unlike the picture psychoanalysis has given us of development in infancy and early childhood, its view of adolescence was not based on observation of normal children in real-life situations interacting with their parents and each other, but was based on clinical experience with deviant and troubled youngsters. It went, depending on your point of view, either too far or not far enough.[65]

It had, however, a tremendous influence on the way society saw its young. Countless popularizations in magazine articles and books told us that they were *supposed* to be troubled, resentful, rebellious.

What's more, if they *weren't,* there was something wrong with them.

Perhaps the second most influential authority writing on adolescence from within scholastically pure psychoanalysis, after Anna Freud, was Peter Blos, who spoke of the "profound reorganization of the emotional life" that takes place during adolescence, "with attendant and well-recognized states of chaos"[66] and of "the typically rebellious adolescent" who turns against his parents in his attempts to detach himself from them, at the same time turning against the view of reality and morality they have taught him.[67]

Blos's work, like Anna Freud's, is full of insights about various aspects of development. It is impossible to write about adolescence without quoting from them. But the question here is whether what they describe as "normal" adolescence actually describes a universal process or only characterizes certain youngsters in our society—the highly sensitive children of sophisticated upper middle-class parents who make up the psychoanalytic patient population and the deviant class of delinquents who come to treatment through the courts and other social agencies. To what extent do those groups resemble the vast number of youngsters who grow up in less self-conscious and less disruptive families and who are never seen in treatment?

Perhaps the psychoanalyst says, "Ah hah!" too soon. Listening to a patient, he has an insight that encapsulates a truth, although a highly particular one, of this person at this time in this place. But sometimes he leaps to form a generalization that will become a learned paper, adding to the sum of human knowledge and, incidentally, to his professional reputation. Corroborative evidence is produced from other patients reported on by other analysts in their papers, and theory is spun on theory that, however well it reflects the facts of certain pathologies of these individual troubled lives, may not reflect the reality of the many quieter lives they never see or hear about.

Other psychiatrists, many of them also psychoanalytically trained and scientifically sophisticated, looking outside the private-practice milieus and public institutions of our urban centers, saw a different picture, and began to suspect that there might be some distortion in the theoretical construct of adolescence promulgated by orthodox analysts and also described by social scientists and celebrated by the media.

For in the years from the early sixties through the mid-seventies, both those influences joined in insistently picturing the young as riotously unsettled and a force for change. On the one hand, many social scientists *became* social scientists because of a strong interest in changing society. They defined the problems and focused on the activities of highly selected groups who held the values they themselves held, and the expectations they brought to the situations and individuals they scrutinized colored their conclusions. And the media, of course, welcomed anything that made a story—any confrontation, anything new, different, violent, strange, or arresting in any way—and made instant heroes of a handful of characters writing their own story. It would be hard to say who was using whom. While sociologists romanticized youth, looking to them for the changes they themselves sought, the media exploited them, finding—and perhaps creating—the excitement that sold papers and built up TV ratings.

Meanwhile, a generation was growing up pretty much as boys and girls always had, relatively calmly becoming much like their fathers and mothers before them. And a few observers decided it was time to consider *them,* to look at some of these large numbers of unremarkable and unremarked youth, and see where they were going, and where they came from.

In the 1960s Chicago psychiatrist Daniel Offer and his colleagues designed and carried out the most systematic study of normal adolescents[68] that had ever been made, an in-depth, through-the-years examination of the behavior, thoughts, and feelings of a group of some seventy well-adjusted nonpatient high-school boys[69] from average middle-class suburban families in the Midwest.

In his report of the study, *The Psychological World of the Teenager,*[70] Offer sums up: "We have not found turmoil to be prevalent in our normal adolescent population,"[71] and suggests that "turmoil should be seen as only one route for passing through adolescence," one that the majority of young people do not follow, and he concludes that what makes for a calm passage through adolescence is "a non-stressful childhood (one in which not very many developmental and accidental 'crises' have occurred prior to reaching adolescence)."[72]

Offer agrees with Erikson, who had told us even before the 1960s that "adolescence is not an affliction but a *normative crisis,*" by which he meant that while there is increased conflict, it carries with it, unlike neurotic conflict, a high potential for growth. While neurotic conflict is inflexible and self-perpetuating, the conflicts of normal adolescence fluctuate and lead on to new and expanded capacities "in the searching and playful engagement of new opportunities and associations." The normal crises of adolescence "prove to be self-liquidating and, in fact, contributive to the process of identity formation."[73]

It would appear, then, that for most middle-class youngsters living normal lives in average homes—and this means most young people in America—adolescence is a transitional period between childhood and adulthood that presents a challenge—an opportunity for growth—and that challenge is met and mastered by these youngsters, unlike the disturbed adolescent, "precisely because their ego [read: "character"] is strong enough to withstand the pressure." In this task the study finds "they are greatly helped by their parents." It is not that they have no problems, are happy all the time, are never depressed, succeed at everything they try, nor is it that they lead sheltered lives; it's that they are flexible enough to adjust to what life throws in their way, are in touch with their feelings, and have good relationships with their parents, from whom they detach themselves gradually rather than asserting their independence in any kind of dramatic confrontation.[74]

Offer found that for the majority of normal teen-agers "there is no major gap of understanding and communication between the generations." They assert their independence in early adolescence, around twelve or thirteen, in terms of such superficial and ritualistic behaviors as how they dress and what music they listen to, what time they come home and whether they make their beds or do their homework on time,[75] but when it comes to moral and political questions, religious and ethical matters, and to life goals, they share their parents' basic values.[76] Most of them see their mothers as warm and understanding, feel respect and distant admiration for their fathers, who were usually the disciplinarians in the family.[77] On the whole, they are proud of their parents and want to be like them.

Their plans include marrying and having families similar to their own.[78] Their ambitions are consonant with their parents' expectations. As for the parents, they praise their sons for being (or wish they were) "conscientious, responsible, studious, obedient, and sensitive"—the values of the American middle class.[79]

It is a class that despite its vast numbers throughout the country has received scant attention from those who study the young or report on them, for reasons we will consider a little further on.

Many of the parents interviewed had misgivings about changes that had occurred between their own adolescence and that of their children, misgivings that suggest something more than nostalgia for the past of one's own lost youth, although there is always something of that present when we remember and compare. They questioned whether their sons were really better off, despite having more things, more knowledge, more opportunities open to them. These parents had grown up during the Depression, had been less affluent, harder working. "The suggestion was that one *should* have to work hard for rewards, that it all should not come as easily as it does to today's young." They said such things as that the world was smaller then "and there was more mystery to things. . . . We were on our own more and were children longer . . . There's more pressure on them now in every way."[80]

Psychologically, stability was the overriding characteristic of these adolescents. Their sexual behavior bore no resemblance to the myth of sexual revolution among the young reported in the popular press. Their aggressive impulses were most often sublimated into competitive sports. They had a sense of humor, not just confined to joking as a way of dealing with hostility but involving the ability to look at the problems of life and at oneself and see the humorous side of things. Their style of coping with crises was more or less what it had been since childhood, leading to the conclusion that it is disturbed children who become disturbed adolescents—or at least children who have not accomplished the tasks of early childhood and latency, of individuation and competency. Youngsters who grow up in stable families where there is open communication and emotional security, who have empathic parents who set limits for them and serve as ideals for them, grow up relatively peacefully. They learn to cope, and they do so largely through identification with their parents, as they have learned all other important matters at all previous stages of life. Eventually, they become independent and responsible adults themselves.

In short, an adolescent's way of separating from his parents reveals the same style—whether stormy or peaceful, disruptive or gradual—that has characterized his life up to now.

Unlike the more dramatic experience of troubled adolescents, the average suburban middle-class teen-ager experiences a relatively long period of adolescence, proceeding through it slowly, mastering its various tasks gradually, and evidencing comparatively little upheaval.

Why is this really rather unsurprising finding such news and why have we heard so little of it before now?

THE TEEN YEARS: CHAOS OR COMMITMENT?

Six years after the publication of *The Psychological World of the Teen-ager* Offer published a follow-up study of his subjects, *From Teenage to Young Manhood: A Psychological Study*,[81] in which he was able to confirm and extend his earlier findings. There was generational conflict in rather superficial matters in the early teen years of these boys but no real generation gap: No rejection of basic parental values, no decisive moment of confrontation was necessary to establish their sense of identity. It developed gradually and without dramatic incident over the years. Slow and steady growth was the rule, with variations correlated with relatively less stable home life (death, divorce, parental discord, poor relationship between father and son, resistance by the mother to letting her son go). These were also the youngsters who were most dependent on the peer culture, possibly, Offer suggests, "because they received less gratifications from their relationships within the family." Most of the subjects were "slow," if we accept what the media tells us is going on, in becoming involved in sexual activities; only about half had had intercourse by the end of the third post-high-school year. If there was a sexual revolution, it was to be found in society's attitudes and not in the behavior of most its young.

If continuity with parental values and parental expectations prevails in these average young people, how do we account for the rebelliousness of that more visible and more vocal part of their generation? The answer is that they, too, functioned as continuations of their parents,[82] gratifying the wishes, fulfilling the fantasies, acting out the values of their elders, who encouraged their activism and admired their idealism.[83] Over and over, studies of protesting youth in the 1960s showed that most adolescent participants in demonstrations came from families where their actions were fully approved.[84]

Offer calls attention to the influence of "the parents and teachers who have implanted the seeds of change," as well as the direction provided "in both blatant and subtle ways by the total society." In the main, the ideas of radical student activists are rediscovered by each succeeding generation, guided by the adults "raising their children to believe in ideas that can be seen as offspring of the adults' ideas."[85] If we have a teen consumer culture and a socially disruptive student movement, it is because they are encouraged by our culture and ourselves, not because our children have invented them out of a void in spite of us.

Even the much discussed teen culture seems to be largely a creation of society's elders. American society has always placed a high value on getting along with others, being part of the group, and parents tend to see it as a sign of successful adjustment that their youngsters are part of the crowd, are accepted by their age mates. "Peer group values themselves," as Offer puts it, "are likely to be extensions of parental values."[86] He reminds us that the differences between various youth groups outweigh their similarities—as well as their differences from the culture as a whole.

The American family, and the American adolescent in particular, have been the objects of intensive scrutiny in recent years. Unfortunately, studies of some disturbed families[87] have been generalized to describe the population at large; studies of a handful of alienated youth at Harvard University[88] have been generalized to apply to an entire generation. Deviance, as Offer points out, is more visible, more interesting to study, and excites the fantasies of the public more than the familiar, routine, and predictable average.

The Offer studies, however, and others like them,[89] point to stability and continuity rather than disruption and change in the development of the individual character (patterns of coping established early in life tend to persist) as well as in the parent-child relationship and in the functioning of successive generations. This generation tends to cope in pretty much the same ways as those of the last few decades, despite alarms and pronouncements of revolutions and gaps, sexual and generational, from the media and social scientists. Evidently the rapid growth of industrial society does not, as we have been warned it would in one best seller after another, cause obsolescence in character types or necessitate radically new psychological mechanisms for dealing with the stresses of everyday life.

Neither the traditional values of our society nor the relationships between the generations are being made irrelevant by technological growth and cultural change. It is not true as Margaret Mead claimed[90] that rapid change has rendered intergenerational communication impossible, that "there are no guides," that "the elders are . . . vastly alienated from the young, who . . . reject their elders' past." It is only true that some reformers see things that way, and they tend to be the ones who, like Mead, Kenneth Keniston,[91] Marshall McLuhan,[92] Alvin Toffler,[93] and other prophets of the late sixties and early seventies, took off without much hard evidence to expound theories of changing man in response to changing society. Their own enthusiasms for what might be, as well as their own discontents with what was, seem to have led them astray, and their fanciful conclusions, feeding a hungry press—television, instant best sellers, magazines, newspaper supplements—led many others to think of the occasional as the inevitable. This is nothing new, for in every generation artists and visionaries, philosophers and social reformers have looked to the young to change the world. For better or worse, it would appear that most of the young would prefer to join it.

This is the conclusion drawn from surveys of large groups of average youngsters from stable backgrounds functioning without apparent difficulties—as distinct from patients seen in treatment, lawbreakers, or seriously disruptive youngsters referred to the courts or other social agencies[94] or leaders of protest movements described by the press or studied by social scientists.

It would seem that we have accepted a view of youth based on a far from typical sample. Most adolescents seem to be able to move with relative flexibility from the dependency of childhood to the independent functioning of adulthood, negotiating the shifts to greater intellectual tasks, nonfamily social relationships, a clearly defined sexual identity, and vocational commitment gradually and without dramatic emotional upheaval. The prerequisites for such a passage through youth seem to be the internalization of parental controls in early childhood and the formation of habits of industry and mastery of basic intellectual skills in latency. The turmoil so often reported of adolescence seems to be more a matter of the particular individuals focused on than a necessary characteristic of the age, an inevitable "rite of passage." The turmoil of adolescence has been exaggerated and extended beyond what the evidence will support, and having brought us this news, Offer urges a better understanding by parents, professionals, and society, all of whom he feels have encouraged adolescent crises by anticipating them and sometimes by enjoying the acting-out of the younger generation.

"The adult in our Western culture," says psychiatrist E. James Anthony,[95] "has apparently learned to expect a state of acute disequilibrium and anticipates the 'storm and stress' in his adolescent child as he once anticipated the negativism of his two-year-old. The expectation has seemingly been incorporated into the literature of psychological development,[96] and it may take methodical research and many years of endeavor to remove it from the textbooks. There is, however, growing anthropological and sociological support for the concept that society gets the type of adolescent it expects and deserves."

What is it we expect and deserve? Having been sold a bill of goods by clinicians generalizing from the deviant to the normal and academics bent on achieving the change they desire through the young and a press always hungry for sensation, we have come to expect our teen-agers to be disaffected, discourteous, hard to live with, hard to understand. We are disappointed if they are not like this, since we have been told that if they work hard and seem reasonably happy, there must be something wrong with them; it's *normal* for adolescents to be miserable and to make everyone around them miserable.

But what if not only we, but they, deserve something different? Let us look at the only things we know are inevitable at this stage of life—the biological bedrock—and see what that can tell us about the age of puberty before going on to consider what that does and does not necessarily imply about the period of adolescence and how we might readjust our expectations for the sake of both our children and ourselves.

PUBERTY: DEVELOPING BODIES . . .

The years from eleven or twelve to about sixteen or eighteen are a time of rapid growth and developmental change equaled only by the months before birth and the first three years of life—with one striking difference. The individual changing is now a self-conscious observer of those changes, a fact that is bound to have some psychological and social consequences, depending on the time of onset, rate of change and the sex of the individual.

What are these changes, and when and how do they occur?[97] At puberty, hormonal secretions trigger a rapid spurt of growth in body size, changes in body shape and in the reproductive organs in particular, and development of the secondary sex characteristics, all of which sharply distinguish males and females. Girls develop earlier than boys, some being sexually mature while male age mates of theirs are still children, and some girls develop earlier than others, while some boys are fully mature before other boys their age have even begun to develop sexually. Thus, while the sequence of anatomical and physiological events is the same for all girls and for all boys, there is great variation in individual biological timetables, a fact that cannot but influence the feelings of the adolescent about self and others.

Any group of young teen-agers (girls of about eleven to thirteen, and boys of about thirteen to fifteen) are likely to be less alike physically than individuals of the same age are at any other time of life, which can complicate things for some of them socially, depending on what society places a value on—brains, brawn, looks, competence—and where the young person excells or falls short of the cultural norm. Menarche, the onset of menstruation, is a critical point in the emotional life of every girl, and how she responds will be a function of her particular mental life, the specific wishes, fears, fantasies and beliefs that make up her own inner world, a construction that began in earliest childhood. Early-maturing girls, like late-maturing boys, may have problems in self-image and social relationships that need to be understood by their parents, their teachers, and themselves. The girl whose body has made her a woman physically before she has time to catch up emotionally or socially may hide herself in wide and flowing clothes her parents find bizarre. The boy whose body has not kept pace with those of his classmates may pretend to be sick rather than appear in the gym locker room.

The uneven pace of development of the various body organs and systems at puberty, together with the striking variation in the rate of maturing in different individuals, means that an adolescent will often feel out of step—with his own changing self as well as with the rest of the world out there. Self-consciousness is a universal feeling of the so-called awkward age as the adolescent experiences the changes in his own body, compares himself with his peers, looks ahead to the adult world he will enter, and gradually defines himself as a person. It is a process that, while not necessarily shattering to the normal youngster, is bound to involve small pains and indignities, some confusion and disappointments. In fact, it is in how the adolescent copes with these inevitable aspects of the biological and social realities of this time of life that he defines himself, creates his identity.[98]

Along the way, he may try on various kinds of personalities to see how they fit. The wisecracking tough guy, the esthetic bohemian, the understanding giver of sympathy, the jock hero, the glamorous sophisticate may succeed each other from day to day in any given boy or girl's seat at school or at the family dinner table. Eventually most of the play-acting in front of the mirror of one's own and others' eyes falls away and the bits of attitude and behavior that remain are what make up the sense of *me, this is what I'm like, this is what I do and don't do, what I avoid and what I enjoy,* that is what we mean by a sense of identity.

Physically, boys' increase in muscle size and in the capacity of their circulatory system in the teen years make them stronger and faster, and give them greater endurance than girls. Where once this adapted them to being hunters, in our society it adapts them to being athletes.

In modern western industrialized societies the young mature physically sooner than they did in earlier times or than they do today in less affluent countries with inherited and persisting nutritional deficiencies. This means they enter earlier on a period of life that is further extended by the requirements of education and training for increasingly complicated working and professional tasks. Adolescence, once a moment between being one of the children fed and one of the hunters and gatherers who do the feeding, is now a period of some ten years stretching between beginning to grow up in biological terms and being considered a grownup by one's family and society.

And while none of these factors—the biological changes, the emotional response to them, or the demands of society—necessarily entail traumatic upheaval for the majority of adolescents, there are minor fluctuations in mood, day-to-day problems in adjusting the changing self to friends and family, little difficulties along the way toward defining one's adult self, and challenges in deciding on a vocation and mastering its prerequisites that face every teen-ager. Parents who have supported a child through the separation and individuation of the earliest years and encouraged learning and diligence in the early school years will naturally be supportive, empathic, and mindful of what limits still need to be set at this age. Family life need not be shattered by the awful fact of a child turning thirteen or fourteen—unless parents expect it to and tacitly encourage such an outcome. When they remain understanding friends, sure of themselves and what they stand for, examples of how to cope in life, their youngsters are too busy living and learning to remember to go crazy.

Being busy—with the body and with the mind—is the greatest need at this age of suddenly increased energy. The delay our complex economy imposes on young people's ability to do productive work, channel their overflowing energies, and feel they contribute something useful to the world is the result not only of the extended education and apprenticeship necessary for certain kinds of careers. It is also, ironically, a result of some of the reforms enacted into laws originally intended to improve the lives of those children who would not enter on a course of higher education leading to a profession but enter the marketplace. The child labor laws, designed to prevent the exploitation of the vulnerable young in factories and on farms, "may also," as L. Joseph Stone and Joseph Church put it, "sometimes impede the adolescent from getting practical experience and a sense of growth, accomplishment and independence."[99]

Physical labor and athletic activities are singularly valuable to the adolescent needing to come to terms with a new body and find ways to channel new energies. And so is learning, making use of other new capabilities. For parallel with the physical changes that begin to make a man or a woman of a boy or a girl are the intellectual changes that occur at around the same period of time.

. . . AND YOUTH: DEVELOPING MINDS

These have been most systematically charted by Piaget in his theory of the development of intelligence in children, which, we saw earlier, begins with the infant's sensorimotor perceptions and culminates in the acquisition of "object permanence," the realization that things outside himself have an existence that persists even when he cannot see them. He realizes that the ball that rolled away might be under the table, that if mother goes away she will return. The acquisition of language at around the age of two ushers in the "preoperational" stage of intelligence. The child has acquired mental images of objects but is still entirely dependent on his own experience, perceptions, and intuition for his understanding of what things are and how they work. His explanations are largely magical. At around the age of seven the child enters what Piaget calls the stage of "concrete operations." This is the beginning of what we usually mean by thinking and the basis of readiness for schooling. The child can now perform mentally where he previously had to perform physically. He can count in his head, without using his fingers or other objects, and this means he can do arithmetic—adding, subtracting, multiplying, and dividing numbers in his mind.

The next stage is to be able to perform operations on abstract concepts.[100] This is the stage of "formal operations," and it begins at around the age of eleven, when the child acquires the ability to formulate hypotheses and reason deductively. He can think about a problem from various points of view and entertain different ways in which it might be solved. He can think about thoughts, "operate on operations" as Piaget puts it, not just on concrete objects or his images of them. He can deal with the ideas of space and time and, by about the age of fifteen, possesses the intellectual tools with which to function as an adult. Experience will add to his understanding, facts to his knowledge, but there will be no further development of basically new mental structures.

"The great novelty that characterizes adolescent thought," according to Piaget, "consists in detaching the concrete logic from the objects themselves, so that it can function on verbal or symbolic statements without other support" and results in "the possibility of manipulating ideas in themselves and no longer in merely manipulating objects. In a word, the adolescent is an individual who is capable (and this is where he reaches the level of the adult) of building or understanding ideal or abstract theories and concepts." He is capable of reasoning on propositions "which are not taken as true or false but are experimentally formulated in order to derive from them all possible consequences, which are then checked by comparison to the facts."[101] "An adolescent, unlike the child, is an individual who thinks beyond the present and forms theories about everything, delighting especially in consideration of that which is not."[102]

These new intellectual capabilities enable the adolescent to be integrated into the social world of adults, to think as they do. They also enable him, in Piaget's words, "to conquer a certain number of fundamental intellectual operations which constitute the basis for a scientific education at high-school level," without which it is not possible to function successfully in our society.[103]

What else is implied by these new mental capabilities of the adolescent? Obviously, now that he can learn and understand more complicated things he can prepare himself for the higher levels of work and for the professions; he can begin to plan for his future. He has a new sense of time. The endless days of childhood have given way to a new perspective on historical time as well as on his own life. Together, these factors lead him to the possibility of a commitment to vocational goals that will signal the end of adolescence.

In addition to a capacity for realistic thinking, however, he has acquired a capacity for idealism. Which will win out—or how they will be reconciled—is very much a matter of the individual's emotional makeup, the direction in which all his past experience has pointed him. The naïve and unrealistic ideals of the adolescent's social thinking, the typically utopian schemes for reforming the world in his own image of right and wrong without regard for the possible, the practical, or the demonstrable nature of human beings, is the other side of the adolescent's sensitivity and self-consciousness. "The adolescent not only tries to adapt his ego to his social environment but, just as emphatically, tries to adjust the environment to his ego."[104]

This characteristic of the adolescent has been fastened on, idealized, and made into the ultimate stage of moral virtue by some educators and would-be social reformers, most notably Harvard's Lawrence Kohlberg and his followers, the proponents of programs in "cognitive moral development" in schools.[105]

179

In Defense of the Family

Drawing on Piaget's theoretical scheme of stages of children's intellectual development and his assumption[106] that their moral judgment follows the same scheme as their cognitive development, Kohlberg has described a series of moral stages[107] proceeding from "blind obedience to authority" to avoid punishment, through the intermediate stages of "instrumentalism," which judges an act in terms of its practical effect and conforms for the sake of rewards, "good-boy" behavior to avoid disapproval, authoritarian conformity to "law and order" to avoid censure by legitimate authority figures, and the "morality of contract," which respects individual rights and democratically accepted law, and acts morally for the sake of the common welfare.

Contrary to what one might suppose, this fifth stage is not the one that characterizes the mature moral character in Kohlberg's view. It is rather a sixth stage, the "morality of individual principles of conscience," in which the individual acts "morally" for reasons that have nothing to do with the judgment of any other individuals or of the community at large, but solely "to avoid self-condemnation." Kohlberg calls this state of mind "moral autonomy" and asserts that this highest stage of moral development is characteristic of late adolescence. Self-chosen universal ethical principles, not laws, religion, or the social contract, are the measure, and laws may be broken in the name of what the individual has decided is a higher principle than that which they serve.[108]

We have commented earlier on some of the implications of Kohlberg's ideas and their wide acceptance by professional educators.[109] Suffice it to point out here that this elaborate structure is erected on the basis of what children say and does not necessarily bear any relation to what they actually do. One must ask what meaning the verbal responses to elaborate "moral dilemmas" posed by interviewers and teachers have—what relation to nonverbal behavior in real life. One must also marvel at the way in which Kohlberg and his followers make use of their scheme to support their own political ideology.

They must admit that only a small fraction of adults in the world are "morally mature" in their terms—that is, have reached Kohlberg's sixth stage. Many people, they tell us, never reach stage six, which, it should surprise no one to learn, is most prevalent among the college-educated upper-middle-class youth most typically found in the cities of the northeast. Even they, it must be reported, sometimes "regress" to earlier stages of development when they leave campus—that is, when they grow up and experience more of the real world, or, as we might put it, when they become not only older but wiser.

It is an example of the circular reasoning of Kohlberg's argument that since individual behavior guided by abstract concepts of justice must be the highest level of morality, those who do not guide themselves by such concepts have either never reached that stage or have regressed from it to some earlier stage. It does not occur to Kohlberg that perhaps it is the individual who remains at a stage characterizing adolescence who is arrested in his moral development.[110] It would not suit his political purpose, which is to treat contemptuously, or at least patronizingly, those who "conform" to society, and to heap praise and encouragement on those who put their own ideals above the laws.

In Kohlberg's view, conservatives and even those we would usually call liberals belong to lower stages than radicals and revolutionaries, although even Kohlberg has to acknowledge that some of the latter belong to his second, "pre-moral" stage, where self-interest and satisfaction of one's own needs and desires are one's guide. "Protest activities, like other acts, are neither virtuous nor vicious; it is only the knowledge of the good which lies behind them that gives them virtue."[111]

Kohlberg wants adolescents to be taught "the idea of justice" rather than a "bag of virtues." His technique is to shake the student up, create a dissatisfaction with his existing values, his ideas of good and bad, right and wrong. Only then can he become receptive to new ideas of right and wrong. Whose? You guessed it. Students will "move up" a stage or two with this kind of exposure, and so, with a wonderful kind of irony, they have learned once again to think as their teachers want them to, the only difference being that it is Kohlberg's way of seeing the world, and not necessarily their parents', with which they are being subtly indoctrinated. Before throwing it out, we ought to take a good look at the contents of that much maligned "bag of virtues" Kohlberg and his followers are so scornful of. It might hold some things we can ill afford to do without, and have a right to want to provide our children with: the middle-class virtues of honesty, decency to others, self-control, cooperation, hard work, and the achievement of goals for oneself, one's family, and one's society.

Kohlberg claims to be helping the young to construct their own autonomous morality, rejecting values imposed from without. In fact, he substitutes one set of values—his own—for another—those of the young person's parents and community. In fact, either one can be chosen freely. All value systems have to come from somewhere. What matters is not where the values originated but that they are adopted willingly. That is what constitutes free choice. And the majority of young people do adopt the morality of their parents and their community willingly—because they want to. It is that free and willing choice that makes for an autonomous morality, not the mere fact of having chosen something other than that which one's parents believe and one's society accepts.

WHEN THINGS GO WRONG: PARENTING AND PATHOLOGY

With his new powers of reasoning and his widening awareness of human experience and sense of the humanly possible, the adolescent inevitably begins to realize that neither the great world nor his own parents are perfect. But the anger that makes him want to shatter the one and turn his back on the other exists only in the troubled adolescent. Most young people are able to come to terms with the limitations of reality, the imperfections of their parents, and their own shortcomings, and to become more tolerant and more mature in the process. The desperate search for new heroes, new values, new ways to fill an emptiness within does not characterize most of the young but only some of the most highly visible. These are the political activists, trying—and sometimes being encouraged—to lead when they should still be learning; the religious fanatics, seeking certainty and a sense of security in a new family and community with unbending rules; and the drug takers, who regress to an infantile state of passivity in the face of the challenges of preparing for adult responsibility.

Drug use has less to do with the search for pleasure and thrills than with the wish to reduce a tension, a state of mental distress, that the individual cannot manage by means of his own efforts of thought or physical activity. To take the attitude that drug use by the young is a normal part of growing up is to do them the same disservice as to lead them to believe they are political saviours, or that they should all be having sexual intercourse—a message clearly implied by "family life and sex education" courses telling them how to do it, with whom to do it, under what circumstances to do it, and in fact offering every kind of advice except not to do it—or that they are expected to be rebelling wildly against home and school, a message clearly spelled out in the picture of teen-agers romanticized in films and on TV.

Many of the young will experiment with drugs and it is better that they do so without parental "understanding" (read: "approval") than that their parents should, in Erikson's phrase, compromise themselves totally. The emotionally healthy adolescent cannot tolerate a dependence on drug use; it conflicts too sharply with his wishes to learn, to master, to be active, to achieve. Those who do become drug dependent are those who have problems that originated in early childhood, a time to which they regress now because they have never really moved beyond it. Most adolescents reject such dependency; those who continue to seek the effects of mood-changing or mind-altering substances—opiates, amphetamines, LSD—are seriously disturbed, and should be offered help, including more structure rather than more permissiveness. Habitual use of any artificial means of controlling one's feeling life is a sign of serious emotional malfunctioning.[112]

In fact, all of the serious disturbances of adolescence have their origins in a childhood derailed or never satisfactorily journeyed through. Among the most severe reactions to childhood deficits experienced as a legacy in adolescence are anorexia in girls and homosexuality in boys. Girls who at puberty respond to menarche and the ripening of their bodies with fear, disgust, and distorted self-images sometimes stop eating, go on severe, even self-abusive diet regimens, and starve themselves, sometimes to the point of death. The histories of such adolescents usually reveal early conflicts between the infant girl and her overanxious and compulsive mother centering around feeding and elimination.[113]

Like those who may experiment with drugs and then abandon their use, not every girl who worries about her new shape and decides to cut out ice cream and cookies until she likes what she sees in the mirror better, and not every boy who experiences tender feelings for another boy is in serious trouble. As always, it depends on the meaning of the behavior in the mental life of the individual. The important thing is to distinguish between the transient behaviors of the adolescent trying out new ways of being himself to see whether they fit and discarding those that don't, and the inflexible grip of the persistent nonadaptive rituals the youngster cannot move beyond.

In the case of homosexuality, there are two important things to keep in mind. The first is that a boy's isolated homosexual experience does not necessarily indicate a fixed proclivity. In early adolescence, what psychoanalysts call "instability in the aim and object of the sexual drive"[114] is not uncommon. Experiment and regression of a transitory nature do not necessarily indicate pathology. By late adolescence, however, a stable pattern of heterosexual adaptation is to be expected. The second important point to keep in mind is that when this heterosexual adaptation has not taken place, the young person has not chosen an alternate route to adult sexuality but an incomplete one. He has been unable to achieve the sense of masculinity that would permit him to function normally as a heterosexual male, and this inability is the result of conflicts arising early in life that interfere with his development and cannot in any rational way be considered a free "choice."

The identification with a strong and confidently masculine father who is admired by a mother who encourages the boy's identification with his father's masculine traits rather than her own feminine ones is the sine qua non of the development of masculinity in boys.[115] Time and again for over half a century clinicians have reported the presence in the male homosexual's past of overpowering, overprotective mothers and inadequate fathers—fathers who are not there actually or in some cases emotionally, or whose overt brutality or subtler hostility interferes with the boy's identification with them as models of what it means to be a man.

To understand that the homosexual response to growing up is a distorted one, determined by early failures of identification within the family, is not a justification of intolerance or persecution. But the understandable wish not to visit suffering on homosexuals does not justify describing homosexuality as just another "life choice" like being an accountant or living uptown.

The homosexual is already a victim—of his past and its failure to release him from the bonds of childhood sexuality to the mature patterns of feeling and behavior characteristic of his biological sex. To maintain otherwise is to do a terrible disservice to the young. The adolescent whose sexual drive remains channeled in pregenital behavior needs help in understanding and dealing with the feelings that determine his behavior. To deprive him of the chance of that help by maintaining—as, unbelievably, many courses in the "family life and sex education" curriculum now established in many of our schools do—that homosexuality is simply an "alternate life style" is to compound one distortion with another.

The homosexual's choice is determined by a pattern of family relationships that interferes with the average expectable course of psychosexual development; it represents a flight from something that is feared more accurately than it does the adoption of something that is desired. The adolescent boy or girl who shows signs of being unable to face growing into a man or woman may be in serious trouble, unable to relinquish the desire for infantile gratification and regressing in the face of that overwhelming need to ways of regulating food or sex that are primitive and can prove destructive if not interrupted.

Girls who are preoccupied with the control of their bodies through depriving themselves of food or overwhelming themselves with it, and boys whose desire for physical intimacy with other males is more than sporadic or transitory, should be firmly guided toward competent professional help. To tolerate or "wait out" such potentially damaging behaviors is as foolish and as much a disservice to the adolescent, his family, and the society as the attitude that tolerates sexual acting-out, delinquency, drug-taking, and the political or religious fanaticism that seeks a meaning for one's life in violence or submerging oneself in a group with a strong leader and a strict discipline—because "kids will be kids" and it's all part of growing up. For most of the young, it is not. And when behavior of this kind occurs, as it does all too frequently, it is a sign that all has not gone smoothly in early childhood and latency and that help is needed—at the very least in the form of not denying that something is wrong, not romanticizing the sickness.

In recent years our society has displayed a tendency to perpetuate its ills by romanticizing them. Instead of helping the poor climb out of poverty through goal-directed efforts, we encourage a dependency that perpetuates the culture of poverty until it is inherited in families that have not retained and cannot transmit strengths of character to their children, who are in any case often the children of no one, of absent fathers and immature mothers. We wonder why there is so much crime, so little sense of community, when the rate of illegitimate births soars and the number of "single-parent families" (surely an oxymoron) increases, while we teach our schoolchildren in "social studies" that all values are relative and in "sex education" that whatever feels good is all right.

Are we so afraid our children won't like us that we haven't the courage to be parents to them? While we enjoy watching them grow we have to remain steady about what we believe is right, what they can and cannot do, what we expect of them now, and what we think they can become in life. To fail to provide such limits and such expectations is to fail to give them what they need in order to go out into the world and manage for themselves. The test of parenthood, after all, is one's own eventual obsolescence. Our children should be able to face life as adults without the need for invented parents to give them the things we failed to provide—a sense of self and a place in the world.

THE PROBLEM OF ADOLESCENCE . . .

At the same time that adolescence as a time of life is extended further and further by the need for prolonged education before the assuming of economic independence in our technically advanced civilization, it is beginning even sooner than it used to. Not only does physiological puberty occur earlier than it did in past times, but a number of pseudoadult forms of behavior such as dating, going steady, wearing makeup and provocative clothing have moved down the age scale all the way to prepuberty and the grade-school scene; and children in our society are constantly exposed to—indeed, bombarded with—sexually stimulating material in the mass media, particularly in films and on television.

None of this helps the young person facing the tasks of growing up—learning about himself, learning about the world, and forging an identity based on a reconciliation between his own nature and that of his family and society—and it is the fortunate child whose parents are able to help him maintain continuity of development and steadiness of direction during the adolescent years.

Contrary to what experts, pundits, and trend-spotters tell us, the enemy is without; it is not "us" as family members. Society creates a good deal of the trouble for adolescents by the demands it makes in the form of the temptations it presents; the trouble doesn't inevitably arise from the inner nature of the child this age or from a need to wrench himself violently from the smothering embrace of parents. Where home life is stable, parents fulfilled and sure of themselves, tasks and goals clearly defined for the adolescent, and affectionate tolerance provided for minor upsets, experimentation, and peccadilloes, the young still grow into solid citizens without liquefying along the way.

But it gets harder all the time for parents to offset the influence of the media and even, in some cases, the schools. The sensation-mongering of the one and government-supported attempts at social engineering in the other have been erecting some heavy obstacles in the way of family life.

Looking recently at adolescents of the late 1970s compared with their predecessors of the early sixties, Daniel Offer makes some disquieting observations about the changes that have occurred over the last twenty years or so.[116] Among the differences he found were that teenagers of the seventies had a less positive self-image, were less self-confident, less controlled, and less trusting of others, spoke less positively about their families and reported lower ethical standards, and felt they were sexually "behind." In short, although the majority felt positively about themselves and their families, there was a decided trend to report more negative self-images among the young. They were less happy than teen-agers a decade or more ago.

What has been going on, and what can we do about it? How can we help our young to hold on to their youth and make the most of it? The answer, not surprisingly, lies with the family itself. And, not forgetting the caveat of the earliest part of this book—take from all advice only what seems right for you and your child, what works in your home and family—here are some thoughts for parents of adolescents in the eighties.

. . . AND SOME SUGGESTIONS

At home, maintain an ordered world in which distinctions between the sexes and between the generations are clearly expressed, values are clearly stated and limits clearly set. Weak parents who abdicate their authority in their children's lives do little to help their children find strengths to identify with in forming their own characters. Discussing the trend toward "permissiveness," a traditional view suggests that the choice of heroes like Che Guevara or Mao Tse-Tung by students of the sixties, as well as such phenomena as religious cults and encounter groups, may spring from the needs engendered in a "fatherless" society. "In former times," we are reminded, "parents considered it their task to teach children moral values. . . . Upbringing was a positive task. In recent decades parents and educators, insecure in this task, have been mainly afraid of harming the next generation and of losing its love."[117]

Try to keep your young adolescent children from environments and events that are overstimulating sexually. Help them resist the trend toward earlier and earlier eroticism of the life of the young. Most of the "crushes" and "love affairs" of adolescence are in reality less of a sexual nature than what Erikson calls "an attempt to project and test one's own diffused and still undifferentiated ego through the eyes of a beloved person in order to clarify and reflect one's own self-concept and ego-identity." It is himself the adolescent is stuck on, and the fickleness with which he moves from one "steady" to another, or she from one "best friend" to another, is like looking in a different mirror to get a better idea of what one is like. "Many a youth," Erikson remarks, "would rather converse, and settle matters of mutual identification, than embrace."[118]

It's too bad that those long conversations about life and love that help establish the basis for learning about intimacy and later practicing it have been displaced by demonstrations of "what it's all about" on TV and at the movies, "rap sessions" in—of all places—school. What is stolen from the young this way can never be replaced. They will learn very little of value, very little that's true, very little that can help them understand what they are like or what they can be to others, in front of the TV screen or at the movies, from a guidance counselor or a sex education course. And adding to the problem is the fact that habituation to incessant sensory stimulation (TV, radio, hi-fi) contributes to reducing what Peter Blos calls "the faculty to be alone with oneself or, in psychological terms, to attend to internalization processes and to the use of fantasy."[119]

Encourage your adolescents to read instead, and help them to identify the literature that mirrors their own concerns. This does not mean the books that seem to be about youngsters just like them in the present, the commercially exploitive books manufactured for the "teen market"—junk food that caters to transitory appetites and doesn't stay with you. There is a valuable perspective to be gained from what shows different facets of age-old feelings experienced in

189

different times and even expressed in unfamiliar vocabularies. The mind is stretched. Adolescence is a time of apprenticeship. If this was once true in terms of occupation, it remains true in terms of relationships and vocation. This makes the nineteenth-century novel— Dickens and George Eliot, for instance—both appealing and enriching to the adolescent, who sees his preoccupations and his tasks, his problems and his goals mirrored in the plots and characters, rich in detail of person and place and absorbing in the presentation of the hero's search for the right way to live among others. And to love. For, despite the absence of explicitly depicted sex acts, the erotic life of men and women is never very far beneath the surface of the stories told in books like *Anna Karenina* or *Hard Times* or *The Mill on the Floss*. It appears, however, not as details of behavior in the bedroom but in the context of the characters' emotional life, from which one learns that fulfillment is preceded by desire and followed by commitment.

All societies have always provided some set of rules for regulating the sexual behavior of adolescents before marriage to insure the continued functioning of the society and its particular institutions, the way marriages are arranged and the way family life is structured within the larger social organization.

Although the media insist the rules are breaking down in contemporary American society, Daniel Offer tells us that "despite the political and ideological influence of the women's movement, traditional sex-role orientations still seem powerful among American youths in the late 1970s and 1980. . . . It is as though, in their minds, the girls are still on the side of home and hearth, while the boys are the conquerors and achievers in the larger society."[120]

Surprisingly, the area in Offer's latest study that showed the least difference between adolescents of the sixties and those of the seventies was sexual attitudes.

Teenagers today are not more liberal in their attitudes with respect to sex than they were in the 1960s. . . . Our guess is that, if nothing else, the sexual revolution has changed expectations and attitudes in the abstract. Ironically, because of the publicity given to the sexual revolution, it may be common-place for a teenager to have the impression that other teenagers are sexually much further along than he is and to believe that other teenagers are much further along than they actually are.[121]

What actually influences adolescent sexual behavior is a combination of factors: hormonal changes, sociocultural expectations, and internalized psychological factors—for example, fantasies about bodily development. It is not just the biology of puberty that matters but what the individual makes of the changes in terms of his or her own perception of society's expectations and judgments and in terms of his or her own mental life.[122]

Both the fantasies and the realities of the sexual life of most girls and women center around the emotional context of the acts performed. Eroticism and arousal depend on romantic commitment. In our culture, the capacity for intimacy is more highly developed in girls; with boys the emphasis is on the achievement of skills and independence. Thus close friendships are more common among adolescent girls, running in packs among boys. These patterns have evolved over long periods of time and seem adaptive for most girls and boys.

Observing that everything typical of middle or even late adolescence seems to be happening at a younger and younger age, Peter Blos cautions that what we ought to be doing instead is to "foster latency development to the fullest as the precondition for a competent entry into adolescence."[123]

The psychological integration of the sexual and aggressive drives that emerge at puberty depends largely on having accomplished the progress in learning, memory, tension tolerance, and the ability to distinguish between reality and fantasy, between action and thought, during latency. The child who has not developed these capacities can only fall back on infantile modes of discharging the intensified drives that beset him at puberty, and many of the disturbances of adolescence result from the failure to fully develop these capacities during the early school years. The child who acts out sexually, for instance, or regresses to dependency through drugs, is the one who is not occupied with learning or cannot tolerate frustration.

But this development, this learning, takes time, and freedom from demands the child is not yet ready to meet. It is this time required to prepare the child for adult functioning in a complex industrial society—for work, for citizenship, for parenthood—that we've bought by the prolongation of childhood and adolescence. And the capacity to persevere in the learning process depends on a certain degree of inhibition, delayed gratification, sublimation of desires into channels removed from immediate instinctual discharge.

"We have ample evidence," Blos reminds us, "to demonstrate that an acceptance of the young adolescent as a self-directing, sexually active 'young person' interferes severely with the preparatory functions of this stage." What is needed is a prolongation, rather than an abbreviation of childhood. "The young adolescent of thirteen—regardless of the status of his primary and secondary sex characteristics—is still, psychologically, a child. This fact should be acknowledged by family, by school, and by society at large. These institutions must continue to extend their containing and protective roles, rather than push the young adolescent ahead under the misleading banner of 'the earlier and the faster, the bigger and the better.' "[124]

In the interests of prolonging childhood instead of extending adolescence downward, Blos takes issue with the received wisdom of the day among feminists and educators alike with the suggestion that "the separation of the sexes in school during the early adolescent years is, psychologically and biologically, well advised," citing "the intellectual, physical, social, and psychological discrepancies that make boy and girl of this age ill fitting companions in work and play."[125] This does not, he insists, deprive the sexes of their normal development. On the contrary, "it is the boy showing a precocious preference for girl playmates who is the one whose maleness proves in later years shakily established, while the young boy who keeps company with boys as a young adolescent tends to settle, later on, more firmly and lastingly in his masculine identity."[126]

Much of the courtship games, exploration and rehearsal of what they take to be adult behavior, is engaged in by adolescents because they think it is expected of them. It may be less an expression of their intrinsic desire for sexual activity at the time than an anxious response to opportunities constantly placed in their way and messages telling them it's what is done by everyone else. The fear of being too different from everyone else leads adolescents into doing all sorts of things—from stealing hubcaps to having intercourse—they might not choose to do if strongly enough supported in their independence of mind. That kind of support—in a society increasingly unable and unwilling to provide clear rules for what is and is not permitted, will and will not be tolerated—can only be given by the family. The answer is not to revert to a more restrictive society but to encourage more expression of values within the family. The young person who knows he is more respected by his parents for following his (and their) own principles of behavior than for being an accepted member of the crowd of his peers is halfway to being able to resist social pressures that go against the grain of his own nature.

Parents have to be clear about discouraging precocious sexual activity, which means sexual activity engaged in without an emotional context, which in turn presupposes time to develop and maturity to do so.

In the past, and in fact until quite recently, moral strictures and the fear of pregnancy served to keep most young people from premarital intercourse. When they are constantly faced with images in film and on television and opinions in the press suggesting that "everyone does it" now that we've undergone a sexual revolution (a perfect example of the self-fulfilling prophecy), when their parents and teachers opt out of taking a strong position for fear of being unloved or out of step with liberal modern thought, and when they are methodically instructed in school in the uses of contraceptives, in case they should be tempted, and just as methodically told not to feel guilty if they do, it can hardly come as a surprise that more adolescents are having sexual relations earlier. Nonetheless, most adolescents continue to hold traditional views on sexual matters.[127] Early sexual experimentation seems to be "embedded in the social context of deviance," correlated with drug use, delinquency, and with estrangement "from those institutions—the family, the church, the school—that [have traditionally served] to monitor and maintain commitments to conventional values."[128]

Parents would do well to keep their children as far away for as long as possible from the media that cheapen and distort human nature, human relationships and human values. Don't hesitate to assume responsibility for deciding which television programs, films and—yes—books they are exposed to. Everyone in a liberal society should be free to write and publish anything, but you should be free to protect your own children from what you believe is harmful or overstimulating to them, both at home and in the schools you entrust them to. Use what influence you can to resist the teaching of relativism in social studies (kids need heroes, not skepticism—that can come later with more experience), of sex education (except for the biological facts of reproduction; sexual behavior is best discussed elsewhere and in a different context), and of values (except as each teacher makes it clear they are his own). It is not the business of the schools you send your children to to teach them that all political and social ideas are equal, that sexual behavior is a matter of taste like cooking, or that there is no right or wrong in human actions.

What are we to think of a curriculum on moral development enthusiastically adopted in schools of education that defines morality so as to exclude everyone not capable of a high level of abstract thinking (and, we might add, talking) and that makes actual deeds less significant than words about them? With its placing of the individual judgment above the traditional values of the culture, it seems designed to contribute to the erosion of confidence in society.

For the followers of Lawrence Kohlberg, the level of morality is neatly tied to the nature of political ideology. A concern with preserving "law and order" is "conventional" and characterizes conservatism. It only rates a four, while the "principled" abstractions of "postconventional" stage six reflect the radical left, critical of everything that is and eager to replace it with the individual's view of Utopia now. Is this the kind of exercise we want our schools to encourage in the young—and then take seriously?

The observable tendency of adolescents to practice their new-found capacity to consider multiple possibilities and verbalize them does not tell us anything about what they actually do now, or what they will do later. Life has not tested them yet, and, for the time being, talk is cheap. Kohlberg seems to have overestimated the value of the amount of it he has collected.[129]

What most of us mean by intelligence is not the capacity for performing formal operations in itself but the ability to do so with a certain degree of wisdom: to use experience to find adaptive solutions to real problems and to act on them. Few adolescents have had enough experience dealing with life to use their intelligence wisely. They are good at conundrums, hypotheses, the strategies of possibilities. Sometimes they are very funny and very charming. But God help us if we are to take our moral instruction from them.

For the fact is that you can't make a judgment about anyone's thinking—their stated thoughts and opinions—unless you know what purpose it serves in their mental life. A verbal espousal of altruistic behavior may be made in order to impress the interviewer; it may bear no relation to what the speaker would do in a real-life situation. Thus, though the capacity for abstract thought makes certain kinds of judgment possible, they're not necessarily "better" or even necessarily "good." We would have to know what relation they bear to a person's actions.

The moral zealots of the youth movements of the sixties were often singularly willing to "resort to" violence, to disregard the feelings of others, in short, to assume virtue without behaving virtuously if by virtuous we mean kind, generous, tolerant, forgiving. Other students participated in political demonstrations for reasons that had to do neither with politics or pathology: to relieve the tedium of hard work and study with a little excitement and fellowship. They were not too different in spirit from other generations of students who cut up in the springtime by swallowing goldfish or crowding into telephone booths. Only to the committed did they seem to be making a serious political statement.

Clearly, those whose experience has not yet reached beyond the school cannot have much to offer the rest of the world in the way of advice. They need to learn before they begin to teach, and to encourage them to think otherwise is only to cheat them of the learning that is so crucial to them now in terms of defining what they will do and how they will live later. Their business now is choosing a vocation, defining educational goals and career expectations. The more they think and talk about it now, the less likely they are to drift or stumble into a decision that will prove ultimately unsatisfying.

Always assuming that parents know the difference between encouraging and pushing, it is important to be encouraging about a young person's indications of interest in a particular kind of work in the world into which they will move from school. They should also be helped to understand that they go on with education as a means of preparing for that eventual place in the world. They enter college to find knowledge, understanding, and, finally, some day, wisdom. They do not bring it with them.[130]

There are those—we may call them the "neo-Eriksonians"—who maintain that neither sex nor independence is the burning issue of adolescence, but the establishment of a sense of identity, and that sexual activity and the assertion of independence in adolescence are aspects of the formation of identity—a self-defined organization of one's history, characteristics, and beliefs that defines an individual's uniqueness as well as his similarities to others, his capacities as well as his limitations.

Identity goes on being constructed throughout the lifetime of an individual, gradually and often unawares, through the choices that open certain paths and lead away from others. There are some moments in the lives of boys and girls, men and women, where critical choices have to be made and upheaval may attend the making of them for those whose previous history has left them unprepared for the task. Most of the time, the decisions about making friends, choosing a course of study, a place to study it, a kind of job, a place to live, a political point of view, are made in a way that feels natural in terms of what has gone before in the individual's life, what seems to fit with the piecemeal accretion of attitudes and behaviors that have constructed an identity since early childhood.

Human beings are creatures of history. Our choices in any moment of the present—whom we love and how our marriage goes, what kind of work we choose and how we do it, how we feel about our children and how we raise them—can only be understood in terms of our past. Since adolescence is a time in which many choices are made, both consciously and unconsciously, about what kind of person we will be and what kind of life we will live, it cannot be understood without reference to the years before it, back to the beginning of life.

Psychoanalysts have turned their attention in recent years to the "pre-oedipal" years, the first three of life, and to the vicissitudes of the young child's earliest efforts at self-mastery and a sense of autonomy. The way in which separation-individuation is achieved then influences the way it is is handled a decade or more later in the individual's life. Adolescent conflict often conceals, beneath the apparent struggle over independence, longings for union with the mother of infancy. Struggling against the lingering wish to be indulged and cared for, the young person may seek solutions in new figures to idealize in place of his parents, as well as in the kinds of friends he makes, the nature of those friendships, both hetero- and homosexual, and their ultimate outcome.

The development of character and personality has to be seen as a continuing and dynamic process, which means that adolescence must be viewed within the entire course of an individual's life, as part of a continuum, not a discrete entity. It does not begin on one day and end on another. It is the patterns laid down in childhood that reveal themselves in adolescence, and the way an individual copes with the stresses of adolescence also carries over into adult life. Crisis and difficulty in coping, storm and stress belong more to the persistence of an ongoing style of personality in an individual's life than they do to a particular stage of development.

This is not a bleak determinist view of human development. The past need not be a prison. It may be more like a storehouse full of resources that can be drawn on when they are needed in the present. In the flux of daily life we are continually faced with new problems. Our repertoire of possible solutions can be limited by rigid adherence to patterns already established or we can respond with variations ranging from the slight to the adventuresome. How we use old feelings, attitudes, experiences in evolving solutions provides opportunities for the kind of reorganization of self we call growth.

The importance of the earliest experiences of life comes home in adolescence. Disturbances in the early establishment of a separate identity—battles over feeding, toileting and other aspects of bodily autonomy, or too prolonged a maternal closeness and dependency— are the precursors at puberty of such problems as anorexia in girls and homosexuality in boys, or severe alienation in either sex, which takes the form of making trouble but little else. When adolescents are permitted, even encouraged to live in a world of their own, the problem is confounded. What they need is not to be separated from the larger society, but to be welcomed into it on every level, from the rituals that signal their coming of age to the tasks that make them part of the household and the obligations that make them part of the family and larger community.

Parenting always calls for a degree of flexibility, by which we mean an understanding of the main developmental thrusts of each stage of life so as to respond to them appropriately. It means knowing when a child needs to be encouraged to move away, when reassured that he has a place at home. In adolescence, it means tolerating a degree of moodiness, inconsistency, and experimentation. It does not mean joining in it, or even necessarily approving of it. Neutrality is often the best stance, and disapproval should not be ruled out in some cases. And it means distinguishing between the ephemeral problems that come and go in the days and nights of the young and those persisting difficulties that require intervention. Tolerating those is not appropriate. It is a distortion of the adolescent experience to say that all aberrant behavior—sexual acting-out, drug use, lack of academic interest and ambition, depression, delinquency—is part of growing

198

up and will disappear with time. None of these are necessarily part of the teen years, none of them characterize the lives of most teenagers, and however painful it may be for parents to recognize pathology and face the fact that a child has somehow failed to come to terms with growing up somewhere along the way up to now, the responsible parent faces reality and gets the best professional help available in the situation. In such situations sooner is always better than later.

It is time we put aside our fantasies about the young and saw them as they are and not as we wish or fear them to be. They are what they have always been—a link in the chain that connects the past with the present and is forged in the family, where they absorb so much of what is inherited and passed on in the culture.

4

Summing Up: The Family and the Future

Parents are always influenced by forces at work in the larger society beyond the family. The question is in what way, and to what extent. It is a question middle-class families in America today are in a better position to answer for themselves than families anywhere ever before.

One always has to consider the part played by culture and commerce, science and technology, in civilized life. One obvious example is the role played by developments in the science and art of medicine, through the decline in infant mortality and the gradual conquest of children's diseases, in the changing patterns of child care of the last two hundred years. Children can be planned for, they do not necessarily threaten the lives of the women who bear them, and

Summing Up: The Family and the Future

they are more likely to grow up than in times when they were routinely swaddled and sent away to be cared for by a wet nurse. Obviously mothers are more likely to take an interest in their babies and to form affectionate ties with them when they have more reason to expect them to live past infancy.

Through most of Europe two hundred years ago an infant had only one chance in four of surviving childhood. Four hundred years ago the chances were even slimmer with recurring waves of famine and plague. Isolated inventions and discoveries—the obstetrical forceps, the pasteurization of milk, the knowledge of what causes rickets and measles and how to prevent them—blend together in a single stream of improvements in the chances of a newborn's surviving birth and infancy, avoiding the ravages of the killer diseases of the past, and emerging into adulthood with a degree of health and intelligence, capabilities and possibilities, that even at their lowest in our society were undreamed of and unattainable by most human beings in the past.

It is a common sentimental assumption, nevertheless, that industrialization was responsible for a breaking up of family ties and erosion of parental control, presumably due to the removal of the father from the household to work elsewhere and the change from working on the land or in cottage industry that united the family in common labor to employment patterns that split the members up and established a division of labor in factory and office.[1]

Interestingly, though, the facts seem to be otherwise. History shows that the pattern in the preindustrial family was to send young people out to live in other families between puberty and marriage; in the nineteenth century they began to stay home longer as apprenticeship in other households declined, schooling was extended, and domestic life included children for a longer and longer period of dependency, all of which actually resulted in a strengthening of generational ties.[2] One historian concludes that "the most pronounced change in family roles caused by industrialization was in enhancing the power of parents and decreasing the independence of teenage boys."[3] It would appear that if there is a villain responsible

201

for any trend toward loosening the ties of the family it is not industrial capitalism, which gets a bum rap on this issue.

Fathers did not lose their moral force when they ceased to be visible to their sons and daughters as they performed the work that sustained the family. One current dirge for the modern family maintains that the father who ran the farm or the family business, because he actually produced the food his children ate and had skills to teach them that they would eventually need, seemed worth emulating; his sons dreamed of surpassing him and his daughters of finding someone like him.

But does moral force, or psychological identification, or respect—different ways of talking about the same thing—become impossible when a man's work is not witnessed by his children? There have been enough hated fathers of rebellious children among the old-fashioned farmers we hear so much about and enough achieving and affectionate sons of fathers who work for organizations quite separated from where they live to suggest otherwise—that children can understand very well it is their father who provides the necessities of life when they are little even though the money may come from "faceless" businesses.

The deciding factor is a man's feeling about himself and his competence, and the attitude his wife has toward him. It is from those, whether he brings home the bacon from a farm or a factory, a shop or an office, that a child forms his idea of a father's effectiveness, and a mental representation of what to try to be like.

Throughout most of history, survival, then enough to eat and a warm shelter, were the goals of most human beings. Now we have exquisite goals for our children—both in terms of character and accomplishments—and only the subtlest interactions between them and us can elicit—and not always, even with the best of understanding care—what we want. How is it possible to expect to be able to train a professional class to accomplish these goals, to "parent"?[4] The exception is the case of children who risk being grossly abused or neglected by their own parents, in which case "professional parenting" is an improvement, but a limited one.

Summing Up: The Family and the Future

In our concern for a better world, what is the most effective kind of social action? It's an old argument, the chicken-egg controversy about which comes first in the improvement of society—the improvement of social institutions or of the individual, some choosing to legislate, others to deal with the nurturance of particular individuals, as parents, teachers, therapists of some kind.

We are all influenced by our environment, by the society we live in, but the most pervasive environment remains the family that shapes us and the most effective form of social action is still arguably the bringing up of children with a sense of self and feeling for others, with goals that give meaning to their lives. The central problem of our time may be how to raise men and women who can withstand the threats to autonomy of the centralized bureaucratic state and the numbing and all-pervasive media that cheapen human experience and deaden human response—how to guard our humanity and transmit it while enjoying the undeniable blessings of technology.

The short and uniquely important time of early childhood never comes back, and there are few other things parents can't do just as well later in life, few things as significant or as rewarding as guiding their own children's growth. Ask any old person looking back on life, even one who feels his children have disappointed him, about parenthood. Chances are he will wish he had it to do over, not that he had never done it.

We begin life helpless, hungry, full of needs and desires that can only be satisfied by those who care for us. The problem is that they inevitably become the source of frustration as well as of satisfaction, setting up feelings in each of us that have to be reconciled as we grow up. It is the vicissitudes of this resolution of conflicting feelings we each make in our own way that creates our particular characters.

Irrationality and violence persist in human life despite greater understanding of natural phenomena and technological innovation. This does not condemn either knowledge or industry per se, but only says something about the human nature that finally directs their uses. There is something dark in human nature that persists, whether it is called instinct or sin. Both psychoanalysis and the Judeo-Christian religions are based not on the idea of inevitable progress or of fatalism either, but on a tragic view of human nature that recognizes the inevitability of conflict, although they deal with it in very different ways.

Institutions can contain but not eradicate the darker impulses. Laws and all the other arrangements of society exist to protect us against the worst in ourselves and in each other. Enlightenment, whether the bringing to consciousness and resolution of mental conflicts or the acquisition of faith, has its limitations.

We cannot prevent emotional problems entirely. Our children are bound to feel anger, hatred, jealousy, envy at times, no matter what we do. The darker passions are one end of the spectrum of human feelings that comes with the territory of being alive. Conflict is ubiquitous in mental life. It is not the avoidance of conflict—that would be impossible—but the way in which it is resolved that determines character. Having come through a successful resolution of conflict, rather than never having experienced it, is what makes for normality, usefulness, and happiness in love and in work.

There are limits to what we can protect our children from, since much of what they experience arises from within, a product of their own mental life, of what they with a unique vision make of experience, and since impulses, wishes, fears, and dreams are always lurking beneath reason and the civilized life. The child needs the assurance that the adults in his life will protect him from the tide of his impulses rather than allow him to drown in it. It is highly questionable whether the young child can best be socialized for life in a democracy by being introduced to egalitarian principles from the beginning of family life. Simple rules and clear authority are more likely to provide the basis for a self with a secure identity. The young child's fear of being overwhelmed by his passions because no one is able or willing to assume the responsibility of "being boss" is more likely to lead to weak character than the opportunity to identify with a benign but firmly in-charge adult. The problem arises when parents are too afraid of losing their child's love to meet its needs for discipline. To spare the child the experience of authority is to deprive him of the opportunity to test himself, to resolve emotional conflict, and to become an autonomous adult himself.

Only in a stable family with strong and affectionate parents does a child grow up with the sense of being protected in a world that makes sense. Such a beginning provides the basis for the flexibility of response that will help him learn and overcome difficulties in later life. Such parents are able to let the child go little by little as he indicates a need and an ability to move out on his own. They instill conscience rather than dependency. The paradox is that only by remaining strong authority figures can they help their child become independent. He learns from what they are, what they do, what it is to be an adult.

If our children are to go us one better in life, to emulate us and perhaps eventually surpass us, they will need our help. We must interpret the world of adulthood for them through what we show them is the way to live, the way to love. If they are to define themselves, we must define ourselves for them, letting them know who we are, what our life history has been, what matters to us, what we believe, what we stand for. To avoid doing so is to confess the worst sort of poverty and to leave our children impoverished after us. It is a confession that we have no values, no pride in ourselves, no interest in the world we have made for ourselves and each other. Why should they want to enter a world that means so little to those already there?

The only answer is to make a world for our children in the family, at home, that provides enough satisfactions and pleasures at the same time that it transmits enough education and sets enough limits so that they won't be drawn elsewhere in search of selfhood.

The answer lies in providing phase-appropriate care, meeting the needs of the child in changing ways as he changes in growing. It is appropriate in early infancy to meet all of a child's needs, but the same behavior becomes smothering and overprotective a few years later. Changing what one gives and how one gives it as the child grows older is the challenge of parenthood.

Each child is also an individual, and even within the same small family one will have a greater need for closeness, another for independence, and the sensitive parent must be able to provide not only what is usually indicated at a given stage but at the time and in the way this particular child needs it. It is not an easy task and not an unimportant one.

Sometimes it calls for new ways of looking at life. For instance, even if you are not religious yourself, think twice before abandoning the idea of a form of religious training for children that stresses the idea of a benign cosmogony and the role of holidays in celebrating community with others and the round of the seasons in nature. A religious outlook, as long as it is not a punitive one, may serve many phase-related needs for the young child, contributing to a sense of security, of belonging with others in an understandable universe. Formal beliefs can be outgrown and discarded later, or adapted in some more personal way, more easily than they can be dispensed with in childhood. It may turn out that Sunday schools have more to do with the emotional needs of young children than progressive schools do.

Ceremony binds people together, is a way of celebrating their connectedness. With the secularization of modern life, and the passing away of many rituals celebrated in the community at large, it becomes increasingly meaningful to observe the family rituals in the home that emphasize the binding of the generations. Whether it's the daily coming together around the dinner table, birthday parties, holidays and religious observances, reading out loud together at bedtime until a certain number of stories and then perhaps a long novel or two have passed into the collective family memory, it is having structured times for coming together in certain roles that creates a family culture, a context for sharing the experiences that become shared memories.

Dostoevsky may seem an odd source from whom to draw maxims about domestic life, but I have always been struck by Alyosha's words to the boys at the end of *The Brothers Karamazov:*

My dear children, perhaps you will not understand what I am going to say to you, but you will remember it all the same, and will agree with my words someday. You must know that there is nothing more important to later life than some good memory, especially a memory of childhood, of home. People talk to you a great deal about your education, but some good memory preserved from childhood is perhaps the best education. If a man carries many such memories with him into life, he is safe to the end of his days; if one has only one good memory left in one's heart, even that may be the means of saving us.

NOTES

1 / The Family

1. Delegates to the White House Conference on Families in the summer of 1980 were unable to agree on just what they meant by a family, "persons related by blood, heterosexual marriage or adoption," or any group of people "living together in a climate of caring."

2. Christopher Lasch, *Haven in a Heartless World: The Family Besieged* (New York: Basic Books, 1977).

3. Edward Shorter, *The Making of the Modern Family* (New York: Basic Books, 1975).

4. Mary Jo Bane, *Here to Stay: American Families in the Twentieth Century* (New York: Basic Books, 1976).

5. J. H. Plumb discusses the nature of toys in "The Great Change in Children," *Horizon* 13 (Winter 1971). Antonia Fraser deals with medieval childhood in *A History of Toys* (London: Weidenfeld & Nicholson, 1966), and Iona and Peter Opie explain the origin and meanings of nursery rhymes in *The Oxford Book of Children's Verse* (New York: Oxford University Press, 1973).

6. Subtitled *A Social History of Family Life* (New York: Knopf, 1962) and originally published in France in 1960 under the title *L'Enfant et la vie familiale sous l'ancien régime.*

Notes

7. Subtitled *The Psychology of Family Life in Early Modern France* (New York: Basic Books, 1970).

8. Erik H. Erikson, *Childhood and Society* (New York: Norton, 1950), one of the most influential works of cultural interpretation of our time.

9. The family, in Wilhelm Reich's phrase, reproduced society—an idea that later theorists of the family would use to explain the development of "the authoritarian personality."

10. David Hunt, *Parents and Children* (New York: Basic Books, 1970), pp. 157–58.

11. Lloyd deMause, ed., *The History of Childhood* (New York: Harper Torchbooks, 1975).

12. Shorter, *The Making of the Modern Family.*

13. Ibid., p. 8.

14. George Masnick and Mary Jo Bane et al., *The Nation's Families: 1960–1990* (Cambridge, Mass.: Joint Center for Urban Studies of MIT and Harvard University: 1980), p. xiv.

15. Ibid., p. 88.

16. Ibid., p. 68.

17. Ibid., p. 70.

18. Ibid., p. 89.

19. Nathan Glazer, "The Rediscovery of the Family," *Commentary*, vol. 63, no. 3 (March 1978).

20. Masnick and Bane, *The Nation's Families*, p. 113.

21. Ibid., pp. 129–130.

22. For an interesting discussion of this period, see Joseph E. Illick, "Childrearing in Seventeenth-Century England and America," in deMause, *The History of Childhood*, pp. 303–350.

23. From a popular book of child-care advice of the time, Samuel Moody's *Discourse to Little Children*, published in 1769 in New London, Connecticut.

24. Eighteenth-century American childhood is discussed by John F. Walzer, "A Period of Ambivalence," in deMause, *The History of Childhood*, pp. 351–382.

25. The title of the history by John Demos, *A Little Commonwealth: Family Life in Plymouth Colony* (New York: Oxford University Press, 1970). In his *Of Domesticall Duties*, William Gouge, a seventeenth-century Puritan preacher, called the family "a little community."

26. In her introduction to the section on Child-rearing Literature in Margaret Mead and Martha Wolfenstein, ed., *Childhood in Con-*

temporary Cultures (Chicago: The University of Chicago Press, 1955, p. 145), Martha Wolfenstein points out that "child-training literature is as much expressive of the moral climate of the time and place in which it is written as of the state of scientific knowledge about children," and in her own contribution to that section, the often-quoted "Fun Morality: An Analysis of Recent American Child-training Literature" (pp. 168–178), she traces the changing pattern of child-care advice in this country from before the First World War until after the Second.

27. Lasch, *Haven in a Heartless World,* pp. 143, 161.

28. Christopher Jencks et al., *Inequality: A Reassessment of the Effect of Family and Schooling in America* (New York: Basic Books, 1972) was widely read and hotly discussed. It was disturbing to those who thought that education could provide a way into the mainstream for everyone in the nation, comforting to those who thought schooling a red-herring means to what should be a state-imposed end, and no particular surprise to those who already had reason to believe that achievement was a product of certain qualities like ambition, effort, and ability that varied in different individuals and were encouraged in different ways by different cultural patterns expressed in family life. Jencks himself maintained (in the *Harvard Educational Review* 43, no. 1 (1973), p. 138) that the point of the book was to show that "equalizing opportunity, especially educational opportunity, would not do much to reduce economic inequality or reduce poverty." In the climate of that establishment it did not need to be said that therefore other means of reducing inequality would have to be found—means that would ensure justice, if not liberty, for all. Justice could not mean that everyone had the same crack at the ultimate rewards; it had to guarantee that everyone would end up with the same amount of them.

29. From the introduction by Donald M. Levine and Mary Jo Bane to *The "Inequality" Controversy: Schooling and Distributive Justice* (New York: Basic Books, 1975), a collection of essays in which various writers responded to the Jencks book, the nature of its data, and the character of its conclusions.

30. Bane, *Here to Stay,* p. 70.

31. Ibid., p. 142.

32. Ibid., p. 35.

33. Ibid., p. 90.

34. Ibid., p. 81.

35. Ibid., p. 84.

36. Ibid., p. 36.
37. Ibid., p. 29.
38. Ibid., p. 91.
39. Ibid., p. 142.
40. That critique was carried even further in the next volume to issue from the Council's deliberations: Richard H. de Lone, *Small Futures: Children, Inequality, and the Limits of Liberal Reform* (New York: Harcourt Brace Jovanovich, 1979). De Lone dismisses all of the accumulated knowledge of child development on the ground that it is not consistent with "the requirements of egalitarian reform." Not the family, inherited traits, or early experience, but the social structure—caste and class—his argument goes, is what determines a child's fate. We must "move beyond an individualistic psychology" to a theory that is based on social structure rather than "genes and environment."

"Implicit in attempts to solve inequality by helping individuals," de Lone tells us, "is the belief that social inequalities are caused by individual differences." The Carnegie Council on Children maintains that this is only "a more sophisticated version of the notion that we are all masters of our fates" and is "a natural companion of market economic theory" (*Small Futures*, p. 173). Efforts to change society by changing individuals are doomed to failure. Instead of trying to change what families *do* we should alter what families *are* by reducing inequality, changing the basic patterns of society through "the redistribution of income and power," thus creating "a more egalitarian setting for development."

This is a bald statement of a political agenda that ignores or denies every single thing we know about the forces that shape character and the dynamics of personality. That knowledge is best represented in the books mentioned and described in the notes to part 2 of the present volume.

41. Kenneth Keniston, *All Our Children: The American Family Under Pressure* (New York: Harcourt Brace Jovanovich, 1977).
42. Ibid., p. 214.
43. Ibid., p. 70.
44. Ibid., p. 137.
45. Ibid., p. 136.
46. Ibid., p. 118.
47. Ibid., p. 214.
48. Ibid., p. 215.
49. Ibid., p. 188.

Notes

2 / The Child

1. In such books as *The First Five Years of Life* (New York: Harper, 1940), *Infant and Child in the Culture of Today* (Harper, 1943), and *The Child from Five to Ten* (Harper, 1946), Arnold Gesell and Frances L. Ilg and their colleagues at the Yale Clinic of Child Development provided a "systematic summary of the characteristics of normal infancy and childhood" that was followed like a blueprint by the post-World War II generation of young parents. Despite the authors' disclaimers to the effect that "every child is an individual," and that "the maturity traits" were *"not* to be regarded as rigid norms," the "behavior profiles" and "maturity traits" ascribed to "the 15-month-old," "the 3-year-old," and so on were so detailed and issued from so obviously authoritative and unimpeachable a source that young veterans' wives on college campuses sat outside their Quonset-hut housing in the late forties comparing notes on how the feeding, finger-painting and sociability of their tots stacked up against the description of their child's age-mate's "behavior day" in Gesell, an activity that continued among young mothers on city park benches and suburban backyards in the fifties. Gesell et al. were important contributors to the understanding of child development. Their fate, partly because of their format, was to be taken more seriously for their timetable than for their description of a process. It is one thing for parents to know that children move from one phase to another. It is quite another for them to expect him to make his move at fifteen months, or eighteen months—and worry when he appears to be deplorably behind schedule.

2. While Gesell and his colleagues described the social behavior of children, Swiss psychologist Jean Piaget was observing children's perceptual and intellectual development and evolving a highly complex and widely influential theory of cognitive process. Piaget's observational studies of infants and children trace the movement from sensorimotor to symbolic-representational intelligence and abstract thought in the mind of the child. A list of titles of some of his major writings, together with their original dates of publication, gives some idea of the nature of his work. Most of these titles are available in various hardcover and paperback editions: *The Language and Thought of the Child* (1926), *Judgment and Reasoning in the Child* (1928), *The Child's Conception of the World* (1929), *The*

Notes

Child's Conception of Physical Causality (1930), *The Moral Judgment of the Child* (1932), *Play, Dreams and Imitation in Childhood* (1951), *The Child's Conception of Number* (1952), *The Origins of Intelligence in Children* (1952), *The Construction of Reality in the Child* (1954), *The Child's Conception of Space* (1956), *The Child's Conception of Geometry* (1960). Piaget's writings, detailed and technical as they are, do not make easy reading for the generalist. A good introduction to the system of his thought, itself a scholarly work and somewhat heavy going for the ordinary reader, but easier to move around in than a dozen specific volumes, is *The Developmental Psychology of Jean Piaget* by J.H. Flavell (New York: Van Nostrand, 1963).

3. Two very different books both of which examine aspects of collective child rearing in our time are *Two Worlds of Childhood: U.S. and U.S.S.R.* by Urie Bronfenbrenner (New York: Russell Sage Foundation, 1970) and *The Children of the Dream* by Bruno Bettelheim (New York: Macmillan, 1969). Bronfenbrenner looks at how communal facilities for child care and education supplement family upbringing in the Soviet Union to produce a child who conforms to the standards of the adult society, less independent than his American counterpart but also less alienated, aggressive, or rebellious. Bettelheim's study of child rearing in the Israeli kibbutzim (see note 22) suggests that—while the typical kibbutz youth, socialized by his peer group rather than his parents, is characterized by a sense of his belonging to his group—comradeship, adaptation, and industriousness may be purchased "at some cost to personal identity, emotional intimacy and individual achievement."

4. It is Bettelheim's contention in *The Children of the Dream* that the relative lack of emotional complexity and spontaneous creativity observed in the well-adjusted kibbutznik is the price paid for avoiding a struggle for individual identity in the family context.

5. See "Lesbian Mother Who Won Child Custody Battle" (*New York Times*, Sept. 5, 1980, p. B9), in which a New Jersey court's decision to award custody of her children to a lesbian living with her lover is described as "part of a pattern in which more and more judges are awarding custody of children to homosexual mothers." The article makes reference to "several studies" (unidentified) purporting to have shown that children of homosexual mothers were not "more prone to become homosexual" and quotes a lawyer who founded an organization called CALM (Custody Action for Lesbian Mothers) after losing custody of her own children: "I know that the

213

children of lesbian mothers aren't any different from any other children."

Scholarship and scientific understanding count for nothing in the unreal world of the media; when the history and context of an idea are ignored, any one is as good as any other, so we might as well fasten on the one that suits the trendy politics of the *Times.* And so to the lesbian child-rearing arrangement is added that of "self-sufficient women in their 30s who are choosing to become unwed mothers, to combine careers with child rearing in a home where there is no father" ("When Motherhood Doesn't Mean Marriage," *New York Times,* November 30, 1981, p. B16). Presumably, these children may enjoy the further advantages of "Children Witnessing Childbirth" (*New York Times,* September 21, 1981, p. B14), in which we are told about the seven-year-old who cuts the umbilical cord of her mother's newborn while her four-year-old brother watches.

In "Pros and Cons of the Family Bed" (*New York Times,* Feb. 20, 1981, p. B4) we are told about a "new philosophy" that "advocates letting a child sleep with his parents until he decides to leave the family bed." Sex, the *New York Times* writer finds, "is not an issue." According to whom? Why, to "most family bed advocates." As for sexual stimulation, incest fantasies (or realities), we get another authoritative opinion. "Sleeping together as a family doesn't inhibit us; we wait until she's asleep," says the mother of a two-year-old. Oh.

This idea proved so intriguing that the once stuffy *Parents* magazine, in the process of trying to update its image and increase its appeal to a new crop of young parents, devoted an entire article in its March 1981 issue to "The Family Bed," which it confidently characterizes as "actually good for all concerned."

6. In a previous book for parents and parents-to-be (Rita Kramer, *Giving Birth: Childbearing in America Today;* Chicago: Contemporary Books, 1978), I dealt with the controversy over the management of labor and delivery in the context of the history of childbirth customs and practices and the art and science of midwifery and gynecology. Many of the thoughts in this chapter originated there.

7. Dick-Read's best-known book was *Childbirth Without Fear: The Principles and Practice of Natural Childbirth* (New York: Harper, 1944).

8. See Kramer, *Giving Birth,* pp. 43–44.

9. The idea that "there is a *sensitive period* in the first minutes and hours after an infant's birth which is optimal for parent-infant

Notes

attachment" was stated by Marshall H. Klaus and John H. Kennell in *Maternal-Infant Bonding: The Impact of Early Separation or Loss on Family Development* (St. Louis, Mo.: Mosby, 1976).

10. Two interesting discussions of the philosophy that informs permissive child-rearing advice are in "Fun Morality: An Analysis of Recent American Child-training Literature" by Martha Wolfenstein, in *Childhood in Contemporary Culture*, edited by Margaret Mead and Martha Wolfenstein (Chicago: University of Chicago Press, 1955) and "Dr. Spock: The Confidence Man" by Michael Zuckerman, in *The Family in History*, edited by Charles E. Rosenberg (Philadelphia: University of Pennsylvania Press, 1975).

11. Organized and summarized in *The Psychological Birth of the Human Infant: Symbiosis and Individuation* by Margaret S. Mahler, Fred Pine, and Anni Bergman (New York: Basic Books, 1975).

12. In addition to the works of Bettelheim, Erikson, Fraiberg, and Piaget cited elsewhere, these pioneer sources include the works of John Bowlby, whose *Maternal Care and Mental Health*, first published by the World Health Organization in 1951 and by Schocken Books in 1966, was the landmark statement of the importance of early mothering to the formation of character and personality, later elaborated in his three-volume study *Attachment and Loss* (vol. 1, *Attachment*, 1969; vol. 2, *Separation: Anxiety and Anger*, 1973; vol. 3, *Loss: Sadness and Depression*, 1980; all, New York: Basic Books); Anna Freud, especially *The Ego and the Mechanisms of Defense*, which first appeared in 1936 (New York: International Universities Press, 1966), and *Infants Without Families*, a study of the effects of wartime separation of children from their parents first published from 1939 to 1945 (International Universities Press, 1973); Phyllis Greenacre (the most literary of the psychoanalysts) whose influential papers include "The Childhood of the Artist: Libidinal Phase Development and Giftedness," which described the exhilaration of the toddler, in *Emotional Growth: Psychoanalytic Studies of the Gifted and A Great Variety of Other Individuals*, her collected papers (International Universities Press, 1971); Heinz Hartmann (the most influential of the post-Freudians) who shifted the emphasis in psychoanalysis from symptoms to character formation in *Ego Psychology and the Problem of Adaptation* in 1939 and whose work is summed up in his *Essays on Ego Psychology* (International Universities Press, 1956); René A. Spitz, who first called attention to the depression and failure to thrive of infants in institutions who received adequate physical care but no affectionate handling or per-

sonal attention, work that was summed up in *The First Year of Life: A Psychoanalytic Study of Normal and Deviant Development of Object Relations* (International Universities Press, 1965); and D. W. Winnicott, whose many original and influential views of the mother-infant relationship included "Transitional Objects and Transitional Phenomena: A Study of the First Not-Me Possession," first published in 1951 and included in *Through Paediatrics to Psychoanalysis,* a collection of his papers (New York: Basic Books, 1975), and "The Ordinary Devoted Mother and Her Baby," one of his BBC broadcast talks reprinted in *The Child and the Family* (Basic Books, 1957).

13. When it comes to the nature of evidence, you pays your money and you takes your choice: the empathic insights of experienced clinicians or the statistical results of what has been studied in ways that can be precisely measured. The first often enriches our understanding, the second too often lays the dead hand of categorization on its "data" and in the end can only tell us that it has not been possible to prove anything—which political interpretation will often tell us is the same as having proven something.

A very different approach from, say, Mahler's or Fraiberg's to such aspects of early child development as sex differences is that exemplified by *The Psychology of Sex Differences* by Eleanor E. Maccoby and Carol N. Jacklin (Stanford: Stanford University Press, 1974). Information-retrieval systems have made it possible to locate thousands of studies on any specific topic and correlate their results. Unlike the clinical impressions of psychoanalysis, the neat numbers of factor analysis do not tell us, It looks as though this happens this way, but over and over again "at present it has not been demonstrated that . . ." (p. 35; all figures in parentheses in this note refer to page numbers in *The Psychology of Sex Differences*), "the existing studies . . . would seem to indicate no difference . . ." (p. 72), no correlation has been found, "we have not been able to document . . ." (p. 150), "the dimensions have not been defined in such a way as to yield a clear picture . . ." (p. 190), ". . . our survey . . . has shown surprisingly little information on some topics . . . and . . . we must remain dissatisfied with the way the disposition in question has been measured" (p. 225), "on the basis of this rather fragmentary evidence, we are inclined to believe . . ." (p. 299). Yet, despite their admission at the outset that they were "constrained by the nature of the tests that have been given and the clusters of abilities that have emerged from them in the course of the psychometric work that has been done (p. 64) (that is, standardized tests can correlate only those variables that can be expressed in numbers, and so impose enormous limitations on exactly what portion of behavior can be studied), or, as they put it elsewhere, have had "to restrict our classifications to the behavioral level" (p. 166), the authors still feel justified in concluding that many "beliefs about the psychological characteristics of the two sexes"—mainly those having to do with their differences—"have proved to have little or no basis in fact" (p. 355). How the problem has to be defined in order to be susceptible to available techniques of measurement is often so reductionistic as to remove human behavior from any context of meaningful social or personal reality. Having failed to prove is not the same as having disproved.

But you would never know that from a perusal of the kind of popular work that bases its statements and recommendations on its interpretation of the Maccoby work and claims it and the kinds of studies it is based on as its authority (along with articles from the press, hardly an impressive fount of scholarship). Such a recent book was the highly promoted *Growing Up Free* by Letty C. Pogrebin (New York: McGraw-Hill, 1980), for whom Maccoby is "the last word" that seems to "settle all the arguments"—in favor, of course, of a feminist politics that asserts that there are few real differences between the sexes and those there are ought to be legislated out of existence when they cannot be made to disappear by means of a child-rearing technique that denies and circumvents them. What it cannot ignore, it distorts. In contrast, the kind of popularization to which the Mahler work has lent itself (see Louise J. Kaplan, *Oneness and Separateness;* New York: Simon and Schuster, 1978), while inevitably losing something in richness of detail and fullness of examples in the original, is still faithful in spirit and significance to the evidence amassed by sensitive observers about what happens in the busy, complicated, changing, different hours of babies' and children's lives—and how they are responding. For without some idea of what they are thinking and feeling about it, we can have very little real understanding of what they are doing. Of course, there has to be some test of what is said about the meaning of experience to those too young to tell us themselves. If self-reporting by older subjects has its pitfalls, so does the reporting of others on the preverbal child. Ultimately the test questions here as elsewhere in science are, Does it explain the events and is it fruitful in leading on to further explanations? Is it consistent with what we already know and

Notes

suggestive about what is still unknown? The conclusions (always tentative: this is *what we know so far*) built on the kinds of observational studies in naturalistic settings described in Mahler's book seem to pass that test better than most experimental studies it is possible to design and carry out on human beings.

14. See Erikson, *Childhood and Society*, pp. 247–251.

15. The behavior of the newborn was described by Peter H. Wolff in *The Causes, Controls, and Organization of Behavior in the Neonate* (Psychological Issues, Monograph 17; New York: International Universities Press, 1966).

16. The understanding of the socializing or "attachment" behavior of infants was greatly enlarged by some of the contributors to the Tavistock Seminars on Mother-Infant Interaction Held in London in September 1961 and published in *Determinants of Infant Behavior*, vols. 1 and 2 (New York: Wiley, 1961 and 1963)—in particular, "Observations on the Early Development of Smiling" by Peter Wolff, and Harry F. Harlow's studies of infant monkeys separated from their mothers and how they responded to the various substitutes provided for them. It was soon common knowledge that Harlow's monkeys preferred a terrycloth mother (one that they could snuggle up to for comfort) to one that merely fed them, and that the monkeys who had no relationship with responsive mothers grew up to be, as Harlow put it in one of his many publications, "hopeless, helpless, heartless" mothers themselves.

17. In a brilliant and moving book that illustrates the empathy that must be part of a truly therapeutic relationship, the late Selma Fraiberg makes it clear how the pain of the unloved child is later translated into the inability to give appropriate care to another child. In *Clinical Studies in Infant Mental Health: The First Year of Life* (New York: Basic Books, 1980) Fraiberg reports on the work she and her remarkably sensitive colleagues have done in their Infant-Parent Program in San Francisco, where they have succeeded against all odds in reaching the core of walled-off feeling in women whose babies' diagnosis was "failure to thrive due to severe maternal deprivation" and freed them from what she calls the "ghosts in the nursery."

Fraiberg explains that the pleasure in social interaction we see in a healthy baby of three or four months of age—the smiles, the cooing, the excited kicking—is elicited by mothering. The exuberance, the animation, the snuggling, the ability to be comforted by the mother when in distress "are not in the innate repertoire of any baby; when we see them we must conclude that his human partners have given him pleasure and a sense of trust" (*Clinical Studies,* p. 36). Maternal deprivation consists not just in the absence of adequate physical care, or even of stimulation, as the behavioral psychologists would have it, but in the absence of constancy of response, without which a child never loses the fear of abandonment. Through a kind of miraculous intervention Fraiberg and her colleagues were able to restore to mothers unable to feel for their own children "what every parent seeks: hope for a rebirth of the self." This is not the language of most professional works on psychiatry, but of literature. Fraiberg was uniquely talented as therapist, thinker, and writer, and her histories have the effect on us of a story by Tolstoy or Joyce; there is an emotional realization of a human truth.

18. Piaget's work traced the development of the concept of object permanence in the mind of the child (see note 2).

19. Winnicott described the function of the "transitional object" (see note 12).

20. A fascinating discussion of how this comes about is in Robert J. Stoller's *Sex and Gender: On the Development of Masculinity and Femininity* (New York: Science House, 1968), especially pp. 97–100, in the description of the consequences of what Stoller calls "too much bliss."

21. See Bruno Bettelheim's *The Empty Fortress: Infantile Autism and the Birth of the Self* (New York: Macmillan, 1967).

22. Even in that most ideally realized and most voluntary of group child-care experiments, that carried out in the Israeli kibbutzim, the results have been ambiguous. The aim of the kibbutzniks was to free the child from the effects of generational conflict, anxiety, and guilt, by means of collective education in age groups. Parents would not impose their values on their children; the peer group, not the parent, would socialize the child, who would thus be liberated from the effects of an intense relationship with his parents of the kind that characterized Jewish family life in the Eastern Europe from which so many of the kibbutz founders came. Even as sensitive and sympathetic an observer as Bruno Bettelheim (in *The Children of the Dream;* see notes 3 and 4) found a certain impoverishment of personality, a diminution of creativity and complexity following from a lack of introspection and of interest in the past, where the child was socialized not in the family but by the peer group and where the ties between parents and children were diluted by the

children's prior loyalty to the larger community as the provider of all of the necessities of life.

Of course it is, like so much in life, a trade-off. Some would willingly pay the price in potential individual achievement and the inner life for the sake of a community of equals bound by ties of loyalty to each other. Most, even in Israel itself, would not. Something most men and women, when given a choice, perceive as uniquely human is their role as shapers of their children's destinies.

23. The phrase "emotional refueling," coined by Margaret Mahler's colleague Manuel Furer, is one of the many expressions in her work—like "hatching," "mutual cueing," "normal symbiosis," "rapprochement crisis," and "shadowing and darting away"—that have entered the language common to all observers of children's behavior, an indication of the aptness with which they describe what we observe or remember.

24. See note 12; note 22, part 3.

25. These observations have been confirmed and systematized by infant researchers Eleanor Galenson and Herman Roiphe and reported in a series of papers by them in the professional literature in recent years, including "The Emergence of Genital Awareness During the Second Year of Life," in *Sex Differences in Behavior*, edited by R. C. Friedman et al. (New York: Wiley, 1974), and "Some Suggested Revisions Concerning Early Female Development," in *Female Psychology: Contemporary Psychoanalytic Views*, edited by H. P. Blum (New York: International Universities Press, 1977), and their book *Infantile Origins of Sexual Identity* (International Universities Press, 1982). Like Money and Ehrhardt and Stoller (see notes 20, 27, and 29), Galenson and Roiphe identify "a critical period for the establishment of gender identity which occurs by the second half of the second year of life," although there are disagreements among them about the factors involved in this early phase of sexual development. Galenson and Roiphe find that after children discover the sexual differences and become aware of genital sensations, some time around eighteen months of age, "there are marked differences between boys and girls in many sectors of their psychological development" ("Early Female Development," p. 55).

26. The life stories of the children in *Truants From Life: The Rehabilitation of Emotionally Disturbed Children* by Bruno Bettelheim (New York: Free Press, 1955), especially that of "John," pp. 271–387, illustrate the disruption of the sense of self in a child who is overpowered and overcome. These are, of course, very extreme

cases but, like those described by Stoller (see note 20), paradigmatic for normal development.

27. In *Sex and Gender* (see note 20) Stoller distinguishes between sex, the genetically determined anatomical and biochemical characteristics that make one a male or female, and gender, the sense of being a man or a woman, masculine or feminine, which is determined by one's life experiences, how one is defined and treated, starting in infancy. Sex is a matter of physiology, a biological given; gender is psychological and is learned. Being a boy or a girl, a man or a woman is a role and an identity. This core gender identity is a fundamental aspect of character structure, the bedrock of the sense of self. It is established by the time a child is two or three years of age, by which time there is no question in his or her mind whether he or she is a boy or a girl, although there are still many questions to be answered in the family and society about what males and females do, about how they differ and about the proper role of each.

28. The connection between gender identity and identification with the parent of the same sex is, like so much else about the mind of the young child, described lucidly in Selma Fraiberg's *The Magic Years* (New York: Scribner's, 1959).

29. Sex differences in aggression are discussed by John Money and A. Ehrhardt in *Man and Woman, Boy and Girl* (Baltimore: Johns Hopkins University Press, 1972) and by Eleanor E. Maccoby and C. Jacklin in *The Psychology of Sex Differences*, vol. 1 (Stanford: Stanford University Press, 1974), pp. 242–247. If anything, these authors are biased in the direction of cultural, rather than biological, forces as determinants of sexual behavior.

30. See Maccoby and Jacklin, *The Psychology of Sex Differences*, p. 275.

31. Such strategies emerge from the agenda of books like *Growing Up Free* (see note 13) with its ludicrous advocacy of a child-rearing program as repressive as anything in Victorian times in its insistence on standing one extreme on its head to create another one and its humorless advocacy of a constant, unremitting pressure on the child to conform—in this case, to nonconformism.

32. Unlike *Growing Up Free*, which tells you quite a lot about the mind of a certain kind of grownup and nothing at all about the mind of a child, Fraiberg's *The Magic Years* deals with this way of seeing the world and what causes things to happen in it that is characteristic of the child of three.

221

Notes

33. In *Every Child's Birthright: In Defense of Mothering* (New York: Basic Books, 1977), Selma Fraiberg coined the phrase "the diseases of non-attachment," disorders the basis for which is laid "during the formative period of ego development, the first eighteen months of life," and which are characterized by "the incapacity of the person to form human bonds." Fraiberg describes "these bondless men, women, and children [who] constitute one of the largest aberrant populations in the world today, contributing far beyond their numbers to social disease and disorder" as "people who are unable to fulfill the most ordinary human obligations in work, in friendship, in marriage, and in child-rearing. The condition of non-attachment leaves a void in that area of personality where conscience should be. Where there are no human attachments there can be no conscience." She adds that while such diseases are difficult to cure, they "can be eradicated at the source, by ensuring stable human partnerships for every baby" (*In Defense of Mothering*, p. 62).

34. Perhaps it is unrealistic to expect legislators to be wise as well as smart, prudent as well as practical. In her introduction to a typical volume about day care (*Child Care—Who Cares*, edited by Pamela Roby; New York: Basic Books, 1973), U.S. Congresswoman Shirley Chisholm urged a program of comprehensive child-care services that would "create healthy and full environments for children," something only a mother and father can provide. And she maintains that discrimination against women—the attitude that "woman's place is in the home"—lies behind opposition to public child-care programs, rather than recognizing that critics of such programs maintain, rather, that a *mother's* place is in the home, with her pre-school-age children. The editor of this volume, a blueprint for boondoggle, bureaucracy, and the weakening of parent-child bonds formed in early childhood, describes child-care programs as "a basic human right," an idea so perverse as to defy analysis. Mothering (see note 33)—if it is children one is talking about—is the basic human right.

A description of programs in other countries with cultures very different from our own, and where the outcome of public policies is far from unambiguous, and of demonstration programs in well-funded university centers in this country, where the adult-child ratio and the quality of the adults participating is far from what we could expect in any huge publicly funded program, provides the "evidence" for the benefits of public day care. These benefits include the editor's aim "to maximize females' contribution to the labor force during the years when they have young children" (*Child Care,* p. 55); child-development programs should also influence the distribution of income in the nation (p. 75).

What politics needs, it justifies and then creates. According to Pamela Roby, a sociologist active in many policy-making organizations, it is important for "the children of the poor . . . to believe that the nation really cares for them," as though any living child could possibly have such a concept. What children need is to believe that their mothers and fathers really care for them.

The historical and humanitarian arguments for day care, that it is necessary in order to socialize the children of the poor, as it once was necessary to socialize the children of immigrants, can be left aside from considerations of whether day care, which may be a necessity in the most fragmented and depriving of families, is necessary or desirable for normal families where mothers are capable of caring for their young children. It should be no surprise that those who urge middle-class mothers to leave the care of their children to others are less concerned with family life or individuality than with the leveling policies of the social philosophy of redistributive egalitarianism. It is the contention of feminist Virginia Kerr in her contribution to the Roby volume that the state owes every woman the right to have someone else take care of her children (*Child Care,* p. 96). Other planners contributing to the volume make it clear that "radicals see child care as a first step toward dramatic social change . . . a first step in the necessary breakdown and broadening of the nuclear family," and quote a 1970 statement of the Women's Caucus of the New University Conference that "through day care we can begin to break down the notion of the child as private property" (pp. 102–2). As a member of the National Organization for Women puts it, "Feminists believe that the rearing of children is a matter for the entire society, not simply for individual parents, or more narrowly, for individual mothers" (p. 117). What kind of children are not reared by individual parents but by "the entire society," history can show us and Selma Fraiberg (see note 33) can explain.

35. Typical of such commentary is "The New Interest in Corporate Day-Care" on the *Wall Street Journal's* editorial page, April 20, 1981: "Today, both Daddy and Mommy often hold paying jobs. Who's minding their kids? Management is helping to mind them." The article considers the issue in terms of labor and management considerations, discusses the economic factors and employment sta-

tistics, and is totally devoid of any suggestion of what meaning such policies might have in terms of children's development—or even of any suggestion that there is such a question to be raised.

36. The psychoanalytic literature on child development is replete with examples and anecdotes illustrating the universality of these responses, most recently the work of Galenson and Roiphe (see note 25).

37. The most comprehensive theory of the development of children's thinking is that of Piaget (see note 2). See, in particular, *The Language and Thought of the Child.*

38. Three important studies in which this issue is discussed are *Homosexuality* by Irving Bieber et al. (New York: Basic Books, 1962), *The Overt Homosexual* by Charles W. Socarides (New York: Grune and Stratton, 1968), and *Sex and Gender, Vol. II: The Transsexual Experiment* by Robert J. Stoller (New York: Aronson, 1976), pp. 159–69.

39. These findings and the research on which they were based were presented in *Perceptual Development in Children,* edited by Aline H. Kidd and J. L. Rivoire (New York: International Universities Press, 1966). See in particular the article by Robert L. Fantz (pp. 143–173).

40. Among the most influential voices were those of psychologists Jerome Bruner and Jerome Kagan and psychiatrist Burton L. White, all of Harvard, each of whom published much research funded by government grants.

41. The phrase is Winnicott's. See note 12.

42. The most thoroughly annotated indictment of television in the lives of children to appear so far is *The Plug-In Drug* by Marie Winn (New York: Viking Press, 1977).

43. See *"Sesame Street" Revisited* by Thomas D. Cook et al. (New York: Russell Sage Foundation, 1975).

44. There are some provocative and still relevant insights into American attitudes toward growing up in "French and American Children as Seen by a French Child Analyst," in *Childhood and Contemporary Cultures* (see note 10). (Ever since de Tocqueville, the French have had a bent for astute observations on American life and the American character.) In the 1955 volume, Françoise Dolot contrasts French children, routinely punished, inhibited, and coerced, who can hardly wait to attain the envied state of adulthood, with their counterparts in America, where parents not only tolerate but actively encourage the indulgence of impulses, and

where children come up against the first direct threat to their freedom when they reach genital maturity. "After an American childhood comparatively free from all coercion, from all threats of corporal violence at the hands of parents, school, and society," in which "the pleasure principle is king" and "the child often seems to perceive the parental couple as a big brother and sister" rather than as powerful and privileged beings, childhood, not adulthood, appears the most enviable stage of life in America, where "the adults dream of their lost childhood—the golden age which they can find only in regression." While the French child's life is one of duties, the chief of which is to prepare for his future, the American child enjoys rights, the chief among which is not to be traumatized by his parents.

This is not an analysis one should take too literally, but it is suggestive of trends that are still discernible thirty years after it was written.

45. Bruno Bettelheim, *The Uses of Enchantment: The Meaning and Importance of Fairy Tales* (New York: Knopf, 1976).

46. See *The Uses of Enchantment,* p. 14.

47. Ibid., p. 51.

48. *The Common Sense Book of Baby and Child Care* was first published by Duell, Sloan and Pearce (and simultaneously by Pocket Books as *The Pocket Book of Baby and Child Care*) in 1946. It has since been revised three times (in 1957, 1968, and 1976, generally in the direction of a somewhat less "permissive" attitude) and gone through hundreds of printings.

49. Among the most popular books for parents in the sixties and seventies were Haim Ginott's *Between Parent and Child* (New York: Macmillan, 1965) and *Between Parent and Teenager* (Macmillan, 1969) and Thomas Gordon's *Parent Effectiveness Training: The Tested New Way to Raise Responsible Children* (New York: New American Library, 1975), otherwise known as P.E.T. Ginott and P.E.T instruct parents in how to avoid confrontation on issues and arguments about rules by confining their encounters with their children to discussions of feelings. In these systems there are no imperatives, only preferences, and no requirements, only requests. The parent can remain a companion, and authority over the child's life can be exerted by other agencies of society—the school, the peer group, the media. Gone is the father of authority, and with him the need to reconcile love and restraint, to master ambivalence by internalization, to take the father's rules (and society's) into oneself

and make them one's own. One just does what "everybody else" is doing.

50. For illustrations of the changing concept of the child in the family and society, see David Hunt, *Parents and Children*, pp. 113–186; deMause, "The Evolution of Childhood," in *The History of Childhood*, pp. 1–73; and Wolfenstein, "Fun Morality," in *Childhood in Contemporary Cultures*, pp. 168–178.

51. A witty and irreverent analysis of Dr. Spock's message is social historian Michael Zuckerman's "Dr. Spock: The Confidence Man" (see note 10).

52. See "Dr. Spock: The Confidence Man," pp. 192–96.

53. See note 12.

3 / Family, Child, and the World Beyond

1. According to Piaget, at around age seven the child enters the stage of concrete operations with the acquisition of the ability to think without acting. He is able to manipulate numbers in his head, classify objects in groups, and see that objects can remain the same even though they look different, that quantities are not necessarily changed because their appearance changes (for instance, that the amount of water in a tall thin glass is the same as was poured into it from a short thick glass, a fact that younger children cannot grasp). These stages are described in detail in such works as *The Construction of Reality in the Child, The Language and Thought of the Child,* and *The Origins of Intelligence in Children* (see note 2, part 2).

2. The physical characteristics of the latency child are described by Gesell in *The Child From Five to Ten* (see note 1, part 2).

3. General works on this stage of childhood are very few in comparison with what is available on the years before and after it, the vast literature on infancy and early childhood and on adolescence. All but impenetrably written, and mentioned more for the record than for its usefulness to parents, Charles Sarnoff's *Latency* (New York: Aronson, 1976) discusses the psychodynamics of the early school years. An overview of the period from many angles, easier to read but flawed by an already-dated attempt to be up on the lat-

est trends in social thinking when it was revised in the early seventies is found in L. Joseph Stone and Joseph Church's *Childhood and Adolescence* (New York: Random House, 1975).

4. The anonymous source was the author's young daughter, whose definition appeared in "The Middle-Aged Child" by Rita Kramer, *The New York Times Magazine,* May 23, 1965, pp. 65–75.

5. From *"Where did you go?" "Out" "What did you do?" "Nothing"* by Robert Paul Smith (New York: Norton, 1957, p. 8), one of the truly evocative pictures, like the one drawn by Mark Twain in *The Adventures of Tom Sawyer,* of the state of boyhood.

6. Jump-rope rhyme, quoted in a somewhat different version in *Children's Games in Street and Playground* by Iona and Peter Opie (London: Oxford, 1969, p. 59), a compilation of games and counting-and-choosing rhymes from the British Isles. This version is from the childhood of the author, ca. 1939, in the American Midwest. Such games and rhymes, along with riddles, jokes, chants, and other rituals, form a culture of childhood that is handed down from one generation of children to another, bypassing adults altogether. Children learn this culture not from their parents—or indeed from any grownup—but from each other, and they play remarkably similar games all over the world, with the same rules and the same phrases turning up in different eras and in different languages on different continents. They are revised and added to as they incorporate the culture of each particular moment (Harry James gives way to Perry Como, who is replaced by Ringo Starr, to be succeeded by someone else already forgotten, ad infinitum, in the rhymes collected by the Opies in the towns and villages of England and Scotland; see the Opies' *The Lore and Language of Schoolchildren;* Oxford, 1959, pp. 115–16), but the theme and the rhythm remain the same as they are passed on from one cohort of children to the next, from the older to the slightly younger, in a sameness that survives wars, television, and even sexual revolution to attest to the staying powers of these rhymes and rituals.

7. See note 29, part 2.

8. Erik H. Erikson, *Childhood and Society* (New York: Norton, 1963), pp. 256, 258.

9. In an early paper, "On Latency" (*The Psychoanalytic Study of the Child,* vol. 6; New York: International Universities Press, 1951, pp. 279–285), child analyst Berta Bornstein wrote, "The child's behavior during the latency period might be described as one of persistent denial of the struggle against the breakthrough of instinc-

Notes

tual impulses, a denial which extends into adulthood as a partial amnesia for this period," which she suggests may be why grownups tend to remember relatively little about this period of their lives.

10. Latency is a creation both of culture and biology. Civilized life requires the suppression of infantile sexuality in all its expressions, wishes as well as behavior, a period of sexual inhibition in which instinctual urges can be sublimated. What makes all this possible are changes in a number of measures of perceptual and neurophysiological development and cognitive organization that take place at around age seven and endow the child with the capacity for "a new set of cognitive strategies to outwit and control his environment." Reasoning and inference take the place of magic, and logical thought supersedes trial and error. See Theodore Shapiro and Richard Perry, "Latency Revisited: The Age Seven Plus or Minus One," in *The Psychoanalytic Study of the Child,* vol. 31 (New York: International Universities Press, 1976, pp. 79–105).

11. One of the ways early latency children deal with their unacceptable instinctual urges (incestuous thoughts, masturbatory impulses) and achieve the degree of calm necessary to sit still, pay attention, and learn while in the classroom is through their "rhythmic, repetitive games and activities . . . the children's solution which they have passed down via psychomotor communication through multitudinous generations of children" (from "Reflections Regarding Psychomotor Activities During the Latency Period" by Elizabeth Bremner Kaplan, *The Psychoanalytic Study of the Child,* vol. 20; New York: International Universities Press, 1965, pp. 220–238).

12. The eight-year-old who bullies his baby brother the way he feels his father has bullied him is identifying with the aggressor in order to exchange his painful feelings of humiliation for a sense of being powerful and effective. When he draws an elaborate machine that emits "poisin pelets" and "deth rays" strong enough to destroy the world in which he has been sent away from the dinner table for misbehaving, he is making use of a fantasy of omnipotence to protect and defend himself against feelings of hurt and loss. See Ted E. Becker, "On Latency," *The Psychoanalytic Study of the Child,* vol. 29; (New York: International Universities Press, 1974, pp. 3–11).

13. This finding is discussed in "The Impact of the First Menstrual Period" in Sarnoff, *Latency,* p. 77.

14. The phrase is Erikson's. In a chapter called "Womanhood and the Inner Space" in *Identity: Youth and Crisis* (New York: Norton,

1968), he attempts a revision of Freudian theory by substituting for the concept of penis envy that of "the productive interior." Erikson speculates that penis envy is more apparent in the patient population in whom the psychoanalytic method "bares truths especially true under the circumstances created by the method, the venting in free association of hidden resentments and repressed traumata," and that in a normative theory of feminine development penis envy would be subordinate to "a sense of vital inner potential." This formulation did not make radical feminists any happier, since proponents of androgyny or "unisex" prefer to believe that there are no real distinctions to be made between the sexes except the obvious anatomical ones, and that these—despite what would seem to be overwhelming evidence to the contrary—have no consequences in mental life that are not culturally induced.

15. The twelve-year-old heroine of Carson McCullers' *The Member of the Wedding,* feeling estranged from her father and her own changing body, longs to join her brother and his bride ("the we of me") in a oneness that, like the infant's with his mother, will assuage the terrors of loneliness. When that proves impossible, she finds a best friend to idealize and identify with. Her emotional journey from being "Frankie" to becoming "Frances" as she accepts her developing femininity is mapped by Katherine Dalsimer in "From Preadolescent Tomboy to Early Adolescent Girl," an article in volume 34 of the always interesting *Psychoanalytic Study of the Child* (New York: International Universities Press, 1979, pp. 445–461). However, the story itself really needs no guide. It stands as one of the most evocative recreations of girlhood, what *The Adventures of Tom Sawyer* is to boyhood.

16. See note 1, part 3.

17. Rubinstein, Eli A. et al., *Television and Social Behavior* (Washington, D.C.: U. S. Department of Health, Education and Welfare, 1972).

18. A study of *The Impact of Head Start* by the Westinghouse Learning Corporation (Washington, D.C.: Clearinghouse for Federal Scientific and Technical Information, 1969) indicated, as expressed by Elizabeth M.R. Lomax, Jerome Kagan, and Barbara G. Rosenkrantz in *Science and Patterns of Child Care* (San Francisco: Freeman, 1978), "that most of the intervention programs did not lead to appreciable intellectual changes and that the cognitive gains revealed by some studies appeared to be only temporary." An explanation for this general fact about early stimulation programs was

suggested by the authors of *"Sesame Street" Revisited* (New York: Russell Sage Foundation, 1975) as they considered the lack of significant or permanent gains in children who had been encouraged to watch many hours of the program. The immediate gains widely publicized at the time were the result of the encouragement itself, not the program material. They resulted from the extra attention the children received and the parental involvement in the project. See *The Plug-In Drug* (note 42, part 2), pp. 38–39.

19. David Riesman put this very nicely when he wrote: "There is always an element of indeterminacy in art; in the relation of a reader to a book many things—many unintended things—can and do happen. It seems possible to argue, for instance, that *Huckleberry Finn* is a more serious book on race relations than any of the recent crop, among other reasons because of the artistic ambiguities in the reflections of Huck on the problem of helping Nigger Jim escape" (from " 'Tootle': A Modern Cautionary Tale," in *Childhood and Contemporary Cultures,* edited by Margaret Mead and Martha Wolfenstein; Chicago: University of Chicago Press, 1955, p. 238). Three examples of the books that were produced and promoted to teach children something about racial integration are *Edgar Allan* by John Neufeld (New York: Phillips, 1968), *Iggie's House* by Judy Blume (Scarsdale, N.Y.: Bradbury Press, 1970), and *The Integration of Mary-Larkin Thornhill* by Ann Waldron (New York: E. P. Dutton, 1975), all popular with teachers and librarians. It is hard not to feel, on reading any of them, that children would have been better off reading *Huckleberry Finn.*

20. In three lectures published as *The Family and Human Adaptation* (New York: International Universities Press, 1963), psychoanalyst Theodore Lidz discusses some positive aspects of the generation gap as well as of what radical feminists see as "sex stereotyping." Drawing on the work of sociologist Talcott Parsons and others, he maintains that the division of the family into two genders and two generations, each with differing functions, directs the structuring of families in all societies and ensures the stability of the individual as well as of the family and of society itself. "Failures to maintain this structure, based essentially upon the different roles and tasks of two generations and the two sexes in the family, lead to pathological family interaction . . . . The spouses need to form a coalition as members of the parental generation maintaining their respective gender-linked roles, and be capable of transmitting instrumentally useful ways of adaptation suited to the society in which

Notes

they live . . . . Security of sexual identity is a cardinal factor in the achievement of a stable ego identity" and "is acquired by role allocations that start in infancy, role assumptions, and identifications as the child grows older" (pp. 48, 53, 67).

21. See note 5, part 3.

22. In her paper "A Consideration of the Nature of Thought in Childhood Play" (in *Separation-Individuation: Essays in Honor of Margaret S. Mahler,* edited by John B. McDevitt and Calvin F. Settlage; New York: International Universities Press, 1971, pp. 41–59), Eleanor Galenson discussed the relation of children's play to creative work later in life, prompting her colleague Phyllis Greenacre to restate her own position in "The Childhood of the Artist" (see note 12, part 2) that "certain characteristics are inborn in the potentially gifted child and may either flower or be stunted by the exigencies in the later development of his personal life. Most important of these special qualities is the increased sensitivity of the sensorimotor equipment permitting earlier and greater intensity and range of responsiveness to external stimulations, including patterns of form and rhythm." Not only what the mother provides but peripheral forms that resemble her or parts of her body, what Greenacre calls "collective alternates," become invested with emotional meaning for the child and "form the seeds of the love affair with the world which, with all its hazardous disappointments, is the fate of the creative individual" (*Separation-Individuation,* pp. 6off).

23. Traditional feminine and masculine attitudes and interests remain remarkably resistant to change, despite the efforts of feminists and proponents of other kinds of egalitarianism to encourage androgyny and to do away with differences of all kinds between individuals. The argument that sexual stereotypes are produced by cultural conditioning alone does not seem to hold water (or perhaps we should say the baby gets thrown out with the water), since they appear to persist despite efforts at cultural deconditioning. Certainly, all of the evidence is not yet in on this subject, but a good deal of relevant evidence is considered in an excellent review of feminist and other recent political critiques of psychoanalytic theory of female sexuality that appeared in the *Journal of the American Psychoanalytic Association's* special supplement on Female Psychology (vol. 24, no. 5, 1976, pp. 305–350). In "A New Female Psychology?" psychiatrist Peter Barglow and Margaret Schaefer point out that writers like Kate Millet, Germaine Greer, Phyllis

231

Chesler, and others who published widely in the early seventies fail to understand the essence of the Freudian perspective they attack. To quote from Juliet Mitchell (in *Psychoanalysis and Feminism;* New York: Pantheon, 1974, p. 8), they "implicitly deny the very notion of an aspect of mental life (expressed in its own 'language') that is different from conscious thought processes . . . and as a result the whole point is missed." In arguing that female psychological characteristics are the result of cultural conditioning alone the environmentalist critics ignore biological, developmental, and intrapsychic influences. As Barglow and Schaefer put it: "The evidence from biology, neurology (and yes, psychoanalysis) indicates that the individual, while enormously modifiable, is not infinitely so. He has inborn drives . . . [a] developmental maturational timetable, and perhaps even inborn cognitive structures." The individual personality is thus seen "as the final end product of multiple complex actions between social institutions, rites, and beliefs, the individual's familial and social milieu, and his own drives, wishes, needs, and fantasies" (p. 320).

"The political critics are much more concerned with social advocacy than they are with broadening our analytic thinking . . . The late Horney, Janeway and other social critics almost completely ignore the likelihood that female as well as male infantile needs might have shaped and still shape the structure of social and cultural institutions as well as female personality . . . that the 'myth' placing women into caretaking and childbearing roles in the home reflects female needs and desires as well as those of the male." Psychoanalytic thinking acknowledges that personality traits are influenced by "family interactions . . . laws, customs, and religion; but they are also shaped by biology and anatomy . . . maturational considerations, and female as well as male infantile wishes . . . needs, and drives" (pp. 321–24).

There is much evidence, reviewed here, demonstrating the existence of constitutional psychomotor differences between boys and girls from birth on. At birth, girls demonstrate greater motoric passivity, greater sensitivity to tactile and pain stimuli, and greater responsiveness to perceptions of human faces. By a year, boys play more aggressively, while girls display earlier language development, and so on. Barglow and Schaefer conclude, "It seems probable that organic factors provide a solid foundation for sexual gender identity," although "parental gender assignment and rearing outweighs biological factors by facilitating various kinds of learning through identification with both parents or through parental conditioning of behavior."

24. Letty Pogrebin, *Growing Up Free;* see notes 13 and 31, part 2.

25. This apt description is from *Latency* by Charles Sarnoff, p. 153. See note 3.

26. Economist Thomas Sowell, in "Choice in Education and Parental Responsibility" (from *Parents, Teachers, and Children: Prospects for Choice in American Education* (San Francisco: Institute for Contemporary Studies, 1977, pp. 165–182), suggests that "parental responsibility is not something to be casually written off by educational 'experts' who may have had an overdose of sociology." Among the beliefs of "experts" Sowell challenges are the value of a special "black" education in a special "black" environment with black teachers and special curricula, teaching methods, and tests; that facilities, budget, and innovative programs are what make for a successful school.

Looking at the records of four outstanding black schools, where academic records and students' later professional achievement were extraordinarily high by any standards, he found they had buildings, books, equipment, and financial support that could only be described as inadequate. They had no "community control" or "student rights." What they did have was dedicated teachers, supportive parents, and continuity of school leadership. "The teachers were men and women educated in intellectual content at the leading colleges and universities in the country—not people trained in 'methods' at teachers' colleges." In addition, "parental support of the school was virtually absolute, as was their exclusion from any role in internal school policy." The parents often made sacrifices to send their children to these schools, were ambitious for their children, respected the school authorities, and were supportive of school discipline. Sowell sums up: "The history of black education— and especially of the *successful* education of black youngsters— refutes almost every fashionable assumption about the education of minorities. The popular litany of small classes, good facilities, 'innovative' teaching methods, racial integration, and community control, lists what most of these schools never had in the days of their greatest success. As for 'role models' with which the students can 'identify': the teachers and principals of these schools have been black and white, men and women, lay and clerical, disciplinarians and warm mothering figures. In short, there is no formula, but there

Notes

is a pattern: hard work, mutual respect, and leadership holding the conviction that it can and must be done."

27. James S. Coleman, Thomas Hoffer, and Sally Kilgore, *Public and Private Schools* (Washington, D.C.: National Center for Education Statistics, 1981).

28. All children, as Piaget has demonstrated (see note 2, part 1), achieve cognitive abilities in a universal and unalterable sequence. The mind of the child is continually restructured by interaction with his environment but can go no further than the stage of his development at the time and, of course, no further than his own natural endowment. The basic potential is in the genes; the extent to which it will be realized depends on interaction with the environment. Experience *can* have an effect on a child's musical or mathematical ability by encouraging him to realize his fullest potential or not, but you cannot make a Mozart or an Einstein out of just any child chosen at random by means of environmental stimulation.

In a landmark study of children's intelligence (*Stability and Change in Human Characteristics;* New York: Wiley, 1964), educator Benjamin S. Bloom demonstrated that intelligence tends to stabilize early in life. By the time they start school at age six, children have 50 percent of the vocabulary they will have at age eight, and at the age of eight their vocabulary is already half of what it will be at eighteen.

The child's repertoire of words and ease in using them is a crucial matter. The better an individual's command of language the more subtly differentiated his perceptions of things and people can be, and the better his grasp of abstractions (problem solving) and feelings (explanations of motivations and relationships). Thus the capacity for language influences the capacity for thought and feeling. (Some basic findings on this subject can be found in Basil Bernstein's "Aspects of Language and Learning in the Genesis of the Social Process," *Journal of Child Psychology and Psychiatry,* vol. 1, no. 4, 1961, pp. 313–24.)

However, intelligence is not the only factor that determines who does well in school. Certain personality traits have been found to correlate with academic success. (See, for instance, Lester W. Sontag et al., "Mental Growth and Personality Development: A Longitudinal Study," *Monographs of the Society for Research in Child Development,* Serial no. 68, vol. 23, no. 2, 1958.) The child who is aggressively inquisitive, initiates activity, is self-confident and competitive at age six will probably do well in school, since these

234

qualities have been found to be good predictors of elementary-school performance. This is consistent with Bloom's findings. Statistical measures of height, general intelligence, school achievement, and aggressivity all indicate that less and less change is likely to take place in any individual after the early school years, by which time a third to a half of his eventual development has usually taken place.

29. In 1966 the U. S. Commissioner of Education issued a statement saying that "the U. S. Office of Education will support family life education and sex education as an integral part of the curriculum from preschool to college and adult levels." And in the late sixties the Department of Health, Education and Welfare (HEW) granted funds for study guides for teachers on sexuality published by SIECUS, which was lobbying for sex education in the schools. HEW also began to fund teacher-training programs as well as some of the actual public school programs in sex education.

In discussing the role of the state and federal governments in promoting ethnic education ("Public Education and American Pluralism," in *Parents, Teachers, and Children,* pp. 95–97), sociologist Nathan Glazer makes several points that apply to programs such as sex education and values clarification as well. In recent years, state legislation, regulation and enforcement, budgetary support and administrative control have replaced voluntary private group organizations and, as Glazer points out, "once government enters . . . we have a tendency in education that is firmly fixed. Government does not easily withdraw from a field once it has entered upon it. In the past, cultural pluralism and intercultural education was the concern of groups of intellectuals, of leaders of voluntary organizations, of organized elements within ethnic groups. Programs had to be developed and advocated without government assistance. Voluntary budgets have to be raised anew each year. But government budgets, once established, possess a dynamic of their own. In the past, when individuals and group leaders lost interest in ethnic education, then activity generally declined: there was no one to keep up the pressure. Once a program is incorporated in legislation and budgets, however, one can expect the program to keep going even if the number and intensity of lobbying activity for it declines: there are now, after all, paid agents of government who have developed an interest in the program and are there to see that it does not die." In sum, "we have moved from *facilitating* to *requiring.*" This has proved the case with "women's studies," minority studies and bilingual education programs. It is also the case with government-sponsored sex-education programs.

30. In "Preparing Today's Youth for Tomorrow's Family: Recommendations of the Wingspread Conference on Early Adolescent Sexuality and Health Care, June 3–5, 1979," *Journal of the Institute for Family Research and Education,* vol. 1, no. 2, October 1979, p. 5.

31. Ibid.

32. See note 33, part 2.

33. Theologian Michael Novak, in his conclusion to the *Parents, Teachers, and Children* volume ("Social Trust," pp. 257–278), discussing the changes that have taken place in the American school system since World War II, points out that "schools have taken on a more complex set of tasks . . . and parents have come to expect more and more of the schools—while providing less educational help in the home . . . . Education has become a specialization left to the experts."

One of the best, and certainly the most entertaining, of the books about sex education is *Oh! Sex Education* by Mary Breasted (New York: Praeger, 1970), which unfortunately has gone out of print. It is no less timely today than it was then, when the author, a young journalist of sophisticated liberal persuasion, investigated the controversy over sex education then raging in the schools of one California community. Her interviews with the "Antis" revealed that although they tended to have less formal education and be less articulate than the "Pros," they were something more than the religious bigots and paranoid anti-Communists they were often portrayed as by the Pros, whom she found often glib and even arrogant in their conviction that they had the right to impose their particular outlook on life—a brand of cultural relativism and moral positivism—on other people's children. She saw that much of the argument on both sides proceeds by ignoring the fact that mystery and fantasy attach to sexual life in the very nature of things and cannot always be dispelled by the dissemination of factual information or prove amenable to rational direction. What makes for sexual deviation, or precocious acting-out, for behavior that results in venereal disease or teen-age pregnancy, is not simply lack of information or even of an attitude that can be implanted in a classroom, like an electrode. On the other hand, ignorance is crippling, and children need and want to know "the facts of life." The question is, who should teach them? And can "family

life and sex education" be taught in a way that is "value free"?
Can anything?

Mary Breasted found what is apparent to anyone who sits in a
classroom where "values" or "behavior" of any kind are being discussed: The course "stressed the virtues of certain views over others" (*Oh! Sex Education*, p. 99). And there is no doubt that they are
not the views of all parents everywhere, nor could they be. The perception of the Antis, scorned in the liberal press for a generation
and deeply concerned about what they perceive as the decline of
moral standards among the young, was that now "they were effectively told that they were not 'qualified' to carry the full responsibility for their children's moral and sexual training" (p. 129). The parental domain, the personal value systems of their families, was
being invaded by a class of professional educators who did not share
their views. One of the Antis put it this way:

I have five children, and I want their outlook on life to be that which is taught
at home. I want the teachers to be supportive to that which I am teaching
. . . . If my child goes to school and his personality characteristics, his attitude,
by whatever name you want to call them, are changed against my will
. . . by someone who has instituted a course to make my children less than
that which I want them to be, then I as a patron have the right to object
(p. 172).

That is not a sophisticated exposition of its point of view, but it is
hard to say that, despite the style, that point of view is entirely unjustified. Sex education, as taught in the schools, *was* a threat to
these parents' authority over their own children—or, to put it another way, to their influence over them. The question, as Mary
Breasted perceived, was who would control the sexual behavior of
the young—which was the actual aim of both the Pros and the Antis.

When newspapers described marathon sensitivity training sessions for future sex education teachers at New York University, this
sounded like "brainwashing" to many parents who feared that government money—their tax money—was being used to undermine
parental authority and supervision in order to effect social change.
Mary Breasted's reaction was that the typical devotee of "group interaction" she observed "had only been brainwashed by the fash-
ions of his time. He was a camp-follower. And I didn't want any
child of mine taking a camp-follower's advice on dating and marriage—or anything else" (p. 286).

Notes

Despite her aversion to the politics and style of the Antis, the Pros seemed to her "people who had spent too much time behind desks and podiums and clinic doors. They fairly oozed that dry and cerebral good will of clinicians or students of behavioral science . . . . It was their new faith in the power of the human relations professions." They were better educated than the Antis, and more eloquent in defending their point of view, but hardly wiser. The "health professionals," teachers, psychologists, social workers and marriage counselors—and even doctors and ministers who do this kind of thing—seemed to her a humorless, self-righteous lot, untouched by the subtleties or profundities of either religion or Freud, promulgating a watered-down philosophy of "normalcy" as defined by current middle-brow social-therapeutic thinking. And paradoxically, she found herself haunted by "the question that the Antis had raised so hysterically again and again and again. Which was: Who gave these people the right to tell us all how to raise our children? Who had conferred upon them their special qualifications for informing us of the best and latest sexual techniques?" (p. 291). Listening to a group of them trying to come up with a noncontroversial title for a sex-education curriculum dealing with masturbation, she became convinced "that educators would try to get round the public on matters that they, the educators, thought themselves better equipped to judge" (p. 315).

34. Federal funding for sex education programs in public schools became a big business under the Carter administration. Mathtech, a private research firm located in Bethesda, Maryland, produced for the U. S. Department of Health, Education and Welfare in 1979 "An Analysis of U. S. Sex Education Programs and Evaluation Methods," a weighty report, reprinted in 1980, that was "designed to improve both the teaching of sex education and the evaluation of that instruction." It is a revealing document, which assumes a consensus on such matters as the desirability of "comprehensive programs" comprising "many courses in many grades" that "focus on the clarifying of values" and "make students more tolerant of the sexual practices of others." In particular, "reduction of sexual guilt, an acceptance of alternative life styles for others, and an acceptance of alternatives to sexual intercourse . . . were rated extremely important by most of the experts" who also agreed that "these are not controversial."

The report describes "exemplary" school programs and provides a 124-page bibliography of "exemplary" curriculum materials designed "to encourage students to question, explore, and assess their sexual attitudes" and "develop more tolerant attitudes toward the sexual behavior of others," and "to facilitate rewarding sexual expression" through "the sharing of experiences and feelings" in the classroom. The quotations are all from the Executive Summary and Volume I of the Mathtech report.

35. From *I Am Not a Short Adult: Getting Good at Being a Kid* by Marilyn Burns (Boston: Little, Brown, 1977), the title of which tells the story. Kids in fifth grade, the age for which this book is recommended, are naturally good at being kids; what they need is help in growing up to be thoughtful and responsible adults.

36. From another widely distributed children's book, *Learning About Sex: A Guide for Children and Their Parents* (New York: Holt, Rinehart and Winston, 1978).

37. Erik Erikson, *Identity: Youth and Crisis* (New York: Norton, 1968, p. 125).

38. See note 2, part 2.

39. In *The Moral Judgment of the Child* (first published in 1932; reprinted by the Free Press [New York] in 1965 and in various paperback editions since).

40. See "Development of Moral Character and Moral Ideology" by Lawrence Kohlberg, in *Review of Child Development Research,* edited by Martin L. Hoffman and Lois W. Hoffman, vol. 1 (New York: Russell Sage Foundation, 1964, pp. 383–431).

41. Writing of the extremist student rebels on campuses in the late sixties and of those professors who abdicated their adult responsibilities by romanticizing and appeasing them, Bruno Bettelheim wrote (in "Obsolete Youth?" *Encounter,* vol. 33, no. 3, September 1969, pp. 29–42): "These are 'true believers' . . . convinced that theirs was the only moral position. Their moral absolutism gives them the right to destroy what they judge to be amoral—the right to break up and take over meetings, shout down or physically assault those not in full agreement with them. Indeed such militance is not only felt to be right, but an obligation." Referring to the excitement many adults experienced at the time in observing the confrontations provoked by the young, discerning a "new consciousness" and admiring their "moral development," Bettelheim was almost alone at the time in seeing—and saying—that "we fail these youth if we do not act on our knowledge of what lies behind the grandiloquent way in which they give voice to their confusion and distress . . . the inner anxieties that power the high-sounding moral pronouncements." See note 83.

42. By Sidney B. Simon, Leland W. Howe, and Howard Kirschen-

Notes

baum (New York: Hart, 1972). One of the authors, Howard Kirschenbaum, has since gone beyond this volume with *Advanced Values Clarification* (San Diego, Ca.: University Associates, 1977). Other books in the same vein, all of them strikingly similar and all of them saturated with the authors' own system of values and subtle and not-so-subtle "strategies" for inculcating them, are *Values and Teaching: Working with Values in the Classroom* by Louis E. Raths et al. (Columbus, Oh.: Merrill, 1966, 1978), *Readings in Values Clarification*, an anthology put together by Kirschenbaum and Simon (Oak Grove, Minn.: Winston, 1973), and *Helping Your Child Learn Right From Wrong: A Guide to Values Clarification*, another Simon product (New York: McGraw-Hill, 1976) with an introduction, appropriately enough, by the father of P.E.T. (see note 49, part 2).

43. Simon et al., *Values Clarification,* p. 16.

44. Ibid., p. 19 (emphasis in the original).

45. Ibid., p. 64.

46. Ibid., pp. 109–110.

47. Ibid., p. 196.

48. Ibid., p. 266.

49. Do these books "tell what it is like to grow up Black in America"—or how that experience was perceived by a particular kind of black with a certain political point of view—each of whom, by the way, became something of a celebrity if not even a great success in America? Millions of middle-class blacks have other views of what it was like to grow up in America. They, of course, are not included here.

50. Simon et al., *Values Clarification,* pp. 267–74.

51. Ibid., p. 17.

52. Ibid., p. 18.

53. Lawrence Kohlberg, "The Cognitive-Developmental Approach to Moral Education," in *Values Concepts and Techniques* (Washington, D.C.: National Education Association, 1976).

54. Michael Silvers, *Values Education* (Washington, D.C.: National Education Association, 1976).

55. William J. Bennett, "Where the Values Movement Goes Wrong" (*Change,* February 1979, p. 5).

56. "Moral Education in the Schools" (*The Public Interest,* Winter 1978, pp. 81–98).

57. Ibid., p. 97.

58. Ibid., p. 98.

59. G. Stanley Hall, *Adolescence: Its Psychology and its Relations*

to *Physiology, Anthropology, Sociology, Sex, Crime, Religion and Education* (New York: Appleton, 1904).

60. Of course, it is the artist's youth that is depicted in works of art, from *The Sorrows of Young Werther* through *A Portrait of the Artist as a Young Man* to *The Catcher in the Rye,* and one may well suggest that the artist like Goethe, Joyce, or Salinger is hardly typical of most people.

61. Anna Freud, "Adolescence," in *The Psychoanalytic Study of the Child,* vol. 13 (New York: International Universities Press, 1958), pp. 255–278.

62. Ibid., p. 267.

63. Ibid., p. 275.

64. Ibid., p. 276.

65. Commenting on the original articles by Anna Freud, Peter Blos, and other analysts written around the 1950s, psychiatrist James F. Masterson, Jr. noted "that the authors shifted from describing a specific clinical problem in a patient to generalizing about adolescence as a process of normal growth and development, without making quite plain to the reader that this transition had taken place. It was not always clear when the writer was talking about his findings in a patient and when he was extrapolating theories about normal adolescence. It appears that the theory of adolescent turmoil, derived presumably from the study of neurotics (although this is not spelled out), has been inconsiderately generalized to all adolescents" ("The Psychiatric Significance of Adolescent Turmoil," *The American Journal of Psychiatry,* vol. 124, no. 11, May 1968, pp. 1549–54.)

66. Peter Blos, *On Adolescence* (New York: Free Press, Macmillan, 1962), p. 73.

67. Ibid., p. 157.

68. "Normal" can be used in different ways to mean different things, and the sense in which it is being used should be made clear in any discussion in which the concept of what is "normal" is a factor. It can mean what most people do, in which case normality is defined as a numerical average, the behavior of the greatest number. It can also be used in the sense of what is thought to lead to the best outcome, in conformity to some view of the world such as adaptation theory, in which case that which confers some biological advantage on the species would be considered normal. Before undertaking the study of normal adolescents Offer considered the meaning of the term in some depth in a study written with Melvin

Sabshin entitled *Normality: Theoretical and Clinical Concepts of Mental Health* (New York: Basic Books, 1966). Offer and Sabshin define the normal adolescent as one who, having mastered previous developmental tasks without serious setbacks, is flexible, able to resolve conflicts with a reasonable degree of success, has good relationships with adults, and feels part of the larger cultural environment and aware of its norms and values.

The issue of flexibility is central to the definition of normality in mental health. As Lawrence Kubie pointed out in "The Fundamental Nature of the Distinction Between Normality and Neurosis" (*Psychoanalytic Quarterly,* vol. 23, 1954, pp. 182–85), the essence of a neurotic act is that it is not influenced by reality or changeable through experience but an unalterable pattern of behavior automatically repeated "irrespective of the situation, the utility, or the consequences of the act" because it is the product of unconscious conflict. When unconscious processes predominate, "the resultant action must be repeated endlessly . . . because unconscious symbolic goals are never attainable . . . they will not be responsive to . . . experience . . . or to logical argument." They will be repeated regardless of their suitability to the immediate situation or their remote consequences. Normal behavior, on the other hand, is subject to conscious processes and motives of which the individual can be aware. Such behavior "will come to rest either when its goal is achieved and satiety is attained, or when the goal is found to be unattainable or ungratifying or both." It is this "freedom and flexibility to learn through experience, to change, and to adapt to changing external circumstances" that is the sine qua non of mental health.

69. One limitation of the early Offer studies, recognized by Offer himself, is that for a variety of reasons having to do with practical considerations at the time the studies were designed, the sample consists only of boys. (In his most recent book, *The Adolescent: A Psychological Self-Portrait* [New York: Basic Books, 1981], Offer and his colleagues survey and discuss adolescent girls as well.) According to Joseph Adelson in his authoritative compendium *Handbook of Adolescent Psychiatry* (New York: Wiley, 1980), a survey of work and thought in the field through the 1970s, "adolescent girls have simply not been much studied," in part, Adelson thinks, because "adolescent boys are more troublesome to society, hence more visible to the caretakers and theorists of disorder" and with the result that "the inattention to girls, and to the processes of feminine development in adolescence has meant undue attention to such problems

as impulse control, rebelliousness, superego struggles, ideology, and achievement, along with a corresponding neglect of such issues as intimacy, nurturance, and affiliation" (*Handbook,* p. 114).

70. Offer, *The Psychological World of the Teen-ager* (New York: Basic Books, 1969).

71. Ibid., p. 179.

72. Ibid., p. 182.

73. Erik Erikson, "The Concept of Ego Identity," in *The Psychology of Adolescence,* edited by Aaron H. Esman (New York: International Universities Press, 1975), p. 191.

Offer distinguishes between what Erikson has described as the "psycho-social moratorium during which the young adult through free role experimentation may find a niche in some section of his society" (*Identity: Youth and Crisis;* New York: Norton, 1968, p. 156) and "a state of affairs in society which seems to encourage rebellion" (*The Psychological World of the Teen-ager,* pp. 188–89). On the one hand Erikson describes "a period that is characterized by a selective permissiveness on the part of society and of provocative playfulness on the part of youth" that eventually ends in "commitment on the part of youth" and "confirmation of commitment on the part of society" (*Identity,* p. 157). Examples range from various kinds of travels and apprenticeships to academic life and pranks that range from breaking the rules about smoking to sporadic stealing. On the other hand is the expectation of rebellion ultimately in the service of alienation from existing society and radical change of its forms and institutions. Offer points to several contributors, not the least of them "the scientific literature on adolescence itself" in which adolescent rebellion is romanticized. The press finds space for the deviant adolescent alongside the major events of the news, while "we in the social sciences likewise glamorize the rebellions that offer us a possibility of change . . . . Social engineers like Paul Goodman [in his highly influential *Growing Up Absurd;* New York: Vintage, 1962] feel that youth *ought* to to change the world."

74. Offer, *The Psychological World of the Teen-ager,* pp. 184–85.

75. Elizabeth Douvan and Joseph Adelson put it in *The Adolescent Experience* (New York: Wiley, 1966, p. 352): "Even when we do find overt conflict one senses that it has an 'as if' quality to it, that it is a kind of war game, with all the sights and sounds of battle but without any blood being shed."

76. *The Psychological World of the Teen-ager,* p. 205.

77. Ibid., p. 194. Elsewhere, Offer adds, "This gives the adolescent not only a worthy adversary but one who can set limits to his strengths" and quotes Erikson at a Children's Bureau seminar on the mass media: "I do not like to fool around with such questions as to whether certain movies, T.V. shows, or comic books are good or bad for children. As a citizen and as a father I would insist that they are ugly and worthless, and I, for one, would tell my children so and would try to restrict their opportunities to see them. If they want to see them anyway, that is up to them. It is better for them to rebel than to have parents with totally compromised values" (ibid., p. 204).

78. Ibid., p. 56.

79. Ibid., p. 63.

80. Ibid., p. 64.

81. Daniel Offer and Judith Baskin Offer (New York: Basic Books, 1975).

82. A major study of the literature on adolescence of the sixties published by the Rand Corporation in 1976 (M. Timpane et al., *Youth Policy in Transition,* p. 48) concludes that "any major differences that might exist between youth and older generations are more apt to be differences *within* the adult group, which are being manifested in the youth group, than between parents and their [own] adolescent children." How was it that we were led to believe differently? An overview of recent studies of adolescence ("Adolescence in Historical Perspective," by Glen H. Elder, Jr., in *Handbook of Adolescent Psychology,* p. 21) notes that "a large number of studies in the 1960s were guided by *expectation* of parent-youth conflict and value differences in student unrest," an expectation which, it is remarked, "received little empirical support." As Joseph Adelson, the editor of the *Handbook,* puts it elsewhere in the volume (pp. 113–14), "When the psychodynamic theorist turns away from the study of the disturbed and looks about him for examples of 'normality,' his eye is likely to fall on those most near and dear— his own children and those of his friends and neighbors or, if he is connected to a university, his students. In short, he will tend to understand the 'ordinary' adolescent through the observation of a narrow social enclave, one which tends to emphasize for its youngsters the values of expressiveness (as against inner restraint), of rebelliousness (as against conformity), and of adversarial indignation (as against the acceptance of social givens). Hence we find a continuing failure to give sufficient weight to those habitual strategies of coping

found among many and perhaps most adolescents—strategies that involve ego restriction and an identification with the values and standards of the family and dominant social institutions."

83. There can be little doubt that some use social action as a way of dealing with their own problems. Offer found "[those] who were concerned with stopping world conflicts were often those who were most concerned with controls for themselves" (*The Psychological World of the Teen-ager*, p. 71).

Bruno Bettelheim made the distinction in *Surviving and Other Essays* (New York: Knopf, 1979, p. 351): "The contradictions of adolescence can create an inescapable desire for confrontations . . . or a wish to rely on acts of terrorism to assert one's own strength and that of one's convictions . . . . Or the adolescent may strive for a more peaceful and constructive, but also more difficult, solution to the problem of discovering one's true self, through an inner process of integration . . . It is the adolescent's past upbringing, and the relations that significant adults establish with him, which will be decisive in his unconscious choice of methods to solve both his conflicts with the world, and the contradictions within himself." Earlier, Bettelheim had written in the heat of the battle in which so many other adults had retreated ignominiously in the face of childish rage masking as idealism: "What makes for adolescent revolt is the fact that a society keeps the next generation too long in a state of dependence . . . in terms of mature responsibility and a sense of place that one has personally striven for and won." It is those who cannot find themselves in study or work who find the university and society irrelevant, and Bettelheim indicts their upbringing for failing to prepare them for the prolonging of adolescence in our society, for failing to provide them with any real authority to internalize and from which to fashion inner controls. They have never been taught to repress their aggression, to express it in thought and not in violence. Although often extremely bright, these extreme militants are equally often emotionally immature; intellectually precocious, they remain "fixated at the age of the temper tantrum." Their espousal of leaders like Mao "suggests their desperate need for controls from the outside, since without them they cannot bring order to their own inner chaos" ("Obsolete Youth?" pp. 32–40).

84. See "Youth and Peace: A Psychosocial Study of Student Peace Demonstrators in Washington, D.C.," *Journal of Social Issues,* vol. 20, pp. 54–73.

85. Offer, *From Teenage to Young Manhood,* pp. 193–94.

Notes

86. Ibid., p. 190.

87. Such as Nathan W. Ackerman's *Treating the Troubled Family* (New York: Basic Books, 1966).

88. See Kenneth Keniston, *The Uncommitted: Alienated Youth in American Society* (New York: Harcourt, Brace and World, 1965).

89. Among the published reports of studies of normal populations that appeared around the same time as Offer's was *The Silent Majority: Families of Emotionally Healthy College Students* by William A. Westley and Nathan B. Epstein (San Francisco: Jossey-Bass, 1969). Westley and Epstein described the Canadian families they studied as "mostly middle-class, well-educated, moderately prosperous people who seemed to be responsible, relatively settled in their ways, and moderate in their views . . . and relatively happy in their lives . . . functioning as successful and responsible members of the community . . . . These were families that had never been and probably would never become problems to the social agencies or appear in mental hospitals. They were, in moral terms, good, honest people, living conventional lives, struggling to meet their problems, and giving no trouble to anyone. Ordinarily, we know little about such people precisely because they present few problems and mind their own business" (p. 17). What Westley and Epstein found in these families was a conventional division of labor (mother and father have separate responsibilities) and pattern of authority (father-led) with a demonstrably warm and affectionate relationship between husband and wife. Their conclusion was that the factor most critical to the emotional health of children was a good relationship between their parents, which provides both a model of heterosexual relationships and of a way of life (pp. 85, 88).

Couples who were emotionally close, meeting each other's needs and encouraging positive self-images in each other, became good parents. Since they met each other's needs, they did not use their children to live out their needs; since they were happy and satisfied, they could support and meet their children's needs; and since their own identities were clarified, they saw their children as distinct from themselves. All this helped the children become emotionally healthy people (p. 158).

90. Margaret Mead, *Culture and Commitment* (New York: Doubleday, 1970), pp. 77–78.

91. Kenneth Keniston, *Young Radicals: Notes on Committed Youth* (New York: Harcourt, Brace and World, 1968).

Notes

92. Marshall McLuhan, *Understanding Media* (New York: New American Library, 1964).

93. Alvin Toffler, *Future Shock* (New York: Random House, 1970).

94. According to Douvan and Adelson, "Most contemporary comment on adolescence focuses on two conspicuous but atypical enclaves of adolescents, drawn from extreme and opposing ends of the social class continuum, and representing exceptional solutions to the adolescent crisis . . . . Paradoxically, these two extremes are alike, and their likeness is in being different from the normative adolescent—the adolescent of the core culture. The extremes are alike in showing an unusual degree of independence from the family; they are alike in disaffection, in acting out or thinking out a discontent with the social order; they are alike, above all, in that they adopt radical solutions to the adolescent task of ego synthesis.

"We want to suggest that one cannot generalize these processes to the adolescent population at large . . . . The great advantage of the survey technique is that it allows us to study these adolescents who make up the middle majority, who evoke neither grief nor wonder, and who all too often escape our notice." (*The Adolescent Experience*, pp. 350–51)

95. E. James Anthony, "The Reactions of Adults to Adolescents and their Behavior," in *The Psychology of Adolescence*, pp. 479–80.

96. With a handy assist from the media. The *New York Times*'s personal health reporter, Jane E. Brody, was writing about "the turmoil of adolescence" in a typical article that ran on September 30, 1981 (p. C10), and her colleague Glenn Collins wrote a story headed "Stressful World of Adolescent" that appeared on December 7, 1981 (p. B18), alongside a long article by the same author, "Paternity Leave: A New Role for Fathers." The new role turns out to be being mothers, and one wonders what effect "increasing male involvement in child rearing" will have on little girls like the one in this story. They may well find the assumption of a mature female identity in their adolescence a stressful time of turmoil.

97. Physiological aspects of adolescence are discussed in *Youth: The Years from Ten to Sixteen* by Arnold Gesell et al. (New York: Harper & Row, 1956) and *Childhood and Adolescence* by L. Joseph Stone and Joseph Church (New York: Random House, 1968). There is much useful information about puberty in "Sequence, Tempo, and Individual Variation in Growth and Development of Boys and Girls Aged Twelve to Sixteen" by J. M. Tanner in *Twelve to Sixteen: Early Adolescence*, edited by Jerome Kagan and Robert Coles (New York: Norton, 1972), pp. 1–24.

Notes

98. Erikson, who gave us the term and focused our attention on the problem of identity, describes it as "certain comprehensive gains which the individual, at the end of adolescence, must have derived from all of his pre-adult experience in order to be ready for the tasks of adulthood . . . . [T]he young individual must learn to be most himself where he means most to others—those others, to be sure, who have come to mean most to him. The term identity . . . connotes both a persistent sameness within oneself and a persistent sharing of some kind of essential character with others" ("The Problem of Ego Identity," *Journal of the American Psychoanalytic Association,* vol. 4, no. 1, January 1956, pp. 56–57). " . . . *Identity formation,* finally, begins where the usefulness of identification ends. It arises from the selective repudiation and mutual assimilation of childhood identifications, and their absorption in a new configuration" recognized by the community "as somebody who had to become the way he is, and who, being the way he is, is taken for granted" (Erikson, *Identity: Youth and Crisis,* p. 159). This mutual recognition of the society and the newly emerging individual is institutionalized in various rituals, religious, educational, familial—in confirmations, bar mitzvahs, graduations, birthday parties.

99. Stone and Church, *Childhood and Adolescence,* p. 441.

100. Bärbel Inhelder and Jean Piaget, *The Growth of Logical Thinking from Childhood to Adolescence* (New York: Basic Books, 1958). See note 2, part 2.

101. Piaget, "The Intellectual Development of the Adolescent," in *The Psychology of Adolescence,* pp. 105–6.

102. Piaget, *The Psychology of Intelligence* (New York: Harcourt, Brace and World, 1947), p. 148.

103. "The Intellectual Development of the Adolescent," p. 108.

104. *The Growth of Logical Thinking,* p. 343.

105. See note 40.

106. See Piaget, *The Moral Judgment of the Child* (1932).

107. Kohlberg's stages were set forth in detail by him in "Development of Moral Character and Moral Ideology" (see note 40) and have been repeated in numerous publications since.

108. Perhaps the best comment on placing self-chosen principles above the law was made by the late philosopher and social theorist Charles Frankel, who wrote, in a chapter titled "The Moral Right to Impose on Others": "We do not commonly ask why anyone should behave legally. We ask, When is it permissible to behave illegally? For there is always a prima facie case to be made for legality.

Notes

The law provides a variety of profound benefits: personal safety; an established and dependable way of settling personal and social disputes; discouragement of the violent tendencies in all individuals; preservation of the entire ongoing system of mutual expectation and confidence on which daily affairs depend. These are not small things, and actions that weaken the framework of law endanger them . . . . Civil disobedience can sometimes be justified. But the tests that it must pass are extremely severe. The evils being combatted cannot be middling evils. In view of the potential damage that can be caused by challenging the law, they have to be shocking, excessive, inexcusable. The damage they do to the social fabric must be greater than the damage that comes from breaking the law. Moreover, it has to be shown that there are no legal remedies, or that the ones that are available have been used and found wanting." (*Education and the Barricades;* New York: Norton, 1968, p. 64) Professor Frankel, one is forced to suspect, would not be admitted by the adherents of Kohlberg's scheme of "cognitive moral development" to have progressed beyond their fifth stage to the hallowed sixth.

109. See part 3, pp. 155–162.

110. Kohlberg himself tells us that the "adolescent revolution in thinking," which involves "the clouding and questioning of the validity of society's truths and its rightness" is not only variable as to when it takes place but "for many people it never occurs at all . . . . [A]lmost 50 per cent of American adults never reach adolescence in the cognitive sense." In fact, "a large proportion of Americans never develop the capacity for abstract thought" ("The Adolescent as a Philosopher: The Discovery of the Self in a Postconventional World," in *Twelve to Sixteen,* p. 158).

It seems that "to have questioned conventional morality you must have questioned your identity as well," and "morally conventional subjects have a considerable likelihood of never having an identity crisis or an identity questioning at all." As a matter of fact, the combination of adolescent identity crisis and questioning of conventional morality fits best "the picture of adolescence in the developmentally elite."

Kohlberg's own values could not be stated more clearly than in this circular reasoning. To "question conventional morality" makes you a member of "the developmentally elite," that is, those who share Kohlberg's own value system, moral relativism or "the rejection of conventional moral reasoning." While maintaining with a

Notes

straight face that his scheme of hierarchical moralities describes objectively observable data, he fails to explain in what sense except in terms of his own ideals and beliefs it can be described as a universal system if it not only doesn't fit everyone but doesn't fit even half of everyone? When Kohlberg goes on about universal abstract principles of justice embodied in adolescents' thinking, one can only think of the spoiled children of the sixties who eventually became vicious criminals of the eighties—robbers and killers in the name of the universal abstract principles of justice their civil-rights-advocate and legal-defense-lawyer parents, their liberal clergymen and social studies teachers had encouraged to challenge "the system"—in which, as it happens, some of them would wind up living supported by welfare. One wonders what system existing anytime, anywhere, except in the fantasies created by their pathological needs, would have treated these lunatic destructive children half so generously. And one cannot help wondering why it is that people like Kohlberg identify with the adolescents rather than seeing them from the perspective of adults.

111. Kohlberg, "Moral Development and the Education of Adolescents," in *Adolescents and the American High School*, edited by R.F. Purnell (New York: Holt, Rinehart & Winston, 1970), p. 159.

112. For an intriguing explanation of the way in which various kinds of drug use relate to different kinds of emotional problems, see "Drug Use in Adolescents: Psychodynamic Meaning and Pharmacogenic Effect" by Herbert Wieder and Eugene H. Kaplan, in *The Psychoanalytic Study of the Child*, vol. 14 (New York: International Universities Press, 1969), pp. 399–431.

113. Two articles in *The Psychology of Adolescence* offer revealing insights into the nature of this bizarre disorder; they are "Anorexia Nervosa: A Psychosomatic Entity" by John V. Waller et al., pp. 376–395, and "Observations on Psychological Aspects of Anorexia Nervosa" by Bernard C. Meyer and Leonard A. Weinroth, pp. 396–400. If one draws the curtain of charity over the novel of the same title that comprises the first half of John A. Sours's volume *Starving to Death in a Sea of Objects* (New York: Aronson, 1980), it offers a thorough review of the history, nature, theory, and treatment of the disorder. Pioneering work in understanding the role of the mother-child conflict in anorexia has been done by Hilde Bruch. See her *Eating Disorders: Obesity, Anorexia Nervosa and the Person Within* (New York: Basic Books, 1973). A briefer version of her thought appears in "The Sleeping Beauty: Escape from Change" in *The Course*

Notes

of Life: *Psychoanalytic Contributions Toward Understanding Personality Development,* vol. 2 (Washington, D.C.: U.S. Department of Health and Human Services, National Institutes of Mental Health, 1980), pp. 431–444.

114. See "A Contribution to the Study of Homosexuality in Adolescence" by Marjorie P. Sprince, in *The Psychology of Adolescence,* pp. 415–432.

115. In addition to the works referred to in notes 20, 25, 27, and 29 of part 2, illuminating aspects of the origins and developmental processes of homosexuality are found in Robert J. Stoller's *Sex and Gender, Vol. II: The Transsexual Experiment* (New York: Aronson, 1976), especially pp. 106–7 and 159–169.

116. In *The Adolescent: A Psychological Self-Portrait* by Daniel Offer, Eric Ostrov, and Kenneth I. Howard (New York: Basic Books, 1981).

117. Henry and Yela Lowenfeld, "Our Permissive Society and the Superego: Some Current Thoughts About Freud's Cultural Concepts," in *The Psychology of Adolescence,* pp. 495–512.

118. Erikson, *Childhood and Society,* p. 228.

119. Peter Blos, "The Child Analyst Looks at the Young Adolescent," in *Twelve to Sixteen,* p. 68.

120. *The Adolescent,* pp. 97–98.

121. Ibid., pp. 106–7.

122. See "The Biological Approach to Adolescence," by Anne C. Peterson and Brandon Taylor, in *Handbook of Adolescent Psychiatry,* p. 134.

123. Blos, "The Child Analyst Looks at the Young Adolescent," in *Twelve to Sixteen,* p. 57.

124. Ibid., p. 64.

125. Ibid. And, earlier, "From the beginning of her adolescence, the girl is far more preoccupied with the vicissitudes of relationships than the boy; his energies are directed outward toward the control of and dominance over the physical world" (p. 61).

126. Ibid.

127. In addition to Offer's conclusions referred to previously, a number of relevant studies are cited in "The Development of Sexuality in Adolescence" by Patricia Y. Miller and William Simon in the *Handbook of Adolescent Psychiatry,* pp. 383–407.

128. Ibid., p. 398.

129. Summing up his studies of hundred of teen-agers in the late sixties ("The Political Imagination of the Young Adolescent," in

Twelve to Sixteen, pp. 106–143), Joseph Adelson arrived at somewhat different conclusions from Kohlberg. Adelson describes the movement from the personal and tangible nature of the latency child's thought to the increasingly social and abstract character of the adolescent's mind, from the child's living almost entirely in the awareness of the present to the youth's capacity for imagining the past and the future, as amounting to a "heightened sense of human complexity," the ability to consider alternative possibilities and their various consequences and to consider motivations in human behavior. The young child's reliance on authority gives way in most cases to the development of political thought that is not utopian or idealistic, but skeptical, sober, and cautious. This is perfectly understandable in the young person anticipating adulthood and rehearsing "mature modes of self-definition, among which is the readiness for citizenship."

In his need to have opinions and make judgments on the world of adult affairs, the youngster begins by taking the direction of political thought from his parents, soaking up the tacit assumptions of his milieu. "The striving toward realism, and the consequent tension between 'idealistic' and 'realistic' modes within the person," Adelson cautions us, "has been much neglected by students of adolescence, so enthralled have they been by the myth of adolescent idealism." Most of the youngsters in his sample, drawn largely "from the more or less contented classes of the community, that vast range of the population extending from the stable working class to the nonintellectual upper middle class . . . are consumed neither by grievances nor by moral passion, and in this respect they are almost certainly very much like their families." Adelson found the impulse to utopian thought among adolescents "who feel themselves despised and rejected" and young intellectuals "feeling in themselves the destiny to innovate and lead," and he concluded that "these, too, are no doubt much like their families. The inclination to utopia, in short, is a matter of class and social position, not fundamentally a youth phenomenon" (p. 131).

130. The last word—and the last note—on this subject belongs to the late Charles Frankel. In commenting on student disruptions and demands at Columbia University in the late sixties he made a statement that applies to the education of the young at all times and in all places, and sums up what so many lost sight of at the time: " 'Relevance' in the university cannot mean that everything the university does should be morally *'engagé'* in some way or other, or 'con-

temporary' or 'useful.' To learn detachment, to learn to recognize the limits and ambiguities of one's ideals, is a purpose of education. To take people out of their own time and place, and out of a demeaning and ignorant preoccupation with themselves, is another purpose. And to learn the uses of the useless is a third. The purely speculative, the purely historical, the purely esthetic, enlarge the mind and intensify the consciousness. And besides, in the pursuit of learning, no one knows what will be useful, even in the most practical, bread-and-butter sense of the term.

"That is why a university cannot, without question, give students what they think they want or need. Students are not the best judges; if they were, they would not have to be students. A college ... does its job only if students learn to live in larger intellectual and emotional habitations than those in which they lived when they entered. An intellectual education is not a process of 'meeting needs,' [but] of transforming needs, both the individual's and the society's." (*Education and the Barricades,* pp. 86–87)

4 / Summing Up: The Family and the Future

1. This point of view is summed up in Rolf E. Muuss's *Theories of Adolescence* (New York: Random House, 1975, p. 260): "First, due to the rapidity of social change, knowledge, skills, and values that parents learned when they were young are obsolete for the world in which their sons and daughters live . . . . Second, economic specialization results in the alienation of father and son. The son has little personal relationship to the father's work and must begin his own vocational training independent of his father . . . . Third, the adolescent no longer contributes substantially to the family economy, and the family, in turn, no longer teaches any particular skills and knowledge that prepare the young man and woman for their places in the adult community."

2. According to Joseph F. Kett, "What strikes most historians about the family in the past is less its strength than its fragility, its vulnerability to disruption by depression, disease, and mortality. Family discipline in our society may be weak, but it is not obviously decaying. . . . Every generation of intellectuals since 1820 has been

convinced that an acceleration of the velocity of social change has disrupted traditional harmony and has had a calamitous effect on youth" (*Rites of Passage: Adolescence in America 1790 to the Present*; New York: Basic Books, 1977, p. 4).

3. See "Adolescence in Historical Perspective" by Glen H. Elder in *Handbook of Adolescent Psychology,* pp. 28–29.

4. A current college textbook widely distributed by one of the largest firms supplying classroom material to our schools, often at government—that is, public—expense, presents a description of parents "as rank amateurs who need to be replaced by professional parents . . . by children's caretakers prepared professionally for the arts and science of children's socialization . . . . In this context, parenting is seen as a fulltime profession in which adults earn their living in services to and with children" (*Sociology of Childhood* by Marvin R. Koller and Oscar W. Ritchie; Englewood Cliffs: Prentice-Hall, 1978, p. 109).

INDEX

Index

Barglow, Peter, 231–32n23
Barron's Educational Series, 145
Battered children, psychohistorical views on, 10–11
Becker, Ted E., 228n12
Bennett, William J., 160, 161
Bergman, Anni, 215n11
Berrigan, Daniel, 161
Bestiality, 146
Bettelheim, Bruno, 53, 100, 101, 213n3, n4, 215n12, 219n22, 220n26, 239n41, 245n83
Bieber, Irving, 224n38
Biographies, 124, 127
Birth: children witnessing, 214n5; attitude toward, 135; psychological, 46; of sibling, 76, 77, 80; see also Childbirth
Blacks: education of, 233n26; middle-class, 240n49
Bloom, Benjamin S., 234–35n28
Blos, Peter, 166, 191, 192, 241n65
Blume, Judy, 126, 230n19
Body: control of own, 79; fears about, 60; sense of integrity of, 61
Body image, changing, 121
"Bonding," 41
Bornstein, Berta, 227–28n9
Bottle feeding, 52
Bowlby, John, 215n12
Breasted, Mary, 236–38n33
Breast-feeding, 52
Brody, Jane E., 247n96
Bronfenbrenner, Urie, 213n3
Brothers Karamazov, The (Dostoevsky), 206–7
Bruch, Hilda, 250–51n113
Bruner, Jerome, 224n40
Burgess, Ernest W., 19
Burns, Marilyn, 239n35

Caesarian section, 35
Calderone, Mary S., 145, 147
Capitalism, 202; laissez-faire, 26
Carnegie Council on Children, 25, 211n40
Carroll, Lewis, 129
Carter, Jimmy, 238n34
Centuries of Childhood (Ariès), 8
Ceremony, function of, 206

Character: in adolescence, 172, 197; conscience and, 107, 109; development of, 29–31; mother's, 56; narcissistic, 105; painful situations and, 81–82; resolution of conflicts and, 104
Chesler, Phyllis, 231–32n23
Child labor, 17
Child labor laws, 177
Childbirth, 33–43; "bonding" and, 41–42; current hospital practices, 39–41; development of medical interventions in, 34–36; natural, 36–38; technology applied to, 38–39
Child-care professionals, 18; see also "Professional parenting"
Child-care services, 15, 222–23n34; corporate, 223–24n35; development and, 32; for newborns, 50
Child-rearing practices: based on beliefs about nature of infants, 9; moral climate and, 210n26; permissive, 20, 45, 215n10; sixteenth-century, 9
Children's Bureau, 244n77
Chisholm, Shirley, 222n34
Choices: encouraging children to make, 139–41; moral, 124, 125
Church, Joseph, 177, 227n3, 247n97
Classics, *see* Literature
Cognitive development, 93–102, 212n2, 234n28; in adolescence, 177–82; in latency, 123–24; morality and, 155, 159; reading aloud and, 100–102; television watching and, 96–99
Coleman, James S., 142
Collective child rearing, 213n3, 219–20n22
Collins, Glenn, 247n96
Colonial period, 15–17
Columbia University, 252n130
Comics, regressiveness of, 125, 126
Concrete operations stage, 123, 178, 226n1
Conflict: in adolescence, 168; avoidance of, 79–80; inevitability of, 204; resolution of, 80, 82, 104; about sexuality, 88, 89; unconscious, 100
Conformity, 137–38; to parental values and expectations, 139
Conscience, 102–11; beginning of, 71, 72; dependency versus, 205; in latency, 123

Index

Index

Index

Index

Maternal deprivation, 103, 218–19*n*17
Maternal love, 12, 13
Mather, Cotton, 15
Mathtech, 238–39*n*34
Mead, Margaret, 172, 209*n*26, 215*n*10
Mealtimes, 153
Medicine: developments in, 200–201; professionalization of, 35
Medieval life, 7–8, 10
Menarche and menstruation, 121–22, 175, 184
Meyer, Bernard C., 250*n*113
Miller, Patricia Y., 251*n*127
Millet, Kate, 231*n*23
MIT-Harvard report, 15
Mitchell, Juliet, 232*n*23
Money, John, 220*n*25, 221*n*29
Moody, Samuel, 209*n*23
Moral choice, 124, 125
Morality, 107; and cognitive development, 179–82; development of, 155–57; sexual, 147, 148, 193; street-gang, 132; *see also* Values
Mother substitutes, 50, 74
Murderous impulses, 78
Muuss, Rolf E., 253*n*1

Narcissistic character, 105
National Organization for Women (NOW), 223*n*34
Nation's Families, The: 1960–1990 (Masnick and Bane), 15, 209*n*14
Natural childbirth, 36–37
Neglectful parents, 50, 202
Neufeld, John, 230*n*19
New University Conference, Women's Caucus of, 223*n*34
Newborns, 28, 44–50; constitutional differences among, 49; needs of, 46–48; perceptual development of, 92–93; smiling response of, 48
New York Times, The, 213*n*5, 247*n*96
New York University, 237*n*33
Normality, concepts of, 241–42*n*68
Novak, Michael, 236*n*33
Novels, 125–26, 129
Nuclear family: developmental process in, 32; modern, 12; as refuge, 135–37;

resolution of oedipal conflict in, 90; traditional definition of, 6–7
Nudity, parental, 86, 131
Nursery school, readiness for, 71, 73

Obedience, inculcation of, 9
Object permanence, 177, 219*n*18
Oedipus complex, 88–91
Offer, Daniel, 167–68, 170–73, 188, 190, 241–42*n*68, 242*n*69, 243*n*73, 244*n*77, 245*n*83, 246*n*89, 251*n*127
Omnipotence, 102; fantasies of, 79, 228 *n*12
Open marriage, 147
Opie, Iona and Peter, 208*n*5, 227*n*6
Overstimulation: in adolescence, 187, 189; during latency, 118, 131–32; in sex education, 151; sexual, 86; vulnerability to, 77

Parents and Children in History (Hunt), 209*n*10
Parents magazine, 214*n*5
Parsons, Talcott, 19, 230*n*20
Pasteur, Louis, 35
Patriarchal agricultural society, 18
Peer group, 13; in adolescence, 170; conformity with, 137–38
Penis envy, 229*n*14
Perceptual development, 92–93
Permissiveness, 20, 45, 215*n*10; in schools, 143
Perry, Richard, 228*n*10
P.E.T., 225*n*49
Phase-appropriate care, 205–6
Phayre, Thomas, 8
Physical activity, discharge of sexual drives in, 119
Physical punishment, 58
Piaget, Jean, 31, 123, 155, 177–80, 212*n*2, 215*n*12, 219*n*18, 224*n*37, 226*n*1, 234*n*28
Pine, Fred, 215*n*11
Planned Parenthood Federation of America, 147, 149

Index

Play: creativity and, 133, 231*n*22; imagination in, 96; during latency, 119–20; and reality, 72; symbolic, 59–60, 63, 67, 69; unstructured time for, 132–35
Plumb, J. H., 208*n*5
Pogrebin, Letty C., 217*n*13
Political activists, 182–83, 186, 195–96, 239*n*41, 252–53*n*130
Poverty, culture of, 186
Practicing subphase, 54
Premarital sexual behavior, 12, 193
"Preoperational" stage, 178
Preschool enrichment programs, 93–94
Privacy, respect for, 85
"Professional parenting," 202, 254*n*4
Projection of aggressive feelings, 78
Psychoanalysis, 44–45, 203; on adolescence, 164–67
Psychohistory, 10
Psychological birth of the infant, 46
Psychological growth, 30–31
Psychological World of the Teenager, The (Offer), 167, 170
Psychosexual development, 88
Puberty, 121–22, 174–77; defined, 163; inner unrest during, 164
Public mothering, 74
Puerperal fever, 35
Punishment: extreme, 107; physical, 58

Quarrels, resolution of, 98

Racial balance in schools, 142
Rand Corporation, 244*n*82
Rapprochement phase, 57
Raths, Louis E., 240*n*42
Reaction formation, strict morality as, 156
Reading, 99–100, 118, 124–29; in adolescence, 189–90; anxiety about, 134; attitudes about, 135; to children, 96–97, 100–102; impulse control and, 131; moral issues and, 159, 161, 162; sex education and, 151
Reality, structuring of, 72
Reality testing, 76, 121

Rebelliousness, 139; adolescent, 165, 166, 171
Regiment of Life, whereunto is added a treatise of pestilence, with the boke of children (Phayre), 8
Reich, Wilhelm, 209*n*9
Relativism, 194
Religious fanatics, 183, 186
Religious training, 206
Repression during latency, 118
Responsibility, need for, 137–39
Riesman, David, 230*n*19
Ritchie, Oscar W., 254*n*4
Rituals: of community, 206; family, 136
Rivoire, J. L., 224*n*39
Roby, Pamela, 222–23*n*34
Roiphe, Herman, 220*n*25, 224*n*36
Romantic love, 12, 13
Romantic movement, 164
Rosenkrantz, Barbara G., 229*n*18
Rousseau, Jean-Jacques, 12, 17, 164
Rules, importance of, in latency, 123

Sabshin, Melvin, 241–42*n*68
Sadistic behavior of parents, 131
Sado-masochism, 146
Salinger, J. D., 241*n*60
Sarnoff, Charles, 226*n*3, 233*n*25
Schafer, Margaret, 231–32*n*23
Schools: function of, 141–44; parental support for, 141, 152–53; sex education in, 145–52; sexually segregated, 192; success in, 234*n*28; values inculcated in, 155–62
Secularization, 206
Seductive behavior of parents, 131
Self: autonomous, 63, 71; gender identity and, 65; primary experience of, 60
Self-control, independence and capacity for, 109
Self-discipline, 64, 83
Sensorimotor stage, 49, 177–78
Separation: capacity to tolerate, 71; fear of, 69
Separation-individuation process, 54–57, 197; ambivalence in, 70
Sex education, 87, 145–52; for adolescents, 183, 185, 186, 194; controversy

261

Index

Index